Lecture Notes in Artificial Intelligence   1534

Subseries of Lecture Notes in Computer Science
Edited by J. G. Carbonell and J. Siekmann

Lecture Notes in Computer Science

Edited by G. Goos, J. Hartmanis and J. van Leeuwen

Springer
Berlin
Heidelberg
New York
Barcelona
Hong Kong
London
Milan
Paris
Singapore
Tokyo

Jaime S. Sichman
Rosaria Conte   Nigel Gilbert (Eds.)

Multi-Agent Systems and Agent-Based Simulation

First International Workshop, MABS'98
Paris, France, July 4-6, 1998
Proceedings

 Springer

Series Editors

Jaime G. Carbonell, Carnegie Mellon University, Pittsburgh, PA, USA
Jörg Siekmann, University of Saarland, Saarbrücken, Germany

Volume Editors

Jaime S. Sichman
Computer Engineering Department, University of São Paulo
Av. Prof. Luciano Gualberto, 158, tv.3, 05508-900 São Paulo SP Brazil
E-mail: jaime@pcs.usp.br

Rosaria Conte
Division of AI, Cognitive and Interaction Modelling, IP/CNR
Viale Marx 15, I-00137 Rome, Italy
E-mail: rosaria@pscs2.irmkant.rm.cnr.it

Nigel Gilbert
Department of Sociology, University of Surrey
Guildford GU2 5XH, UK
E-mail: N.Gilbert@surrey.ac.uk

Cataloging-in-Publication Data applied for

Die Deutsche Bibliothek - CIP-Einheitsaufnahme

Multi-agent systems and agent based simulation : first international workshop ;
proceedings / MABS '98, Paris, France, July 4 - 6, 1998. Jaime S. Sichman ...
(ed.). - Berlin ; Heidelberg ; New York ; Barcelona ; Hong Kong ; London ;
Milan ; Paris ; Singapore ; Tokyo : Springer, 1998
 (Lecture notes in computer science ; 1534 : Lecture notes in artificial
intelligence)
 ISBN 3-540-65476-3

CR Subject Classification (1998): I.2.11, I.2, C.2, I.6, J.4, H.5

ISBN 3-540-65476-3 Springer-Verlag Berlin Heidelberg New York

© Springer-Verlag Berlin Heidelberg 1998
Printed in Germany

Typesetting: Camera ready by author
SPIN 10692956   06/3142 – 5 4 3 2 1 0   Printed on acid-free paper

Preface

Fifteen papers were presented at the first workshop on *Multi-Agent Systems and Agent-Based Simulation* held as part of the *Agents World* conference in Paris, July 4–6, 1998. The workshop was designed to bring together two developing communities: the multi-agent systems researchers who were the core participants at *Agents World*, and social scientists interested in using MAS as a research tool. Most of the social sciences were represented, with contributions touching on sociology, management science, economics, psychology, environmental science, ecology, and linguistics.

The workshop was organised in association with *SimSoc*, an informal group of social scientists who have arranged an irregular series of influential workshops on using simulation in the social sciences beginning in 1992.

While the papers were quite heterogeneous in substantive domain and in their disciplinary origins, there were several themes which recurred during the workshop. One of these was considered in more depth in a round table discussion led by Jim Doran at the end of the workshop on 'Representing cognition for social simulation', which addressed the issue of whether and how cognition should be modelled. Quite divergent views were expressed, with some participants denying that individual cognition needed to be modelled at all, and others arguing that cognition must be at the centre of social simulation.

Another theme which was repeatedly mentioned in the presentations was the idea of 'emergence': that features observable at the level of a group or society should emerge from individual behaviour. Some participants (like Servat et al.) argued that it was appropriate to model macro-level features directly and then study ways in which individual agents could discover and adapt to those macro-level features.

Over 50 abstracts were received in response to the call for participation, but time constraints meant that only 16 could be accepted. This volume presents the revised versions of the papers presented in this workshop. In addition, we have provided an introduction pointing out several similarities and differences between these research fields and showing that they are complementary in several aspects, so that each one can benefit from results that emerge from the other. We finish this introduction by presenting and classifying the contributions in this volume.

We would like to thank the organisers of *Agent World* for the invitation to organise the workshop, hoping that it could be the first one of a fruitful series.

São Paulo, October 1998

Jaime Simão Sichman
Rosaria Conte
Nigel Gilbert

Program Committee Members / List of Reviewers

Nigel Gilbert (University of Surrey, Guildford, UK)
Rosaria Conte (Institute of Psychology/CNR, Rome, Italy)
Jaime Simão Sichman (University of São Paulo, São Paulo, Brazil)

H. Van Dyke Parunak (Center for Electronic Commerce, Ann Arbor, USA)
Cristiano Castelfranchi (Institute of Psychology/CNR, Rome, Italy)
Scott Moss (Manchester Metropolitan University, Manchester, UK)
Martine Antona (CIRAD, Montpellier, France)
David Sumpter (University of Manchester, Manchester, UK)
Juliette Rouchier (CIRAD, Montpellier, France)
Takashi Hashimoto (Brain Science Institute, Saitama, JAPAN)
David Hales (University of Essex, Essex, UK)
Mahdi Hannoun (Ecole des Mines, Saint-Étienne, France)
David Servat (ORSTOM, Bondy, France)
Harko Verhagen (Stockholm University, Kista, Sweden)
Leonardo Garrido (Instituto Tecnológico de Monterrey, Monterrey, Mexico)
Edem Fianyo (ORSTOM, Bondy, France)
Mark D'Inverno (University College London, London, UK)
Giuliano Pistolesi (Institute of Psychology/CNR, Rome, Italy)

Contents

MAS and Social Simulation: A Suitable Commitment

Rosaria Conte[1], Nigel Gilbert[2], and Jaime Simão Sichman[3]

(1) Div. of AI, Cognitive and Interaction Modelling, Inst. of Psychology/CNR, Rome, Italy
rosaria@pscs2.irmkant.rm.cnr.it
(2) Department of Sociology, University of Surrey, Guildford, UK
N.Gilbert@surrey.ac.uk
(3) Department of Computer Engineering, University of São Paulo, São Paulo, Brazil
jaime@pcs.usp.br

Abstract. The goal of this introduction is to point out several similarities and differences between the research fields of multi-agent systems and social simulation. We show that these fields are complementary in several aspects, thus each one can benefit from results that emerge from the other. We finish the introduction by presenting and classifying the contributions in this volume.

1 Multi-Agent Systems and Social Simulation: Objective Affinities

The research fields of multi-agent systems and social simulation have some interesting points in common. We characterize each of the fields next, stressing their mutual influences in the last years.

1.1 Multi-Agent Systems

The field of Multi Agent Systems (MAS) is a well-established research and applied branch of AI, which has taken its impetus from the problems encountered in the implementation of tasks on distributed computational units interacting with one another and with the external environment (Distributed AI). A report on the results achieved within DAI, and a synthesis of the reasons underlying the development of the MAS field, is beyond the scope of this introduction (for a quite comprehensive picture, see O'Hare and Jennings 1996). Suffice it to say that distributed AI systems soon revealed a need for autonomy. The more autonomous the local units of the system from a central one, the more efficient the task distribution and execution, and the lower the computational load of the overall system. This discovery stimulated AI researchers and designers to turn their attention to intriguing and apparently philosophical issues, such as how to conceive of an autonomous system and how to design it. In turn, the development of autonomous systems brought about another perhaps even trickier question, i.e. how to obtain coordination and cooperation among autonomous systems executing a common task?

Application-oriented solutions to these questions have often been attempted (e.g. blackboard architectures, master-slave and benevolence assumptions; see Huhns, 1987). Nevertheless, in the last decade, the conceptual question of autonomy has increasingly become a focus of AI scientists' attention. This is shown by several scientific events: from mainly European gatherings such as the early Modelling Autonomous Agents in a Multi-Agent World (MAAMAW) events which characterized the MAS field in its early days (see, Demazeau and Mueller, 1990, Demazeau and Werner, 1991), a larger community has grown (e.g. the International Conference on Multi-Agent Systems, ICMAS; for the last one, see Demazeau, 1998).

The MAS field is increasingly characterized by the study, design and implementation of societies of artificial agents. Fruitful contributions are made by other AI sub-fields. Among these, one which deserves particular attention for its recent developments and increasing popularity is the Agent field with its highly reputed scientific events (the ATAL workshops, the Autonomous Agents Conference, etc.) and journals (the Journal of Intelligent Systems).

If the AI, logic-based and cognitive science approaches have contributed considerably to developments of MAS, the social sciences have exerted relatively less influence. An exception to this rule is offered by economics and game theory, which have rapidly invaded the MAS field (for a critical review, see Castelfranchi and Conte, 1998). The hegemony of these fairly specific areas of the social sciences on MAS is essentially due to the attention paid by economists and game-theorists to the study of the evolution of cooperation from local interactions among self-interested agents, also the quintessential problem of MAS scientists.

The role played by economics has prevented the MAS field itself from taking advantage of the whole range of theories, models, and conceptual instruments that abound in the social sciences and that have received a great impulse thanks to the spread of computer simulation.

1.2 Social Simulation

The computer simulation of social phenomena is a promising field of research at the intersection between the social, mathematical and computer sciences. The use of computer simulation in the social sciences ranges from sociology to economics, from social psychology to organization theory and political science, and from demography to anthropology and archaeology. The use of computers in some social scientific areas can be traced back to the fifties (Halpin, 1998). In its early days, and up to the seventies, computer simulation was essentially used as a powerful implementation of mathematical modelling (Troitzsch, 1997). More recently, computer simulation is more often used in its own right, "as a means of manipulating the symbols of programming languages" (Troitzsch, 1997: 41). Nowadays, the computer simulation of social phenomena and processes can be considered a well established field of research, as is witnessed by a large numbers of publications and scientific events and its own journal, the Journal of Artificial Societies and Social Simulation (for a review, see Gilbert and Troitzsch, 1999). In particular, in the last two decades, the field of computer simulation has been able to benefit from a number of increasingly accessible facilities such as the development of high-level languages; the appearance of learning algorithms and systems; etc. DAI and the MAS have provided architectures and platforms for the implementation of relatively autonomous agents. This greatly contributed to the establishing of the agent-based computer simulation, an approach which has produced a vast body of simulation research, including rebuilding the Cellular Automata tradition, thanks to new technical and theoretical instruments (for a good example of simulation studies based on Cellular Automata modelling, see Hegselmann, 1996).

The agent-based approach enhanced the potentialities of computer simulation as a tool for theorizing about social scientific issues. In particular, the notion of an extended (multiple) computational agent, implementing cognitive capabilities (cf. Doran 1998), is giving encouragement to the construction and exploration of artificial societies (Gilbert and Conte, 1995; Epstein and Axtell, 1996), since it facilitates the modelling of artificial societies of autonomous intelligent agents.

If the MAS field can be characterized as the study of societies of artificial autonomous agents, agent-based social simulation can be defined as the study of artificial societies of autonomous agents. One could argue that the operation result should not be affected by the operators' order. However, the two fields are far from self-sufficient, as the following discussion will try to show. In particular, we shall argue that:

1'. despite their evident affinities, the two fields in question have suffered and still suffer from an inadequate interface;
2. their cross-fertilisation would encourage research in both fields and at the same time stimulate innovative research arising at the intersection between them.

2 MAS and Social Simulation: An Unwarranted Gap

MAS and social simulation differ in terms of the formalism used (logic- and AI-based in the MAS domain, and mathematically based in the social simulation domain). But they also differ in other, more substantial ways.

2.1 Background Theory

Although decision and game theory have had a significant influence on both, theoretical differences between the two fields abound. MAS has inherited a large share of the AI and cognitive science conceptual and theoretical endowment, which entailed (a) long experience with the design and implementation of integrated architectures, rather than elementary automata; (b) a strong emphasis on the whole agent, rather than solely on its actions; (c) careful attention paid to the process of plan-construction, not just decision-making and choice; (d) familiarity with the normalization and implementation of agents mental, as well as their behavioral states; (e) a tendency to provide the social agent with specific capacities for actions answering social requests and tasks (e.g., obligations, commitment and responsibility, etc.), rather than modelling social processes as mere emerging properties of agents' interaction.

The area of social simulation, benefited from the social sciences to a far greater extent than MAS. Among others, the following factors contributed to the field's progress: (a) a tendency to use computer simulation to test theoretical hypotheses, rather than the computational system's efficiency; (b) more familiarity with the interpretation of real-life social phenomena; this in turn implied (c) the production of vast bodies of data relative to artificial large-scale populations. All these features converged to consolidate the scientific methodological reputation of computer simulation, and lessen the toy-world character of its applications. Arising at the intersection of several social sciences, the field of social simulation could profit from their most recent and significant advances, such as (d) the development of the paradigm of complexity, facilitated by a close interaction with the sciences of physical and biological systems; and, in particular, (e) the development of theories, models and techniques for implementing and exploring social dynamics and evolution: social learning (cf. Macy and Flache, 1995), evolutionary game theory (cf. Weibull, 1996), cultural evolution (cf., for one example, Reynolds, 1994) and memetics (see the Journal of Memetics), etc.

2.2 Objectives

In the field of social simulation, objectives vary as a function of the discipline of interest. Applied objectives prevail in political, economical and management science, and especially in the science of organizations, which aims to optimize certain effects (for instance, international cooperation, resource allocation and distribution, or organizational performance). Other disciplines such as archaeology and anthropology are more clearly aimed at increasing scientific knowledge by formulating and testing interpretative models of existing phenomena through computational reconstruction. Overall, therefore, objectives vary between the purely normative in application-oriented disciplines like economics and the descriptive in interpretation-oriented disciplines like sociology, anthropology and archaeology.

In MAS, scientific objectives are unfortunately increasingly subordinate to producing software for various applications such as (micro-) robotics for manufacture and surgery, air traffic control and military defence. Nevertheless, this field has already contributed to improve our understanding of social intelligence and agent modelling by means of its architectural approach. By this is meant the integrated design of the modules, or "specialists", responsible for the different competencies involved in action. In particular, an intelligent autonomous agent architecture should respond in an intelligent adaptive way to a complex environment such as an agent society.

While it can hardly be doubted that social structures are created by interaction among agents, it is also true that the latter are in turn shaped by the social demands that they are supposed to meet. Good MAS theories (see, for the best-known example, the Belief-Desire-Intention (BDI) architecture proposed by Rao and Georgeff 1991) have attempted to model the traits and competencies that enable autonomous agents to cooperate and coordinate with one another for a common task (citations abound; see any volume of proceedings of the ICMAS conference); elaborate and execute multi-agent plans; communicate with and influence one another; form and pursue collective intentions; commit themselves to a given action in a flexible intelligent way; assume and eventually abandon given social responsibilities; and so on.

2.3 Outstanding Issues

Despite the results achieved separately within the two fields, the potential of the computational study of social phenomena has not yet been fully exploited. Several questions are still unanswered and several points are still missing. Generally speaking, these fall into three related areas:

1. How should one combine a more sophisticated agent model and design with the simulation of qualitatively and quantitatively significant social phenomena? While multi agent systems are aggregates of small number of computational units, social simulators obtain data about large-scale populations. Is it possible to obtain a significant volume of data on, say, a BDI platform?

2. What is the role of the agent in the science of complexity? Should we accept the "trendy" view shared by physicists, mathematicians and some social scientists that complex systems can be described with the vocabulary and models of physics and biology only? Or should other vocabularies be developed to describe independently the various levels of complexity that are displayed in any reality of interest (be it natural or artificial)? And if the latter option is preferred, what are the specific vocabularies of social and mental complexity, and how should they be related to one another? In other words, how are the paradigm of emergence and the study of (social) intelligence to be related?

3. How is the two-way micro-macro link, from behaviors to social structures to be explained? The emergent paradigm is insufficient: it accounts for one direction only, namely from behaviors to social structures. What about the other direction? Cultural evolution and memetics try to give an account of the diffusion of so-called second-order emergent properties (mental representations of social constructs). Somehow this paradigm tries to model the way back from social structures to mental representations. However, how can this process be reconciled with agents' autonomy? Why, when and how do agents decide to form, accept and disseminate these representations? The agent's mind seems to play a mediator role here. How is the mediator role of cognition to be explained?

The above questions are intimately intertwined as is shown when one considers some more specific questions:

1. Agents make rational choices; they decide among alternatives for action in a way that is consistent with their internal criteria (rationality, utility maximisation, goal

satisfaction, or any other). How do they form such alternatives? We need to integrate models of social decision-making with planning and problem solving.

2. This integration leads to another more crucial confrontation, between activation and goal-directed action, on one hand, and rationality and utility-maximisation, on the other hand. The social scientific view of the agent is strongly, if not uniquely, influenced by the economic interpretation of rationality. But this view has little to say about how agents should be constructed or how they concretely act. The mechanisms that activate agents are not yet clearly connected with the principles which govern action and decision-making.

3. The emergent paradigm aims to explain social convergence on given behavioral regularities (spatial segregation) on the grounds of a rather simplified characterization of the agents' motivations (for example, the attitude to be next to and imitate in-groups). The same characterization has been applied to explain the emergence and diffusion of conventions (Lewis, 1969). However, if social learning elucidates some mechanisms responsible for the spread of conventions, it does not seem to provide a sufficient account of innovation: how can new rules and conventions break the customary ones? How should one reconcile stability and innovation? Genetic algorithms bridge this hiatus by introducing mutation (for a discussion on different mechanisms for obtaining innovation, see DeJong and Spears, 1995) also the co-learning algorithm introduced by Shoham and Tennenholtz, 1994). However, the view of innovation as accidental mutation does not do justice to the agents' active role in the establishment of conventions. Agents' representations and interpretations seem to have a fundamental part in such a phenomenon.

4. This raises the more general problem of the connection between learning and reasoning. Social dynamics are not only an effect of learning and evolution. Social agents modify their behavior and that of their fellows by means of reasoning, planning and influencing. How should one combine the flexibility and social responsiveness of the agent with its autonomy and intelligence?

5. The emergent paradigms explain conventions in terms of the diffusion of behavioral regularities. Apparently, there is no relationship between conventions on one hand, and obligations, prescriptions, moral rules, etc. on the other. Therefore, either the existence of the latter is denied, or these two phenomena are claimed to be unrelated. However, the former is counter-intuitive. The latter is anti-economical: why should one ignore the relationships between phenomena so evidently intertwined? And, moreover, how is the "mandatory" character of conventions to be accounted for without a model of the agent where that character is somehow represented?

3 A Fruitful Cooperation

Cross-fertilisation among the two fields is needed. This would strengthen the agent-based approach in social simulation, add dynamics into MAS and reinforce simulation as a means of testing MAS systems. More specifically, a number of

positive consequences can be expected from a closer interaction between the fields in question. MAS are likely to:
1. profit from the more refined and well-established theories, concepts and models of social organizations and institutions developed within the social sciences;
2. adopt the more dynamic approach shared by the social scientists using computer simulation;
3. acknowledge the importance of theory-driven computational studies even in addressing applied objectives;
4. import an approach to computer simulation from the social sciences which sees it as a tool for making and testing theories, rather than applications.

Social scientists interested in computer simulation, in their turn, are likely to:
1. give up both the static view of the agent as proposed by some rationality theories, and the behavioral view as proposed by theories of social learning,
2. refine their view of the agent and start to conceive of it as a computable although complex entity,
3. discover the role of the mind as a necessary intermediate between social structures and social behaviors;
4. familiarise themselves with more sophisticated agent architectures.

4 The Contributions in this Volume

Fifteen papers were presented at the first workshop on Multi-Agent systems and Agent-Based Simulation, which was organized by the editors of this volume and held as part of the Agents' World conference in Paris, July 4-6, 1998. Most of the social sciences were represented, with contributions touching on sociology, management science, economics, psychology, environmental science, ecology, and linguistics. There were a total of 69 registered participants. The workshop was organized in association with SimSoc, an informal group of social scientists who have arranged an irregular series of influential workshops on using simulation in the social sciences beginning in 1992.

Over 50 abstracts were received in response to the call for participation, but time constraints meant that only 16 could be accepted. The program included:
1. papers considering the value of agent-based approaches to social simulation compared with other techniques better known in the social sciences such as system dynamics and the implications for methodology (Parunak; Moss);
2. modelling the dynamics of markets (Terna) and the interactions between markets and natural resources such as tropical forests (Antona et al.);
3. explaining the emergent behavior of macro-level entities (e.g. groups and societies) from the actions of individuals (Sumpter, whose paper was on honey bee colonies; Hashimoto on the emergence of language; and Servat et al on water runoff processes);
4. group formation based on cultural evolution (Hales);

5. explorations of social dependency, agent interaction and organisational problem-solving (Conte and Pedone; Hannoun et al; Verhagen; Garrido et al);
6. and a study of how best to represent time in a multi-agent simulation (Fianyo et al).

While the papers were quite heterogeneous in substantive domain and in their disciplinary origins, there were several themes which recurred during the workshop. One of these was considered in more depth in a round table discussion led by Jim Doran at the end of the workshop on 'Representing cognition for social simulation', which addressed the issue of whether and how cognition should be modeled. Quite divergent views were expressed, with some participants denying that individual cognition needed to be modeled at all, and others arguing that cognition must be at the center of social simulation.

Another theme which was repeatedly mentioned in the presentations was the idea of 'emergence': that features observable at the level of a group or society should emerge from individual behavior (although Servat et al argued that it was appropriate to model macro-level features directly and then study ways in which individual agents could discover and adapt to those macro-level features).

Multi-Agent Based Simulation may be a good occasion for social scientists, on one hand, and AI and cognitive scientists, on the other, to meet on a level ground. Let us hope this volume makes the interested reader willing to take advantage of such an occasion.

References

Castelfranchi, C. and Conte, R. (1988) Limits of economic rationality for agents and MA systems. *Robotics and Autonomous Systems*, Special issue on Multi-Agent Rationality, Elsevier Editor, (in press).

DeJong, K. and Spears, W. (1995) On the state of evolutionary computation, *Proceedings of the Sixth Conference on Genetic Algorithms*, 618-23.

Demazeau, Y. (ed.) (1998) *Proceedings of the Third International Conference on Multi-Agent Systems (ICMAS 98)*. IEEE Press.

Demazeau, Y. and Mueller, J.P. (eds.) (1990) *Decentralized AI*, Elsevier, North-Holland.

Demazeau, Y. and Werner, E. (eds.) (1991) *Decentralized AI - 2*, Elsevier, North-Holland.

Doran, J. (1998) Simulating Collective Misbelief, *Journal of Artificial Societies and Social Simulation*, vol. 1, no. 1, <http://www.soc.surrey.ac.uk/JASSS/1/2/4.html>.

Epstein, J. M. and Axtell, R. L. (1996) *Growing Artificial Societies: Social Science from the Bottom Up*. The Brookings Institution Press: Washington D.C. The MIT Press: Cambridge, Mass.

Gilbert, N. and Troitzsch, K. G. (1999) *Simulation for the Social Scientist*. Milton Keynes: Open University Press, (in press).

Gilbert, N. and Conte, R. (eds.) (1995) *Artificial Societies: the Computer Simulation of Social Life*. UCL Press: London.

Halpin, B. (1998) Simulation in Sociology: A review of the literature. Paper read at the Workshop on "Potential of the computer simulation for the social sciences", Centre for

Research on Simulation in the Social Sciences (CRESS), University of Surrey, 14-15 January.

Hegselmann, R. (1996) Modelling social dynamics by cellular automata. In K.G. Troitzsch, U. Mueller, N. Gilbert, and J. Doran (eds.) *Social Sience Microsimulation*. Heidelberg: Springer.

Huhns, M.N. (ed.) (1987) *Distributed Artificial Intelligence*. Pitman, Morgan Kaufmann, San Mateo, CA.

Lewis, D. (1969) *Convention*. Cambridge, MA: Harvard University Press.

Macy, M. and Flache, A. (1995) Beyond rationality in models of choice. *Annual Review of Sociology*, 21, 73-91.

O'Hare, G. and Jennings, N. (eds.) (1996) *Foundations of Distributed AI* ,Wiley Inter-Science.

Rao, A. S. and Georgeff, M. P. (1991). Modelling rational agents within a BDI architecture. In J. Allen, R. Fikes, and E. Sandewall (eds.), *Proceedings of the International Conference on Principles of Knowledge Representation and Reasoning*, San Mateo, CA: Kaufmann, 473-485.

Reynolds, R.G. (1994) Learning to cooperate using cultural algorithms. In N. Gilbert, and J. Doran (eds.) *Simulating Societies: the computer simulation of social life*. London: UCL Press.

Shoham, Y. and Tennenholtz, M. (1994) Co-Learning and the Evolution of Social Activity, CS-TR-94-1511, Stanford University.

Troitzsch, K.G. (1997) Social science simulation - Origin, prospects, purposes. In R. Conte, R. Hegselmann, P. Terna (eds.) *Simulating social phenomena*, Heidelberg: Springer.

Weibull, J.W. (1996) *Evolutionary Game Theory*. Cambridge, MA: The MIT Press.

Agent-Based Modeling vs. Equation-Based Modeling: A Case Study and Users' Guide

H. Van Dyke Parunak*, Robert Savit**, Rick L. Riolo**

*Center for Electronic Commerce, ERIM, 2901 Hubbard Road, Ann Arbor, MI 48105 USA
**Program for the Study of Complex Systems, Randall Laboratory, Univ. of Michigan, Ann Arbor, MI 48109-1120 USA
vparunak@erim.org, savit@umich.edu, rlriolo@umich.edu

Abstract. In many domains, agent-based system modeling competes with equation-based approaches that identify system variables and evaluate or integrate sets of equations relating these variables. The distinction has been of great interest in a project that applies agent-based modeling to industrial supply networks, since virtually all computer-based modeling of such networks up to this point has used system dynamics, an approach based on ordinary differential equations (ODE's). This paper summarizes the domain of supply networks and illustrates how they can be modeled both with agents and with equations. It summarizes the similarities and differences of these two classes of models, and develops criteria for selecting one or the other approach.

1. Introduction

In many domains, agent-based modeling competes with equation-based approaches that identify system variables and evaluate or integrate sets of equations relating these variables. Both approaches simulate the system by constructing a model and executing it on a computer. The differences are in the form of the model and how it is executed. In agent-based modeling (ABM), the model consists of a set of agents that encapsulate the behaviors of the various individuals that make up the system, and execution consists of emulating these behaviors. In equation-based modeling (EBM), the model is a set of equations, and execution consists of evaluating them.[1] Thus "simulation" is the general term that applies to both methods, which are distinguished as (agent-based) emulation and (equation-based) evaluation.

Understanding the relative capabilities of these two approaches is of great ethical and practical interest to system modelers and simulators. The question is important ethically because the duty of simulators ought to be first of all to the domain being simulated, not to a given simulation technology, and the choice of technology should be driven by its adequacy for the modeling task as well as its intrinsic interest to the modeler. The question is important practically because most funding sources are driven by domain-dependent agendas and want to put their resources behind the simulation technology that will provide the best results.

---

[1] When "ABM" and "EBM" are arthrous or plural, 'M' means "model" rather than "modeling."

This paper explores the question in the problem domain of manufacturing supply networks, and giving examples of both ABM's and EBM's (Section 2). It discusses the relation between these two approaches at a high level (Section 3), and then compares their practical performance in three specific areas (Section 4). A concluding section includes recommendations for advancing and propagating ABM's.

2. The DASCh Experience

In our laboratory, the contrast between the two broad categories of models arose in the context of the DASCh project (Dynamical Analysis of Supply Chains) [12, 13], which explores the dynamical behavior of a manufacturing supply network. This section describes the application area, summarizes the structure and behavior of the agent-based model that was the focus of our research, and exhibits a system dynamics model of the same system to exemplify an equation-based approach.

2.1 What is a Supply Chain?

Modern industrial strategists are developing the vision of the "virtual enterprise," formed for a particular market opportunity from independent firms with well-defined core competencies [10]. The manufacturer of a complex product (the original equipment manufacturer, or "OEM") may purchase half or even more of the content in the product from other firms. For example, an automotive manufacturer might buy seats from one company, brake systems from another, air conditioning from a third, and electrical systems from a fourth, and manufacture only the chassis, body, and powertrain in its own facilities. The suppliers of major subsystems (such as seats) in turn purchase much of their content from still other companies. As a result, the

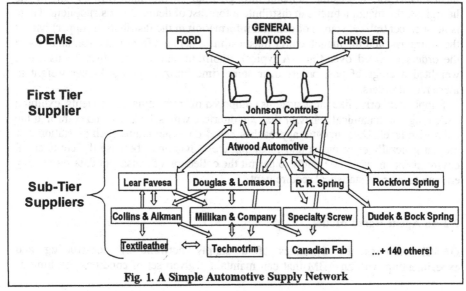

Fig. 1. A Simple Automotive Supply Network

"production line" that turns raw materials into a vehicle is a "supply network" (more commonly though less precisely called a "supply chain") of many different firms.

Fig. 1 illustrates part of a simple supply network [1, 8]. Johnson Controls supplies seating systems to Ford, General Motors, and Chrysler, and purchases the components and subassemblies of seats either directly or indirectly from over one hundred fifty other companies, some of which also supply one another. Issues of product design and production schedule must be managed across all these firms in order to produce quality vehicles on time and at reasonable cost.

In general, supply networks form an hourglass (Fig. 2), with an OEM at the center. Raw materials, parts, and subassemblies move up through the lower half of the hourglass to reach the OEM, and finished goods make their way through the upper half to the final consumer.

Fig. 2 is over-simplified. Linkages among firms are not restricted to the hierarchical patterns shown, and a single firm may appear in both halves of the hourglass. Still, the general pattern is one of convergence of

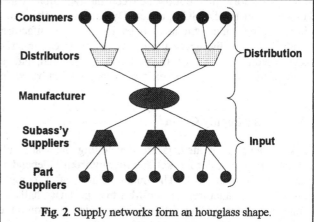

Fig. 2. Supply networks form an hourglass shape.

materials to the OEM, and then distribution of the product out to end users. The two halves of the hourglass exhibit different dynamical behavior, driven by different mechanisms for forecasting demand through time. In the input (lower) half of the hourglass, the manufacturer can distribute a forecast of demand to its suppliers. There is no such centralized source of demand information in the distribution (upper) half of the hourglass, and the manufacturer must estimate demand from statistical analysis of the orders received over time. A typical algorithm, and the one that we use, is a weighted average of past orders over some time horizon, giving higher weight to more recent orders.

Supply networks, like most systems composed of interacting components, exhibit a wide range of dynamical behavior that can interfere with scheduling and control at the enterprise level. Data analytic approaches based on assumptions such as stationarity are not generally effective in understanding these dynamics, because the commercial environment changes too rapidly to permit the collection of consistent data series long enough to support statistical requirements.

2.2 An Agent-Based Model

DASCh explores the dynamics of a supply network by constructing and experimenting with an ABM that can maintain a given set of conditions as long as desired, permitting the collection of statistically relevant time series. Though artificial, this environment allows us to explore the dynamical nature of the supply network and can lead to important insights of great practical significance.

Model Structure. DASCh includes three species of agents. *Company agents* represent the different firms that trade with one another in a supply network. They consume inputs from their suppliers and transform them into outputs that they send to their customers. *PPIC agents* model the Production Planning and Inventory Control algorithms used by company agents to determine what inputs to order from their suppliers, based on the orders they have received from their customers. These PPIC agents currently support a simple material requirements planning (MRP) model.[2] *Shipping agents* model the delay and uncertainty involved in the movement of both material and information between trading partners.

The initial DASCh experiments involve a supply chain with four company agents (Fig. 3: a boundary supplier, a boundary consumer, and two intermediate firms producing a product with neither assembly nor disassembly). Each intermediate company agent has a PPIC agent. Shipping agents move both material and information among company agents.

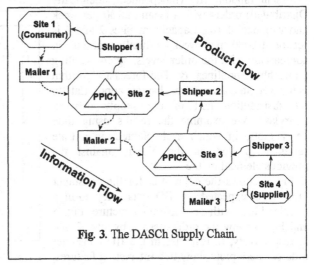

Fig. 3. The DASCh Supply Chain.

This simple structure was intended as a starting point. We expected it to exhibit relatively uninteresting behavior, on which the impact of successive modifications could be studied. In fact, it shows a range of interesting behaviors in terms of the variability in orders and inventories of the various company agents: amplification, correlation, persistence, and generation of variation in the orders and inventory levels in the system. In general, these phenomena introduce strong structural distortions into the order stream. Such disturbances obscure the suppliers' view of the top-level consumer's demand.

---

[2] The basic MRP algorithm includes developing a forecast of future demand based either on past demand or on customer forecast (depending on location in the hourglass), estimating inventory changes through time due to processing, deliveries, and shipments, determining when inventory is in danger of falling below specified levels, and placing orders to replenish inventory early enough to allow for estimated delivery times of suppliers.

Amplification and Correlation of Order Variation. As the demand generated by the top-level consumer propagates to lower levels, its variance increases, so that lower-level suppliers experience much more variability than higher-level ones. This amplification phenomenon is widely discussed in the literature. Not as well recognized is the correlation imposed on an originally uncorrelated series of random orders by the PPIC algorithms in the supply network.

To explore this dynamic we set all batch sizes to one, so the economic order quantity does not introduce a nonlinearity. The consumer generates Gaussian random IID (Independent, Identically Distributed) orders with a mean of 100 per week and variance of 10. Capacity at Sites 2 and 3 is set at 10,000 per week, virtually infinite in comparison with the order levels, again avoiding a threshhold nonlinearity. The forecast algorithm is the weighted average mechanism appropriate to the distribution half of the supply network hourglass. We examine the results using time delay plots, in which each element in a time series is plotted on the Y-axis against the previous element on the X-axis.

Fig. 4 shows the delay plot for the consumer orders. As expected for IID data, they form a circular blob, with no apparent structure. Fig. 5 and Fig. 6 show the orders issued by sites 2 and 3, respectively, in response to the IID consumer orders. These plots show two interesting features. First, although plotted to the same scale, the clouds of points are larger, reflecting amplification of order variation in successive tiers of the supply chain. Second, the clouds are no longer circular in shape, but are stretched along the line X = Y. This stretching indicates that these sites are more likely to follow a large order with another large one, and a small order with another small one. In other words, their orders have become correlated in time, and increasingly so as we go deeper in the supply chain.

Persistence of Order Variation. A single modest change at the top of the chain generates

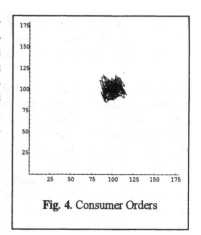

Fig. 4. Consumer Orders

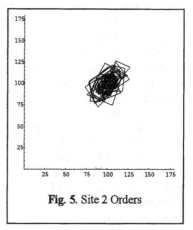

Fig. 5. Site 2 Orders

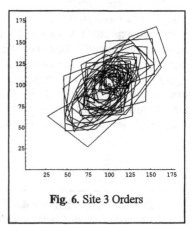

Fig. 6. Site 3 Orders

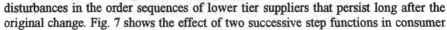

disturbances in the order sequences of lower tier suppliers that persist long after the original change. Fig. 7 shows the effect of two successive step functions in consumer orders (the solid line) on the orders issued by site 3 to the supplier (the dashed line), using weighted average forecasting. In both cases, the consumer increases its order level by 10 orders per time period. Though the change in consumer orders is a one-time phenomenon, its effect persists in the orders that site 3 issues to the supplier. The persistence time is of the same order as the forecast window over which the manufacturer averages past orders to estimate future demand.

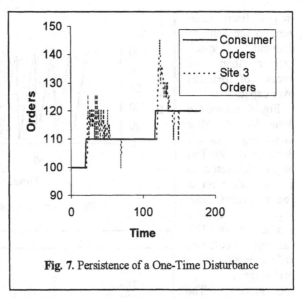

Fig. 7. Persistence of a One-Time Disturbance

For the first step increase in consumer orders, the forecast window is 39 weeks and the disturbance in site 3 orders persists for between 31 weeks (to the last upward spike over the new demand level) and 47 weeks (to the downward spike). The amplitude of the variability in site 3 orders ranges from a high of 125 to a low of 100, or a total range of 25.

Before the second increase, we reduce the forecast window in both PPIC modules from 39 to 20. The period of variability lasted fewer time steps (between 22 to the last order above 120, and 29 to the final downward spike). But shortening the forecast window has the effect of increasing the amplification. Thus the second set of peaks is taller than the first (ranging from 110 to 145, or a total range of 35).

Thus the weighted forecasting algorithm has the effect of imposing a memory on the system. The longer the forecasting period, the longer the memory, but the lower the amplitude of the variations generated.

Generation of Inventory Variation. Even when top-level demand is constant and bottom-level supply is completely reliable, intermediate sites can generate complex oscillations in inventory levels, including phase locking and period doubling, as a result of capacity limitations.

The consumer has a steady demand with no superimposed noise. The bottom-level supplier makes every shipment exactly when promised, exactly in the amount promised. Batch sizes are still 1, but now we impose a capacity threshold on sites 2 and 3: in each time step they can only process 100 parts, a threshhold nonlinearity. As long as the consumer's demand is below the capacity of the producers, the system quickly stabilizes to constant ordering levels and inventory throughout the chain. When the consumer demand exceeds the capacity of the producers, inventory levels in those sites begin to oscillate.

Fig. 8 shows the inventory oscillation that arises when demand exceeds capacity by 10%. Site inventories oscillate out of phase with one another, in the form of a sawtooth that rises rapidly and then drops off gradually. The inventory variation

16

ranges from near-zero to the level of demand, much greater than the excess of demand over capacity

Fig. 9 shows the dynamics after increasing consumer demand to 150. The inventories settle to a sawtooth with a shorter period. Now one cycle's production of 100 can support only two orders, leading to a period-three oscillation. The inventories of sites 2 and 3, out of synch when Demand/Capacity = 110/100, are now synchronized and in phase.

The transition period is actually longer than appears from Fig. 9. The increase from 110 to 150 takes place at time 133, but the first evidence of it in site 2's dynamics appears at time 145. The delay is due to the backlog of over-capacity orders at the 110 level, which must be cleared before the new larger orders can be processed.

Fig. 10 shows the result of increasing the overload even

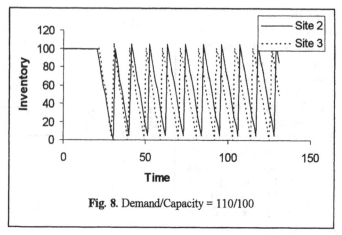

Fig. 8. Demand/Capacity = 110/100

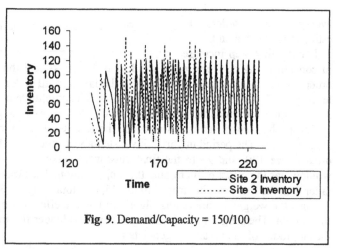

Fig. 9. Demand/Capacity = 150/100

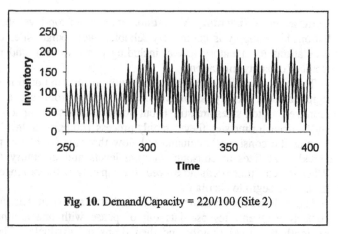

Fig. 10. Demand/Capacity = 220/100 (Site 2)

further. (Because of the increased detail in the dynamics, we show only the inventory level for site 2.) Now the consumer is ordering 220 units per time period. Again, backlogged orders at the previous level delay the appearance of the new dynamics; demand changes at time 228, but appears in the dynamics first at time 288, and the dynamics finally stabilize at time 300.

This degree of overload generates qualitatively new dynamical behavior. Instead of a single sawtooth, the inventories at sites 2 and 3 exhibit biperiodic oscillation, a broad sawtooth with a period of eleven, modulated with a period-two oscillation. This behavior is phenomenologically similar to bifurcations observed in nonlinear systems such as the logistic map, but does not lead to chaos in our model with the parameter settings used here. The occurrence of multiple frequencies is stimulated not by the absolute difference of demand over capacity, but by their incommensurability.

Details of these behaviors are discussed in [13].

2.3 An Equation-Based Model

Following the pioneering work of Jay Forrester and the System Dynamics movement [5], virtually all simulation work to date on supply chains integrates a set of ordinary differential equations (ODE's) over time. It is customary in this community to represent these models graphically, using a notation that suggests a series of tanks connected by pipes with valves. Fig. 11 gives a simple example of the flow of material in the DASCh network as it appears in the VenSim® simulation environment [15].

The *rectangular boxes* ("Finished2," "WIP2," "Finished3," "WIP3") are "levels," or variables whose assignments change over time. In this particular model, they

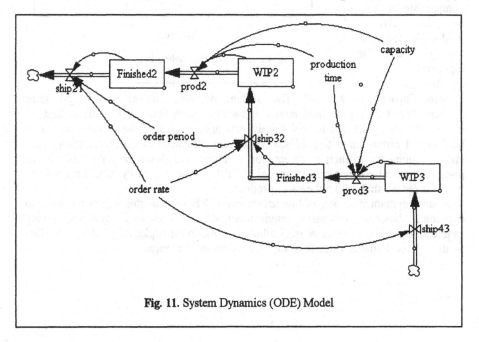

Fig. 11. System Dynamics (ODE) Model

represent the four critical inventory levels in DASCh sites 2 and 3, a work-in-process inventory and a finished goods inventory for each of the sites.

The *arrows with valve symbols* (shaped like hour-glasses: "ship21," "prod2," "ship32," "prod3," "ship43") are flows between the levels that they connect, and the valves are "rates," variables that determine the rate of flow. For example, the rate "prod2" is the rate at which site 2 converts work-in-process to finished goods.

The *cloud shapes* at the upper-left and lower-right corners represent external sources and sinks. In this case, the upper-left corner represents the end consumer (DASCh site 1), while the lower-right corner represents the supplier (DASCh site 4).

The *legends* associated with neither a box nor a valve ("order rate," "order period," "production time," "capacity") are auxiliary variables.

Single-bodied arrows show the dependency of rates on other variables (both levels and auxiliaries) in the model. The exact mathematical form of the dependency is not shown in the graphical representation, but is encoded in the rate. For example, the arrows show that the rate "prod2" depends on the level "WIP2" and the auxiliaries "production time" and "capacity." The actual dependency is prod2 = min(capacity, WIP2/production_time).

This particular model shows the interplay between site capacity and order rate. When the order rate exceeds the site capacity, it demonstrates oscillations comparable to those in the DASCh model. For example, Fig. 12 shows the biperiodic oscillations for

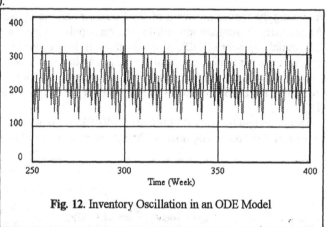

Fig. 12. Inventory Oscillation in an ODE Model

Demand/Capacity = 220/100. The system dynamics model shows the same periodicities as the agent-based model. It does not show many of the effects that we observe in the ABM and in real supply networks, including the memory effect of backlogged orders, transition effects, or the amplification of order variation. Such effects require the explicit representation of levels and flows for orders as well as parts. In particular they require a model of PPIC in the system dynamics formalism, which is (as we shall see) not easy to produce.

System dynamics models of this nature are widely used in studying organizational dynamics, business processes, environmental and ecological systems, policy implications, and a wide range of similar domains. In principle, ABM can be applied to all of these domains, often in a way that seems more natural.

3. Agents vs. Equations: A High-Level View

ABM and EBM share some common concerns, but differ in two ways: the fundamental relationships among entities that they model, and the level at which they focus their attention.

Both approaches recognize that the world includes two kinds of entities: individuals and observables, each with a temporal aspect.

Individuals are bounded active regions of the domain. In some domains, the boundaries that set individuals apart are physical, as when we are studying ants, or bees, or people. In other domains, the boundaries may be more abstract, as in the case of DASCh's sites, each representing a business firm. In any case, the boundaries are such that those who are interested in the domain recognize the individuals as distinct from one another. They are "active regions" because those interested in the domain conceive of the individuals as having behaviors. Individuals "do things" as time passes.

Observables are measurable characteristics of interest. They may be associated either with separate individuals (e.g., the velocity of gas particles in a box) or with the collection of individuals as a whole (the pressure in the box). In general, the values of these observables change over time. In both kinds of models, these observables are represented as variables that take on assignments.

Each of these sets of entities invites us to articulate the relationships that unify it and show how those relationships predict the behavior of the overall system through time. The first fundamental difference between ABM and EBM is in the relationships on which one focuses attention.

EBM begins with a set of equations that express relationships among observables. The evaluation of these equations produces the evolution of the observables over time. These equations may be algebraic, or they may capture variability over time (ODE's, as used in system dynamics) or over time and space (partial differential equations, or PDE's). The modeler may recognize that these relationships result from the interlocking behaviors of the individuals, but those behaviors have no explicit representation in EBM.

ABM begins, not with equations that relate observables to one another, but with behaviors through which individuals interact with one another. These behaviors may involve multiple individuals directly (foxes eating rabbits) or indirectly through a shared environment (horses and cows competing for grass). The modeler pays close attention to the observables as the model runs, and may value a parsimonious account of the relations among those observables, but such an account is the result of the modeling and simulation activity, not its starting point. The modeler begins by representing the behaviors of each individual, then turns them loose to interact. Direct relationships among the observables are an output of the process, not its input.

Fig. 13 summarizes the critical relationships:

- Individuals are characterized, separately or in aggregate, by observables, and affect the values of these observables by their actions.

- Observables are related to one another by equations.
- Individuals interact with one another through their behaviors.

A second fundamental difference between ABM and EBM is the level at which the model focuses. A system is made up of a set of interacting individuals. Some of the observables of interest may be defined only at the system level (e.g., the pressure of an enclosed gas), while others may be expressed either at the individual level or as an aggregate at the system level (e.g., location of an organism vs. the density of organisms per unit space of habitat). EBM tends to make extensive use of system-level observables, since it is often easier to formulate parsimonious closed-form equations using such quantities. In contrast, the natural tendency in ABM is to define agent behaviors in terms of observables accessible to the individual agent, which leads away from reliance on system-level information. In other words, the evolution of system-level observables does emerge from an agent-based model, but the modeler is not as likely use these observables explicitly to drive the model's dynamics as in equation-based modeling.

These two distinctions are tendencies, not hard and fast rules. The two approaches can be combined [4]: within an individual agent in an ABM, behavioral decisions may be driven by the evaluation of equations over particular observables, and one could implement an agent with global view whose task is to access system-level observables and make them visible to local agents, thus driving an ABM with system-level information. Furthermore, while agents can embody arbitrary computational processes, some equation-based systems (those based on PDE's, but not the simple ODE's used in system dynamics) are also computationally complete [11]. The decision between the two approaches must be made case by case on the basis of practical considerations.

4. Agents vs. Equations: Practical Considerations

A practitioner is concerned with the underlying *structure* of a model, the naturalness of its *representation* of a system, and the *verisimilitude* of a straightforward representation. This section discusses these considerations with special reference to modeling supply networks. Some of these issues have been discussed by others in the domains of social science [2, 3] and ecology [9, 16] (where ABM's are usually called "Individual-Based Models").

4.1 Model Structure

The difference in representational focus between ABM and EBM has consequences for how

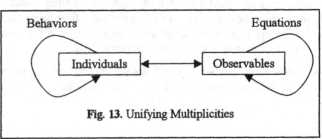

Fig. 13. Unifying Multiplicities

models are modularized. EBM's represent the system as a set of equations that relate observables to one another. The basic unit of the model, the equation, typically relates observables whose values are affected by the actions of multiple individuals, so the natural modularization often crosses boundaries among individuals. ABM's represent the internal behavior of each individual. One agent's behavior may depend on observables generated by other individuals, but does not directly access the representation of those individuals' behaviors, so the natural modularization follows boundaries among individuals.

This fundamental difference in model structure gives ABM a significant advantage in commercial applications such as supply network modeling, in two ways.

1. In an ABM, each firm has its own agent or agents. An agent's internal behaviors are not required to be visible to the rest of the system, so firms can maintain proprietary information about their internal operations. Groups of firms can conduct joint modeling exercises while keeping their individual agents on their own computers, maintaining whatever controls are needed. Construction of an EBM requires disclosure of the relationships that each firm maintains on observables so that the equations can be formulated and evaluated. Distributed execution of EBM's is not impossible, but does not naturally respect commercially important boundaries among the individuals.

2. In many cases, simulation of a system is part of a larger project whose desired outcome is a control scheme that more or less automatically regulates the behavior of the entire system. The agents in an ABM correspond one-to-one with the individuals (e.g., firms or divisions of firms) in the system being modeled, and their behaviors are analogs of the real behaviors. These two characteristics make agents a natural locus for the application of adaptive techniques that can modify their behaviors as the agents execute, so as to control the emergent behavior of the overall system. The migration from simulation model to adaptive control model is much more straightforward in ABM than in EBM. One can easily imagine a member of a supply network using its simulation agent as the basis for an automated control agent that handles routine interactions with trading partners. It is much less likely that such a firm would submit aspects of its operation to an external "equation manager" that maintains specified relationships among observables from several firms.

More generally, ABM's are better suited to domains where the natural unit of decomposition is the individual rather than the observable or the equation, and where physical distribution of the computation across multiple processors is desirable. EBM's may be better suited to domains where the natural unit of decomposition is the observable or equation rather than the individual.

4.2 System Representation

The variety of EBM with which we have experimented (ODE's) most naturally represents the process being analyzed as a set of flow rates and levels. ABM most naturally represents the process as a set of behaviors, which may include features difficult to represent as rates and levels, such as step-by-step processes and conditional decisions. ODE's are well-suited to represent purely physical processes. However, business processes are dominated by discrete decision-making. This is only one example of representational advantages of ABM's over EBM's. More generally:

1. ABM's are easier to construct. Certain behaviors are difficult to translate into a consistent rate-and-level formalism. PPIC algorithms are an important example. In our attempts to duplicate DASCh results using VenSim®, we were unable to construct a credible PPIC algorithm using the rate-and-level formalism. [17] comments on the complexity of such models, and we have been unable to find an actual example of such a model in the system dynamics literature. Recent enhancements to ithink® reflect such difficulties. The most recent release of this popular system dynamics package includes "black boxes" for specific entities such as conveyors or ovens whose behavior is difficult to represent in a pure rate-and-level system [6]. One suspects that the only realistic way to incorporate complex decision algorithms such as PPIC in system dynamics models will be by implementing such black boxes, thus incorporating elements of ABM in the spirit of [4].

2. ABM's make it easier to distinguish physical space from interaction space. In many applications, physical space helps define which individuals can interact with one another. Customer-supplier relationships a century ago were dominated by physical space, leading to the development of regional industries, such as the automotive industry in southeast Michigan. Advances in telecommunications and transportation enable companies that are physically separate from one another to interact relatively easily, so that automotive suppliers in Michigan now find themselves in competition with suppliers based in Mexico or the Pacific rim. Such examples show that physical space is an increasingly poor surrogate for interaction space in applications such as commerce. ODE methods such as system dynamics have no intrinsic model of space at all. PDE's provide a parsimonious model of physical space, but not of interaction space. ABM's permit the definition of arbitrary topologies for the interaction of agents.

3. ABM's offer an additional level of validation. Both ABM's and EBM's can be validated at the system level, by comparing model output with real system behavior. In addition, ABM's can be validated at the individual level, since the behaviors encoded for each agent can be compared with local observations on the actual behavior of the domain individuals. (A balancing consideration is that the code needed to represent an agent's behavior in ABM is often longer and more complex than a typical equation in an EBM, and thus potentially more susceptible to representational error.)

4. ABM's support more direct experimentation. Managers playing "what-if" games with the model can think directly in terms of familiar business processes, rather than having to translate them into equations relating observables.

5. ABM's are easier to translate back into practice. One purpose of "what-if" experiments with a model is to identify improved business practices that can then be implemented in the company. If the model is expressed and modified directly in terms of behaviors, implementation of its recommendations is simply a matter of transcribing the modified behaviors of the agents into task descriptions for the underlying physical entities in the real world.

4.3 Verisimilitude

In many domains, ABM's give more realistic results than EBM's, for manageable levels of representational detail. The qualification about level of detail is important. Since PDE's are computationally complete, one can in principle construct a set of PDE's that completely mimics the behavior of any ABM, and thus produce the same results. However, the PDE model may be much too complex for reasonable manipulation and comprehension. EBM's (like system dynamics) based on simpler formalisms than PDE's may yield less realistic results regardless of the level of detail in the representation.

One example in the case of extremely simple agents is the Ising model of ferromagnetic phase transitions in statistical physics. The agent in this model is a single atom in an N-dimensional square lattice of similar agents. Its behavior is to change the orientation of its spin to minimize the energy in its environment. One common and generally useful approach to such systems employs mean field theory, analyzing the behavior of a representative atom under statistical averages over the states of neighboring atoms [14, pp. 430-434]. In some dimensions, this mean field EBM approach may miss the order of the phase transition, predict a phase transition where there is none, or yield an inaccurate temperature for the transition. (In one and two dimensions, the equations defining the Ising model can be solved exactly and analytically without the homogeneity assumptions that lead to the errors of the mean field approach, but such solutions are intractable in higher dimensions.) ABM models that emulate the behavior of individual atoms can be developed for arbitrary dimensions, and are more accurate both qualitatively and quantitatively than the mean field approximation.

In a more complex domain, researchers in the dynamics of traffic networks have achieved more realistic results from traffic models that emulate the behaviors of individual drivers and vehicles, compared with the previous generation of models that simulate traffic as the flow of a fluid through a network [7]. The latter example bears strong similarities to the flow-and-stock approach to supply chain simulation, and encourages us to develop an agent-based approach for this application as well.

Wilson [18] offers a detailed study that compares ABM and EBM using the same system (a predator-prey model). He develops a series of EBM's, each enhancing the previous one to rectify inconsistencies between the ABM and the EBM. The study assumes that the ABM is the more realistic model, and that the EBM is the appropriate locus for making adjustments to bring the two models into agreement. The initial ODE EBM describes reactions between the two species, but representing dispersal through space requires extending it to a set of spatio-temporal integro-differential equations. These equations, modeling both individual characteristics and dispersal using population averages, lead to qualitatively different behaviors than do ABM's. For example, ignoring local variation in dispersal leads to limit cycles rather than the extinction scenarios that dominate ABM's. To correct for these lumped parameter effects, the EBM is interrupted at each iteration of the integration to add a random perturbation to the population parameter at each location and to zero local population levels that fall below specified threshholds.

The disadvantages of EBM in these examples result largely from the use of averages of critical system variables over time and space. They assume homogeneity among individuals, but individuals in real systems are often highly heterogeneous. When the dynamics are nonlinear, local variations from the averages can lead to significant deviations in overall system behavior. In business applications, driven by "if-then" decisions, nonlinearity is the rule. Because ABM's are inherently local, it is natural to let each agent monitor the value of system variables locally, without averaging over time and space and thus without losing the local idiosyncrasies that can determine overall system behavior. The EBM for our toy four-firm supply network (Fig. 11) does not use averages over individuals, and so does not suffer from this disadvantage. However, real-world supply networks are much larger. The total number of shipping points in the U.S. automotive industry is on the order of 40,000, and it is difficult to see how a parsimonious EBM of such a system could avoid the use of lumped parameters.

5. Conclusion

ABM is a relatively new approach to system modeling and simulation. In many domains, it faces entrenched competition from EBM methodologies such as system dynamics. Our experience with both approaches leads to three general recommendations.

First, ABM is most appropriate for domains characterized by a high degree of localization and distribution and dominated by discrete decisions. EBM is most naturally applied to systems that can be modeled centrally, and in which the dynamics are dominated by physical laws rather than information processing.

Second, researchers in agent-based modeling should be aware of the long history of EBM, and should consider explicit case comparisons of their ABM's with existing or potential EBM's where relevant. Such comparisons are particularly valuable in simple systems in which one can trace the causes of divergence between the models. The sketch of the relative advantages and disadvantages of the two approaches presented in this paper is preliminary. Our ability to adopt the best modeling approach for a given problem depends on developing a collection of cases that demonstrate the respective strengths and weakness of the two approaches.

Third, the widespread popularity of EBM is due in large measure to the availability of several intuitive drag-and-drop tools for constructing and analyzing system dynamics models. Widespread realization of the advantages of agent-based modeling will depend on the availability of comparable tools for this approach, and the ABM community should encourage the development and refinement of such tools.

Acknowledgements

DASCh was funded by DARPA under contract F33615-96-C-5511, and administered through the AF ManTech program at Wright Laboratories under the direction of James Poindexter. The DASCh team includes Steve Clark and Van Parunak of ERIM's Center for Electronic Commerce, and Robert Savit and Rick Riolo of the University of Michigan's Program for the Study of Complex Systems. Sections 2.1

and 2.2 report on joint work of this team, drawn from [13]. This paper has benefited considerably from the detailed comments of Robert Axtell.

References

[1]   AIAG. Manufacturing Assembly Pilot (MAP) Project Final Report. M-4, Automotive Industry Action Group, Southfield, MI, 1997.

[2]   R. Axtell. Three Distinct Uses of Agent-Based Computational Models in the Social Sciences. Brookings Institution, Washington, DC, 1997.

[3]   M. E. Epstein and R. Axtell. *Growing Artificial Societies: Social Science from the Ground Up*. Boston, MA, MIT Press, 1996.

[4]   P. A. Fishwick. *Simulation Model Design and Execution: Building Digital Worlds*. Englewood Cliffs, NJ, Prentice Hall, 1995.

[5]   J. W. Forrester. *Industrial Dynamics*. Cambridge, MA, MIT Press, 1961.

[6]   High Performance Systems. ithink - The Premiere Business Simulation Tool from High Performance Systems, Inc. http://www.hps-inc.com/products/ithink/ithink.html, 1997.

[7]   K. R. Howard. Unjamming Traffic with Computers. *Scientific American*, (October), 1997.

[8]   T. Hoy. The Manufacturing Assembly Pilot (MAP): A Breakthrough in Information System Design. *EDI Forum*, 10(1):26-28, 1996.

[9]   O. P. Judson. The Rise of the Individual-Based Model in Ecology. *Trends in Ecology and Evolution*, 9(1 (January 1994)):9-14, 1994.

[10]   R. N. Nagel and R. Dove. *21st Century Manufacturing Enterprise Strategy*. Bethlehem, PA, Agility Forum, 1991.

[11]   S. Omohundro. Modelling Cellular Automata with Partial Differential Equations. *Physica D*, 10:128-134, 1984.

[12]   H. V. D. Parunak. DASCh: Dynamic Analysis of Supply Chains. http://www.iti.org/~van/dasch, 1997.

[13]   H. V. D. Parunak, R. Savit, R. Riolo, and S. Clark. Dynamical Analysis of Supply Chains. ERIM/University of Michigan Preprint, 1998. To be submitted for publication. Available at http://www.erim.org/cec/projects/dasch.htm.

[14]   F. Reif. *Fundamentals of Statistical and Thermal Physics*. New York, McGraw-Hill, 1965.

[15]   Ventana Systems. Ventana Systems Home Page. http://www.vensim.com, 1997.

[16]   F. Villa. New Computer Architectures as Tools for Ecological Thought. *Trends in Ecology and Evolution*, 7(6 (June 1992)):179-183, 1992.

[17]   M. E. Warkentin. MRP and JIT: Teaching the Dynamics of Information Flows and Material Flows with System Dynamics Modeling. *Proceedings of The 1985 International Conference of the Systems Dynamics Society*, pages 1017-1028, International System Dynamics Society, 1985.

[18]   W. G. Wilson. Resolving Discrepancies between Deterministic Population Models and Individual-Based Simulations. *American Naturalist*, 151(2):116-134, 1998.

Simulating with Cognitive Agents: The Importance of *Cognitive Emergence*

Cristiano Castelfranchi

IP - CNR National Research Council

Group of "Artificial Intelligence, Cognitive Modelling and Interaction"

Viale Marx, 15 - 00137 ROMA - Italy
E-mail: {cris, falcone}@pscs2.irmkant.rm.cnr.it

Abstract

When the micro-units of emerging dynamic processes are cognitive agents, a very important and unique phenomenon arises, called Cognitive Emergence (CE). We argue that: CE characterises the theory of Sociological dynamics with respect to other forms of emergence at different level of organisation (ex. physics, biology, etc.); CE has a very strong influence on the process of emergence, changing it, and should be taken into account in simulating and modelling social phenomena; certain important emerging social phenomena, like social norms cannot be explained at all without CE; CE has critical consequences on the process of "immergence" i.e. the process through which the macro-level emerging structure or global result 'feedbacks' into the micro-level re-shaping the "elementary" behaviours. We examine the case of dependence relationships.

1 Premise

> *"... The most important fact concerning human interactions is that these events are psychologically represented in each of the participants"*
> (Lewin, K. *A dynamic theory of personality*, N.Y. MacGraw, 1935)

The main concern and interest of Social Simulation [11] is the experimental study and the modelling of compound and unpredictable effects of a population of agents in a common world, i.e. the study of complexity, emergence [15], self-organisation, and dynamics deriving from agents' behaviours.

When those agents are "cognitive" agents [1], a very important and unique phenomenon arises, called Cognitive Emergence (CE).

There is "cognitive emergence" [2] [8] *when agents become aware, through a given "conceptualisation", of a certain "objective" pre-cognitive (unknown and non deliberated) phenomenon* that is influencing their results and outcomes, and then, indirectly, their actions.

This phenomenon of CE:

a) has a very strong influence on the process of emergence;

b) characterises the theory of social dynamics with respect to other forms of emergence at different level of organisation (ex. physics, biology, etc.);

---

[1] Cognitive agents are agents whose actions are internally regulated by goals (goal-directed) and whose goals, decisions, and plans are based on beliefs. Both goals and beliefs are cognitive representations that can be internally generated, manipulated, and subject to inferences and reasoning. Since a cognitive agent may have more than one goal active in the same situation, it must have some form of choice/decision, based on some "reason" i.e. on some belief and evaluation.

Notice that we use "goal" as the general family term for all motivational representations: from desires to intentions, from objectives to motives, from needs to ambitions, etc.

[2] For a broader view see [4] where it is claimed that emergence and cognition are not incompatible: they are not two alternative approaches to intelligence and cooperation, two competitive paradigms. and "they must be reconciled:

- first, considering **cognition itself as a level of emergence**: both as an emergence *from sub-symbolic to symbolic* (symbol grounding, emergent symbolic computation), and as a transition *from objective to subjective* conditions (awareness) - like in our example of dependence relations - and from *implicit to explicit knowledge*;
- second, recognizing the necessity of going **beyond cognition**, modeling emergent unaware, functional social phenomena (ex. unaware cooperation, non-orchestrated problem solving) also among cognitive and planning agents. In fact, *mind is not enough for modeling cooperation and society*. We have to explain how collective phenomena emerge from individual action and intelligence, and how a collaborative plan can be only partially represented in the minds of the participants, and some part represented in no mind at all."

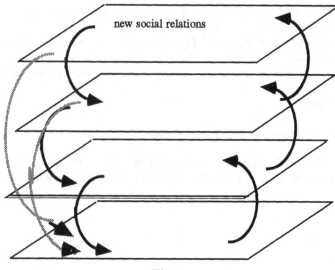

new social relations

Fig.1

c) has critical consequences on the process of "immergence" i.e. the process through which the macro-level emerging structure or global result 'feedbacks' into the micro-level, re-shaping the "elementary" behaviours (Fig 1).

In the following we will illustrate the notion of CE that has been introduced in [8]; its consequences on the process of emergence at the social macro-level, with some examples; its pertinence for the process of *immergence*.

2 Cognitive agents and representation-driven behaviours

Let us first summarise some crucial features of cognitive agents and of their behaviour (action):

i. *Cognitive agents have representations of the world*, of the actions' effects, of themselves, and of other agents. *Beliefs* (the agent explicit knowledge), *theories* (coherent and explanatory sets of beliefs), *expectations, goals, plans*, and *intentions*, are relevant examples of these representations.

ii. *The agents act on the basis of their representations*. More precisely they act on the basis of:
   - their beliefs about the current state of the world, and about their abilities and resources;

- their expectations about the effects of their possible actions, and about possible future events (including the actions of other agents);
- their goals and preferences; and
- the plans they know ("know how") for these goals.

iii. In other words, those representations are not just reflection about the action, or an epiphenomenon without any causal impact on the agent behaviour; they *play a crucial causal role*: the action is caused and guided by those representations. The behaviour of cognitive agents is a teleonomic phenomenon, directed toward a given result which is pre-represented, anticipated in the agent's mind (that is why we call it "action" and not simply "behaviour").

Given these properties of the micro-level entities and of their behaviours, strange consequences follow at the macro-level and for the emergence process.

3 Cognitive Emergence, what is it?

As we have said, there is "cognitive emergence" *when agents become aware, through a given "conceptualisation", of a certain "objective" pre-cognitive (unknown and non deliberated) phenomenon* that is influencing their results and outcomes, and then, indirectly, their actions.

Consider for example, interference and dependence relations that are "objective" relations, i.e. they *hold independently of the awareness of the involved agents*.

There is "interference" (either positive or negative) between two agents if the actions of the former through their effects can affect (favour or damage) the goals/outcomes of the other. There is "dependence" when an agent needs an action or a resource of the other agent to fulfil one of its goals (see 3.1).

The "cognitive emergence" (through experience and learning, or through communication) of such "objective" relations, strongly changes the social situation: from known interference, relations of competition/aggression or exploitation can rise; from acknowledged dependence, relations of power, goals of influencing and asking, possible exchanges or cooperation, will arise (see 5.1.).

In other words with CE *part of the macro-level expression, of the emerging structures, relations, and institutions* [25], *or compound effects*:

- is explicitly represented in the micro-agents minds, is partially *understood*, known by (part of) them;

- there are opinions and *theories about* it [3] ;

---

[3] They may be either correct beliefs and theories -true emergence of the objective phenomenon at the subjective level- or incorrect bielefs and theories; this is misconception about social

- there might be *goals and plans about* it, and even a deliberated construction of it (either centralised or distributed and cooperative).

3.1 A kind of 'emergence'

In which sense CE is 'emergence'? We should worry about the bad conceptual and epistemological state of the triumphant notion of 'emergence'. There are in fact different meanings of this term -used in the same domain and discipline- that create a serious confusion and would require some conceptual discussion. This is particularly important since I think that only computer simulation of emerging phenomena (including social phenomena) can finally provide us with clear notions of "emergence".

"Emergent" is a common sense word whose meaning components and connotations play an important role in orienting us to use it in extended, non well-defined ways. "The original meaning of the term derives from the idea of rising from a liquid, and by extension it connotes *the appearance of something previously hidden, submerged at a lower level*" [18]. It is a transition related to sight and view: from invisible to *visible*. It "implies both *revelation* and *a change of level*" (ibid.).

In the "revelation" connotation also the idea of "interesting", "important" is implied, and the idea of "something which is *unexpected*" (being submerged and then unaware or unperceived or unready). This "surprising" aspect is for example related - in current technical use- to the "unpredictability" aspect of both chaotic and complex systems.

Clearly enough the passage from unknown to knowledge, from unawareness to awareness, from subconscious to conscious, from implicit to explicit that characterises CE, corresponds quite well to this idea. But the use of 'emergence' for CE seems also appropriate in a more technical perspective.

For example, an additional important feature of 'emergence' comes from the reductionism-anti reductionism debate: *there should be some property of the emergent phenomenon that is not predicable of its source or components or elements, and that is not predictable on the basis of the properties of the source components.* Awareness and knowledge seem to be such properties.

Moreover, cognition, mental representation is considered a new level of complexity in nature and behaviour. Now also the fact that a given phenomenon becomes object of cognition, becomes 'represented' is in a sense a transition from one level of reality (mere objectivity) to another level of organisation (subjectivity).

In our perspective on emergence, not only global or collective effects, but also micro, individual phenomena can "emerge" as the result of a *co-evolutionary process* with macro-phenomena [8]. In this sense for example the "individual" as we conceive it in modern cultures is a historical product, not designed but emerging from our cultural, economic and political history.

---

reality, some sort of false-emergence. Of course also misconceptions have important effects on social actions and emergence (see for ex. Doran's research on misbeliefs [13])

However, one might prefer to reserve the term 'emergence' only for macro-level, collective phenomena. In this case one should consider that CE is in fact especially interesting and significant as a distributed and collective phenomenon: the fact that several agents become partially aware of their collective effects produces new collective effects.

In any case, it is true that CE is quite a special form of 'emergence'. It is representational emergence: some aspects of a phenomenon become represented, arrive at a representational level (in some mind).

Currently there are several notions of 'emergence' and it is not yet clear how to manage all the associations, connotations and features of this word to arrive at some well-defined technical uses. Here we just start to disentangle different meanings of the word in our domain (that, however, show important similarities) in order to place CE in this framework.

Diachronic emergence

There is an emergence along time: either developmental, or evolutionary, or historical. Let's call it "diachronic emergence". To see developmental phenomenon as "emergent" you need to think that certain components, or ingredients, of forerunners of that phenomenon were already present in previous stages of the evolutionary process, but were insufficient (as quantity, type or as organisation) to "form" the emergent phenomenon. You have also to consider different periods of the time as *levels, phases*. So there is some sort of phase transition in time.

Synchronic emergence

There are emergence processes that are just relative to different ways of looking at a given information from one level to another; they are relative to different levels of description, abstraction, or interaction. Let me call these cases of "synchronic emergence". Consider for example the relation between the temperature or the pressure of a gas and the movement of its molecules. Or consider the emergence that I will call "Gestalt".

Gestalt emergence

"Gestalt emergence" is the emergence of a significant pattern, structure, form, from the point of view of a given observer. Gestalt psychology's "laws" (proximity, similarity, good continuation, closure, etc.) are just principles for the emergence of "forms" (Gestalts). The most beautiful example is our perception of star "constellations": we know that stars in our perspective (subjectively) form a group with a special structure, but they have no special relation at all among themselves (objectively), and they are distant billions of kilometres from one another (they "interact" just on our retina).

Gestalt emergence is particularly far-reaching for a couple of reasons. Unbelievably enough it *does not require "complex" or "chaotic" system.* [4]

---

[4] I adopts the following informal definition of complex and chaotic systems [23] A system is "complex" when the number of the interacting objects is great, while the interaction rule among

Though in many domains the idea of emergence is even identified with that of "complexity", no complexity is needed for the emergence of some "irreducible" properties, like Gestalts or like "to be a couple", or "to be a herd". The second reason is that Gestalt emergence is very clearly subjective, *"observer relative"*, and this might not be true for other forms of emergence.

We claim that also in Social Simulation what has been called an "emergent" solution, be it intelligence, cooperation, or whatever, is frequently enough just a structure the observer-designer tried again and again to build up, or that she found interesting for her purposes; but it is a merely observed structure, with *no causal effects on the phenomenon itself, not really self-maintaining and self-reproducing*, or acquiring objectivity and independence from the observer-designer. What in these cases people call "emergent" are just "accidental" (but interesting) results; for ex. accidental cooperation. But accidental results are really interesting only when they can be "reproduced", and when they are preconditions for learning or for functions.

The "Gestalt emergence" can be seen as a subtype of a wider category that encompasses also the "descriptive emergence".

Descriptive emergence

Complex systems, consisting of many active elements, can be described either in terms of the actions/properties of their components or at the level of the system as a whole. At this level it may be possible to find out a concise description using new predicates for new properties and regularities which are "emerging" because they are only at the global level.

This descriptive view of emergence is like Gestalt emergence, although not related just to perception but to the observer's conceptualisation and description. In any case, the interest and the goodness of the emerging phenomena is only relative to the observer's aims.

Thus the main question about "emergence" is:
is this notion necessarily relative to an observer and to her "view" and evaluation; is it necessarily subjective? Or is it possible to provide *a scientific notion not based on perception, description and interest of the observer but on the self-organisation of the phenomenon in itself?* And, in particular, what kind/notion of emergence do we need to model social behaviour? The notion of emergence which is simply relative to an observer (who notices something interesting or some beautiful effect looking at the screen of a computer running some simulation [23]) or a merely *accidental* cooperation, are not enough for a social theory and for artificial social systems. We need a more objective notion [12, 5], an emerging structure *playing some causal role in the system* evolution/dynamics; not merely an epiphenomenon. This is for example

---

them is relatively simple. Its microscopic description is too long and impractical. A "chaotic" system can be simple, it can be a system with a few elements, but its macroscopic behavior is complicated.

the case of the emergent dependence structure (see 3.1) and this is also the case of CE. CE is a paradoxical case, since the 'observer' [5] is part of the game and its subjectivity, its perception of the phenomenon 'feedbacks' in the phenomenon itself and plays a causal role in it.

Possibly we need even more than a structure or a global property playing a causal role: we need really *self-organising emergent structures*. Emergent organisations and phenomena should reproduce, maintain, stabilise themselves through some feedback: either through evolutionary/selective mechanisms or through some form of learning. Otherwise we do not have a real emergence of some causal property (a new complexity level of organisation of the domain); but simply some subjective and unreliable global interpretation. It is not clear yet whether one can conceptualise or not CE also in this strong form, i.e. as self-organising and reproducing at least at the social level.

3.2 Emergence as opposed to intelligence?

The emergentist approach to social behaviour (usually based on methodological individualism) tries to deal with the emergence of collective institutions while avoiding CE. Moreover, it is frequently the case that an emergentist and evolutionary approach is seen as an alternative paradigm to cognition and deliberation. For example, *conventions* in game theory or social division of labour in economics are accounted for just in terms of equilibria that can be established also among simple rule-based agents, by learning or selection, without the contribution of some agents' understanding of what is happening.

Also in Artificial Intelligence the emergent view is arbitrarily opposed to cognition and planned behaviour [3, 17, 22]. Emergent social functions, or cooperation, or collective intelligence are modelled only among reactive non-intelligent agents, as opposed to deliberative agents able to reason about their joint intention, and planning and negotiating for all their collective activities.

Our claim [7, 4] is that this opposition is wrong and that collective intelligence, unaware cooperation, and emerging functionalities must also be modelled among cognitive agents who -obviously- have limited knowledge and rationality, and are not able to *understand, predict, and dominate all the global and compound effects of their actions at the collective level*.

Modelling this is precisely the main challenge for Social Simulation; its major theoretical contribution to the social sciences [5].

For sure there are types of social functions and institutions that emerge unnoticed, like the division of labour, or the formation of "conventions" in a game-theoretic sense. In this perspective, Lewin's claim, we cited in the Premise, is too strong.

---

[5] CE is objective in the sense that is not simply in the eye of the beholder, in the view of the observer of the social world; it is a phenomenon independent from the observer and playing a causal role in the dynamics of the observed field. Of course, it is a subjective phenomenon in the sense that it is about the subjectivity of the observed agents. However, we shouldn't mix up the methodological subjectivity of the observer, with the fact that observed entities can have a subjective/mental life.

However, there are other important social phenomena that cannot be understood and modelled in the same way. They cannot emerge and work without also passing trough their CE [2].

Conte and Castelfranchi [8] for example claim that true social norms cannot be reduced to what game theory call "conventions". Social norms cannot emerge and work without the involved agents (partially) understanding what is emerging among them (see later 4.).

To be concise and obvious (but later we will provide some further argument) no Polis and in general no politics would be possible without some CE of collective phenomena, in terms both of beliefs and evaluations, and of goals and projects [2] [6] .

3.3 The inadequacy of physic and biological models

Clearly enough such a form of emergence (and immergence) is unique to the social level among cognitive agents. It doesn't concern other kinds of interacting elements and other forms of emergence. This has quite serious consequences:

- the fundamental models inspired by physics (for ex. synergetics) or provided by biology (ex. evolutionary theory) about emergence and complexity are inadequate for modelling emergence in human (and in general in cognitive agents') societies.

They are incomplete in an important way: not only are they unable to model some aspect of reality and need additional concepts, but the models of the crucial process of emergence and of immergence themselves have to be changed.

Consider also that those models from physics tend to conceptualise and stress only the moment of the emergence. They do not pay comparable attention to the reverse *immergence* process; that is

how the emergent structure or global property changes back (even in time) the properties and then the behaviour of the elements (micro-units).

Indeed immergence is as important as emergence. More precisely *true emergence is based on immergence*.

- As we have said, by true emergence we mean the emergence not simply relative to an observer (some "interesting" figure or pattern), or simply consisting in some resulting equilibrium, but a complex and global result playing a causal role in the process, and self-organising and *reproducing* (actively *maintaining*) itself independently of the observer.
- This kind of emergence self-organises, reproduces and maintains itself precisely through its feedback at the micro-level by shaping the behaviour of the elementary units.

---

[6] Consider for example some interesting anthropological data. In his very detailed study of warfare among the Mae Enga of New Guinea, .. "Meggitt comes up with an important finding: the natives are consciously aware that warfare lends itself to the acquisition of territory. Meggitt himself evaluates this indigenous theory as being both rational and in keeping with the assumptions of "cultural materialist" evolutionists" (Cited in [2]).

Thus, no theory of true emergence is possible without an explicit model of this feedback at the micro-level, i.e. without an explicit theory of *immergence*.

• Since, among cognitive agents, behaviours are controlled by mental representations, *any feedback able to shape the behaviour must pass through some effect on and change of mental representations.* [7] CE is precisely one aspect and one way of this feedback from the macro to the micro.

4   CE from objective to subjective: Dependence and Interests

We will now examine an important example of the CE of objective social structures, and of its effects.

Some social structures are deliberately constructed by the agents (at least partially; for example role structures in organisations); others emerge in an objective way.

Let us focus in particular on one structure: the network of interdependencies. Not only because it is the more basic one for social theory, but also because it emerges before and beyond any social action, contract, and decision of the involved agents.

4.1   An emergent objective structure: the dependence network

In this section we give an example of the spontaneous emergence of the dependence structure, while in section 5.1 we show how such an emergent global phenomenon or structure 'feedbacks' to change the mind (and the behaviour) of the involved agents.

The structure of interference and interdependence among a population of agents is an *emergent* and *objective* one, *independent of the agents' awareness and decisions*, but it constrains the agents' actions by determining their success and efficacy.

Given a number of agents in a common world, and given their goals and their *different* and *limited* abilities and resources, they *are* in fact interdependent on each other: a dependence structure emerges. Consider an agent A with its goal Ga and its plan Pa for Ga, and assume that this plan requires the actions a1 and a2 and the resource r1. If the agent A is able to do a1 and a2 and possesses the resource r1, we say that it is self-sufficient relative to Ga and Pa. When on the contrary A either is not able to perform for ex. a1, or cannot access r1 (thus it has not the power of achieving Ga by itself) while there is another agent B which is able to do a1 or disposes of r1, we say that A *depends on* B as for a1 or r1 for the goal Ga and the plan Pa. A is *objectively* depending on B (even if it ignores or does not want this): actually it cannot achieve Ga if B does not perform a1 or does not make r1 accessible [20].

---

[7] This does not mean that in cognitive agents the feedback is necessarily based on their understanding or becoming aware of their social products, i.e. on CE. This is just one and a partial way.

There are several typical dependence patterns. In [8] the *OR-Dependence*, a disjunctive composition of dependence relations, and the *AND-dependence*, a conjunction of dependence relations, are distinguished. To give a flavour of those distinctions let us just detail the case of a two-way dependence between agents (*bilateral dependence*). There are two possible kinds of bilateral dependence:

• **Mutual dependence**, which occurs when x and y depend on each other for realising a common goal p, which can be achieved by means of a plan including at least two different acts such that x depends on y's doing ay, and y depends on x's doing ax:
Cooperation is a function of mutual dependence: in cooperation, in the strict sense, agents depend on one another to achieve one and the same goal [24]; they are co-interested in the convergent result of the common activity.

• **Reciprocal dependence**, which occurs when x and y depend on each other for realising different goals, that is, when x depends on y for realising x's goal that p, while y depends on x for realising y's goal that q, with p ≠ q.
Reciprocal dependence is to *social exchange* what mutual dependence is to cooperation.

The Dependence network *determines* and *predicts* partnerships and coalition formation, competition, cooperation, exchange, functional structure in organisations, rational and effective communication, and negotiation power, and there is some simulation-based evidence of this [20, 9]. Notice that this emerging structure is very dynamic: by simply introducing or eliminating one agent, or simply changing some goal or some plan or some ability in one agent, the entire network could change. Moreover, after the feedback of the network itself on the agent mind (5.1), and the consequent dropping of some goal or the adoption of new goals, the dependence relations change.
When A is depending on B for its goal Ga, B gets an (objective) *"power over"* A as for Ga. This power over - which is the power to allow or prevent the achievement of A's goal, the power of giving A positive or negative reinforcements and incentives, the power to punish or to reward A- pnce known, is the most important basis for the *power of influencing* A [6].

4.2   From objective interests to conflicts or collective action

A very important "objective" notion is that of "interest", not in the sense of "A is interested in q" or "q interests A" but in the sense of "q is in the interest of A" or "A's interest is that q". A may ignore its interest, i.e. what kind of situation would be good/favourable for itself. We say that *a pre-social relation of interest occurs between an agent A with his mental states and some external state of affairs, when a given state of the world q implies another world state p, and the latter is a goal or sub-goal of the agent A* (when p is a sub-goal, it often coincides with a precondition for a sub-plan) [8]. In other words, q (or, better, the event which produced it) is in A 's interest.

On the contrary, a world state which goes against an agent's interests is a *counter-interest* of that agent's.

Given this interest relation between a world state or event q and an agent A relative to its goal p, relevant objective social relations of interest follow.

In fact A and B may have a "common interest" (even ignoring this): it might be that the same q is both in the interest of A and in the interest of B. Notice that this is true when A and B have a common goal (p), but it can be true also when they have different goals which are favoured by the same world state q. So, A and B are in an important social relation (*communality of interests*) that they may ignore, but that has important effects on their success, failure, interference, and behaviour.

Similarly, they may be in an objective and unaware situation of *conflict of interests*: q being in the interest of A, and Not q being in the interest of B; i.e. the interest of A is a counter-interest of B. They are objectively competing, but not subjectively.

Since, if an agent becomes aware of its interest that q (relative to p), q becomes a (sub)goal of it (although not necessarily a chosen and pursued goal: that is an intention), it follows that the CE of common interests is likely to produce common goals, common intentions, some collaboration and collective action (consider for example the theory of class movement as based on class consciousness of common objective interests).

On the contrary, the CE of competition and conflicting interests will possibly produce conflicting goals, antagonism and deliberated conflict (struggle) (consider the theory of class conflicts).

Social relations of interest objectively and spontaneously emerge from a set of agents, with their goals and constraints and living in a common world. These social relations can cognitively emerge, and this will change the individual and the collective (coordinated) behaviours of the agents; then new unintended social effects and relations will emerge; and so on.

5 The case of Social Norms and Social Functions: the necessity of CE Vs the necessity of Non-CE

Not all important social phenomena, structures or institutions pass through CE. Let us compare for example social norms and social functions.

While for a social norm to work as a social norm and be fully effective, agents should understand it as a social norm, on the contrary the effectiveness of a social function does not depend on the agents' understanding of this function of their behaviour: social functions require an *extra-cognitive* emergence and functioning.

5.1 True social norms require cognitive agents and CE

A norm N emerges *as a norm* only when it emerges as such *into the mind* of the involved agents; not only *through* their mind (like in approaches based on imitation or behavioural conformity). [8] In other words, it works as a N only when the agents *recognise* it as a N, use it as a N, "conceive" it as a N [10].

Norm emergence and formation implies "cognitive emergence" (and then cognitive agents): *a social N is really a N after its CE.*

As long as the agents interpret the normative behaviour of the group merely as a statistical "norm", and comply by imitation, the real normative character of the N remains unacknowledged, and the efficacy of such "misunderstood N" is quite limited. Only when the normative (which implies "prescriptive") character of the N becomes acknowledged by the agent the N starts to operate effectively as a N through the true normative behaviour of that agent. Thus *the effective "cognitive emergence" of N in the agent's mind is a precondition for the social emergence of the N in the group, for its efficacy and complete functioning as a N.*

Notice that this CE is partial: for their working it is not necessary that social Ns as a macro-phenomenon be completely understood and transparent to the agents. What is necessary (and sufficient) is that the agents recognise the prescriptive and anonymous character of the N; the entitled authority, and the implicit *pretence* of the N to protect or enforce some group-interest (which may be against particular interests). It is not necessary for example that the involved agents (for ex. the addressee or the controller) understood or agree about the specific function or purpose of that N. They should respect it because it is a N (or, sub-ideally, because of surveillance and sanctions), but in any case because they understand that it is a N, and do not mix it up with a diffuse habit or a personal order or expectation. Norms, to work as norms, cannot remain unconscious to the addressee, but the agent can remain absolutely ignorant of the emerging effects of the prescribed behaviour in many kinds of Norm-adoption [8] [9] . Normative behaviour has to be intentional and conscious: it has to be based on knowledge of the norm (prescription), but this does not necessarily imply consciousness and intentionality relative to all the *functions of the norm* [5].

5.2 Social Functions and CE

While for a social norm to work as a social norm and be fully effective, agents should understand it as such, on the contrary the effectiveness of a *social function* does not depend on the agents' understanding of this function of their behaviour. Social functions emerge -they are not designed- but they should not cognitively emerge to work. They work without being understood.
Not only

     - a function can rise and maintain itself without the awareness of the agents;
but

---

[8] For ex. [1].

[9] In some forms of Norm Adoption, at least some of the functions of the Norm are conscious and pursued by the agent [8].

- if the agents intend the results of their behaviour, these would no longer be "social functions" of their behaviour but just "intentions". Let us shortly illustrate this complex point (pointing to another specific paper for its argumentation [5]).

As Elster remarked [14], if a behaviour is reproduced *thanks to* its good effects, that are "good" relatively to the goals of the agent (individual or collective) who reproduces them by acting intentionally, there is no room for "functions". If the agent appreciates the goodness of these effects and the action is replied in order to reproduce these effects, they are simply "intended". *The notion of intention is sufficient and invalids the notion of function.*

To account for functions, we should admit some mechanism that reproduces the intentional action thanks to (some of) its effects, *bypassing the agent understanding and planning these effects* (that can even be good for its goals and reproduced for that). The problem is that not simply reactive or routine behaviours have functions but also *intentional actions have functions.* We must account for the functional character of intentional actions: i.e. goals, finalities that go beyond the intended goals, beyond the mental teleonomy, and succeed in maintaining -unconsciously- the behaviour.

6   CE effects on immergence

Since CE implies a modification of the mental representations of the agents (the micro-elements of the emergent macro-phenomenon) we can also see it as a process of immergence. It is in fact a feedback effect of the emergent phenomenon on its ground elements (the agents): the emergent phenomenon changes their representations in a special way: it is (partially) represented in their minds. At the individual level CE is immergence, while globally is a new emergence [10].

More importantly, once CE holds, it will modify the behaviour of the micro-units (agents): they will behave also on the basis of their representations (beliefs and goals) of the emergent effects. The goals/plans of the agent change and consequently their behaviour changes, producing either a negative or a positive feedback on the original behaviours (see 6.):

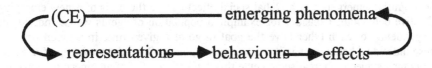

[10] When CE is shared or diffuse among several agents, this creates a new level of macro emergence, which has important consequences. Consider for example the theory of *class consciousness* and of its effect in history, or consider politics.

Let us give a couple of examples of this: how CE of dependence relations leads to social actions; how the perception of some emerging global effect (like crowding) leads to new behaviours and new global effects.

6.1 From subjective dependence to social goals, from "power over" to "influencing power"

The pre-cognitive structure we illustrated in 3.1 can "cognitively emerge": i.e. part of these constraints can become known. The agents, in fact, may have beliefs about their dependence and power relations.

Either through this "understanding" (CE) or through blind learning (based for example on reinforcement), the objective emergent structure of interdependencies 'feedbacks' into the agents' minds, and changes them. Some goals or plans will be abandoned as impossible, others will be activated or pursued [21]. Moreover, new goals and intentions will rise, especially social goals. The goal of exploiting or waiting for some action of the other; the goal of blocking or aggressing against another; the goal of influencing another to do or not to do something; the goal of changing dependence relations. For example if A understands that achieving its goal Ga depends on B performing a1, it will derive the new (social) goal that B performs a1, and it will try to induce B to do this. A may even have the goal of creating a new dependence relation (making B dependent on itself) in order to get some power over B and induce it to do a1. So, dependence relations not only spontaneously and unconsciously emerge and can be understood (CE), but they can even be planned and intended (CE).

Analogously, when B becomes aware of its "power over" A, it will have the goal of using this power in order to influence A to do or not to do something: *influencing power*. It might for example promise A to do a1, or threaten A of not doing a1, in order to obtain something else from A [6].

Without the emergence of this self-organising (undecided and non-contractual) objective structure, and usually without its CE, social goals would never evolve or be derived.

6.2 The cyclic emergence: from crowding to panic and tragedy

The cognitive emergence of a global social effect can be the basis of a new emerging collective behaviour. Consider for example a population of agents whose individuals independently of each other have the goal to go at a given time in a given place x. These individual behaviours will produce a compound effect: the crowding of x. Some agents may subjectively realise/perceive this "crowding": CE of an emerging objective global result. The subjectively perceived crowding may activate in some agents a sensation of danger, and anxiety and alarm that will be expressed. But there is an emerging effect also of this behaviour: in fact the anxiety and the alarm is confirmed, reinforced and *diffused* by the observation/perception that it is diffuse, i.e. that also other agents are feeling this. So it is a self-reinforcing and self-spreading collective phenomenon. This will create new individual goals in the agents (to escape as soon as possible), and the compound effect of these behaviours will be a (new collective emergence) panic, chaos and a disaster.

Without this continuous feedback between micro-and macro, internal and external, and -in this case- without a (partial) CE, perception, awareness of the collective compound result, this phenomenon (panic due to crowding) would not be possible.

7 Positive and negative feedback: an urbanistic example

The feedback from the CE into the individual mind and behaviour and thus into the reproduction of the collective phenomenon itself, is not necessarily a positive feedback. Let us consider two opposite cases.

- The awareness of the phenomenon can be an incentive for it (*positive feedback*).

Let's start from the individual goal: I want to stay close to people of my own language and culture in order to meet friends more easily and to feel more confident [19]. When this goal is widespread, common to several agents, there will be a non-intended and sometimes unexpected or non-understood effect: ethnic concentration in a quarter, the spontaneous formation of a potential ghetto.

At this point there may be CE i.e. partial awareness of this ethnic character of a territory; this may becomes a Goal: this is "our" territory! The individual goals may change: one might have precisely the goal of concentrating in an "owned" area with its similar; or one might have a goal of active persecution and expulsion of people of different cultures.

- The awareness of the phenomenon can dis-incentive it (*negative feedback*).

Let's develop the previous example. Suppose that some people of the same cultural group perceive the emerging effect of a ghetto formation and decide of not going or living there because either they are against ghettos or they do not like to live in a ghetto. Depending on the number of such a people this decision might even stop or counter-balance the phenomenon.

Or suppose that some political authority becomes aware of the incoming phenomenon and that is against the formation of ethnic areas in the town; it could try to create incentives , so that people will not go and concentrate there.

We do not believe that it is possible to fully understand and simulate urban dynamics, without considering the representations that the individual agents or groups have about the urban development itself. This does not mean collective decision (although it is a pre-condition for collective decisions), but it means individual decisions about collective affairs and effects.

8   Concluding remarks

When the micro-units of emerging dynamic processes are cognitive agents, a very important and unique phenomenon arises, called Cognitive Emergence (CE). We have argued that:

- CE characterises the theory of Sociological dynamics with respect to other forms of emergence at different level of organisation (ex. physics, biology, etc.);

- CE has a very strong influence on the process of emergence, changing it, and should be taken into account in simulating and modelling social phenomena like demographic or urban phenomena;

- certain important emerging social phenomena, like social norms, or social politics (and political action in general), cannot be explained at all without CE;

- CE has critical consequences on the process of "immergence" i.e. the process through which the macro-level emerging structure or global result 'feedbacks' into the micro-level re-shaping the "elementary" behaviours, since in fact part [11] of the "immergence" process within cognitive agents' populations consists of the (partial) CE of the objective results, i.e. of the agents opinions, theories, and illusions about them.

We believe that it is both possible and important to set out a research agenda for introducing elements of CE in future Agent-Based Social Simulation. If it is true that CE is a crucial process in several social phenomena, this would be an important advantage of Agent-Based simulation, and in particular of the use of cognitive agents that act on the basis of their mental representations, beliefs and goals.

References

[1] Bicchieri, C., 1990. Norms of cooperation. *Ethics*, 100, 838-861
[2] Boehm C. Rational Preselection. From Hanadryas to *Homo Sapiens*: the Place of Decisions in Adaptive Process. American Anthropologist, vol. 80, 2, 1978, 265-85
[3] Brooks, R. A. 1991. Intelligence Without Representation. *Artificial Intelligence* 47, 139-59.

---

[11] No less important are possible forms of reinforcement learning that do not imply any understanding or explicit representation of the phenomenon.

[4] Castelfranchi, C. 1997a. Modeling social action for AI agents. *IJCAI'98*, Nagoya, Japan

[5] Castelfranchi, C. 1997b. Challenges for agent-based social simulation. The theory of social functions. IP-CNR, TR. Sett.97; invited talk at *SimSoc'97*, Cortona, Italy

[6] Castelfranchi, C., 1990. Social power: a point missed in Multi-Agent, DAI, and HCI. In Y. Demazeau and J. P. Muller, *Decentralized A. I.*, North-Holland, Amsterdam, 1990

[7] Castelfranchi C. and Conte R. 1992. Emergent functionalitiy among intelligent systems: Cooperation within and without minds. *AI & Society, 6,* 78-93.

[8] Conte R. and Castelfranchi C. 1995.*Cognitive and Social Action*, UCL Press, London.

[9] Conte R., Castelfranchi C. and Veneziano, V., (in press) The Computer Simulation of Partnership Formation. *Computational and Mathematical Organization Theory.*

[10] Conte R. and Castelfranchi C. (in press) From conventions to prescriptions. Towards a unified theory of norms. *AI&Law.*

[11] Conte R. and Gilbert, N. 1995 . An introduction to *Artificial Societies: the computer simulation of social life*, London, UCL Press.

[12] Crutchfield, P. 1994. The Calculi of Emergence: Computation, Dynamics, and Induction. *Physica* D, 75: 11-54.

[13] Doran, J. Simulating Collective Misbeliefs. *JASSS*, I, 1, 1998

[14] Elster, J. 1982. Marxism, functionalism and game-theory: the case for methodological individualism. *Theory and Society* 11, 453-81.

[15] Gilbert, G.N. 1995. Emergence in social simulation. In G.N. Gilbert & R. Conte (eds) *Artificial societies: The computer simulation of social life*. London: UCL Press, 1995

[16] Haken, H. 1991. *Synergetics, computers and cognition*. Berlin, Springer-Verlag.

[17] Mataric, M. 1992. Designing Emergent Behaviors: From Local Interactions to Collective Intelligence. In *Simulation of Adaptive Behavior 2*. MIT Press. Cambridge.

[18] Memmi, D. and Nguyen-Xuan, A., 1994, Learning and Emergence: An Introduction . LIMSI-CNRS, Orsay, TR.

[19] Purtugaly, J., Benenson, I. Omer, It. 1997. Agent-based simulation of city dynamics. *SimSoc'97*, Cortona, Italy

[20] Sichman J. and Conte, R. DEPNET: How to benefit from social dependence. *Journal of Mathematical Sociology*, 2, 1-17.

[21] J Sichman, Du Raisonnement Social Chez les Agents. PhD Thesis, Polytechnique - LAFORIA, Grenoble,1995.

[22] Steels, L. 1990. Cooperation between distributed agents through self-organization. In Y. Demazeau and J.P. Mueller (eds.) *Decentralized AI* North-Holland, Elsevier.

[23] Virasoro, M.A., 1996. Interview on Complexity, by Franco Foresta Martin. Trieste, SISSA, TR.

[24] Werner E. 1988 Social Intentions. In *Proceedings of ECAI-88*, Munich,1988, WG, 719-723. ECCAI.

[25] Weisbuch G. 1997 Societies, cultures and fisheries from a modeling perspective. *SimSoc'97*, Cortona, Italy

Acknowledgements

These ideas are the result of a common research project with Rosaria Conte. I would like to thank the anonymous referees for their references and criticisms, and Mark D'Inverno and Maria Miceli for their comments. This work has been conduced within the research agreement between the University of Trento and CNR, and within the PSSB-Project for the Simulation of Social Behaviour.

Social Simulation Models and Reality: Three Approaches

Scott Moss[1]

Director, Centre for Policy Modelling, Manchester Metropolitan University, Aytoun
BuildingManchester M1 3GH, United Kingdom
s.moss@mmu.ac.uk
http://www.cpm.mmu.ac.uk/~scott

Abstract. Theories in the social sciences are informed either by sociology or by
economics. That is, they either draw generalizations from verbal descriptions of
social interaction or from mathematical representations of interacting agents as
constrained maximizers. The three models discussed in this paper are not less
rigorous than economic models and, because they are validated relative to a
formal logic rather than mathematics alone, capture much more of the richness
of sociological analysis than does the economics approach. Moreover, each has,
in its own way, been developed to capture salient characteristics of observed
regularities in specific social interactions. Together they exemplify a set of
modelling techniques and an integrated methodology which capture the rigour
and precision of the economist's approach to the social sciences while, at the
same time, capturing the suggestiveness and richness of the sociologist's
approach.

1 Introduction

It is only a little simplistic to say that theories in the social sciences derive either from
sociology or from economics. That is, they either draw generalizations from verbal
descriptions of social interaction or from mathematical representations of interacting
agents as constrained optimizers. The three models discussed in this paper are not less
rigorous than economic models and, because they are validated relative to a formal
logic rather than mathematics alone, capture much more of the richness of
sociological analysis. Moreover, each has, in its own way, been developed to capture
salient characteristics of observed regularities in actual social interactions.

The purpose of this paper is to present these models as examples of an integrated
methodology which captures the rigour and precision of the economist's approach to
the social sciences and while preserving the suggestiveness and richness of the
sociologist's approach to the social sciences. The construction and experimentation of
these models is related explicitly to their validation and verification.

All of the models described below were developed for the analysis of some kind of
policy. One informs marketing policies; the second informs the development of

---

[1] An anonymous referee corrected a mistake in the previous draft and also made several of
constructive (and/or kind) comments. I thank that referee.

organizational structures and channels of communication for containing critical incidents in an ecologically sensitive industry and the third is concerned with communications essential to production and exchange in a transition economy.

The models differ in that the first, concerned with marketing issues, does not attempt to represent agent cognition while such a representation is essential to the other two models. The absence of any representation of cognition in the first model is natural because the behaviour modelled there is concerned with groups of agents acting in particular contexts. In the other models, agents are learning to cope with changing environments so that the representation of learning is a central issue.

2 Model validation and verification

Validation is the process of ensuring that a computer program will not crash and also that it will perform in the manner intended by its designers and implementors. Verification is the process of assessing the goodness of fit to the characteristics of the models empirical referents. These two topics are considered in turn.

Validation

If a program runs without error in any computer programming language, then that program is consistent and sound relative to that language. That is, the program does not generate or entail mutually contradictory statements and it does not generate statements which the language does not support.

If the programming language corresponds to a logical formalism, then any program viewed as a set of statements or sentences which runs in that language will necessarily be sound and consistent relative to that logical formalism. One such language, implemented precisely to capture this feature of programs, is SDML [1] which corresponds to a fragment of strongly-grounded autoepistemic logic [2].

Programming languages generally make it easier to do some things than others. Fortran is optimized for numerical calculation; LISP for functional programming, PROLOG for backward-chaining deduction, and so on. Numerical calculations, functional programming and backward chaining can all be programmed in any of these languages though, as stated, there is a clear correspondence between the ease of programming in any of these styles and the language used.

The immediate advantage of programming in a language which corresponds to a logical formalism is that there are no hidden assumptions in the form of unstated axioms or rules of inference. In SDML, and therefore in the models reported below, each agent is defined on a rulebase and database for each period of time. Every rule in the rulebases and every clause asserted to the databases is sound and consistent relative to strongly grounded autoepistemic logic. This is not to imply that agents are individually represented as a logical formalism as in, for example, BDI agent-based models - only that the whole model is sound and consistent relative to the formalism to which SDML corresponds.

Verification

Verification by comparing model output with statistical data series is too well established to warrant detailed consideration here. Numerical forecasting models have been shown on a number of occasions to be improved by expert intervention ([3],[4],[5]). Integrating statistical forecasting models with rulebases incorporating expert judgement has been shown by Collopy and Armstrong [6] and by Moss, Artis and Ormerod [7] to improve forecasts while making the interventions explicit. Moss, Artis and Ormerod, in particular included in their system an explanations facility which provided the user with a qualitative account of the reasons for interventions by the rulebase. These qualitative reasons were couched in much the same language as that given by model operators for making similar interventions by hand.

There is therefore some precedent for including qualitatively expressed, domain expertise in models of social or economic processes and verifying the qualitative elements of such models through assessment by domain experts. A further development in this area is to integrate well verified theories from other disciplines into our computational models.

One such theory, used in two of the models reported below, is Alan Newell's unified theory of cognition [8]. The theory itself was guided by the requirement to mimic the time required by humans for cognitive acts of varying degrees of complexity. The Soar software architecture[9] is an implementation of the Newell theory which performs well when assessed against the performance of subjects in a large number of psychological experiments.

Cooper, Fox, Farringdon and Shallice[10] showed that Soar is not the only possible implementation of the Newell theory. Moss, Gaylard, Wallis and Edmonds [1] found that reimplementing Ye's and Carley's Radar-Soar model [11] in SDML reduced the number of computations and the time required to run the model by two to three *orders of magnitude* while replicating the Radar-Soar results.

An important issue which remains is the extent to which further verification can be obtained by comparing numerical outputs from simulation models with appropriate statistical data series. The argument of this paper is that the verification of computational models with qualitative elements can and should include empirical tests of the behavioural elements of the models, assessments by domain experts and, when possible, statistical tests of the model's numerical outputs. The descriptions of the three models are used to investigate the limits to such verification for different applications of social simulation.

3 Relating Qualitative Domain Expertise to Statistical Evidence: An Intelligent Market Modelling System

A social simulation model which perfectly matched the criteria of the preceding section would represent individual agent cognition in a manner which was well validated by cognitive theory and independent experimental evidence, which was implemented in a declarative programming language corresponding to a known logical formalism and which produced numerical output series corresponding to some reliable statistical series generated by the modelled social interaction. The model reported in this section lacks the representation of individual cognition. Instead it incorporates the qualitative judgements of domain experts whose professional expertise involves some, usually highly informal and qualitative, assessment of the social conditions in which the customers for branded goods will seek one or another set of perceived brand attributes.

These attributes have no objective meaning. Examples in markets for alcoholic beverages are "special", "traditional", "imported" (though usually produced domestically), "unique". The first models reportedMoss and Edmonds [12] were based on marketing practitioners' assessments of the different reasons why agents might buy such beverages. For one such market, the reasons given were that they sought the "physiological effect" — this was called "functional drinking" or that they were buying drink for social occasions such as parties or for self-reward or because they sought new and distinctive drinks. Moss and Edmonds devised a distribution function relating brand characteristics as specified by the marketing practitioners to the requirements of consumers in different social contexts. They were therefore called context-dependent attribute preference (CDAP) functions. The differences between CDAP functions and the utility functions used by economists is that utility functions relate to individual preferences and purport to mimic the decisions of individuals while CDAP functions describe the mean preferences, the importance of individual brand attributes and their tolerances to deviations from the ideal attributes for all consumers in particular social contexts. For example, the purchasers of beverages for a party will want something special but not very distinctive so that the beverages will be attractive to a wide range of tastes. On the other hand, the same individuals buying beverages to celebrate (say) a career advancement will either want or certainly be more tolerant of distinctiveness in their purchase since it will be primarily for their own enjoyment. Specialness will still be an important consideration. Moreover, some attributes will be more important in some circumstances than others.

The function which captured these *desiderata* is given in fig. 1 where the value on the vertical axis is the contribution to the strength of demand by consumers in the particular context and the horizontal axis is the intensity of the particular attribute associated with a brand. The parameters of the CDAP functions for each brand and each attribute are obtained from the marketing practitioners who enter the values on a five-point Lickert scale. So the presence of an attribute could be taken to be "highly critical", "moderately critical", "not very critical", "hardly matters" or "does not matter". The ideal value is specified in similarly qualitative terms.

The model was constructed so that, given the various CDAP functions, including functions for the parameters "relative price" and "expensiveness", the relative attractiveness of each brand together with the extent to which each brand differed in its attributes from other brands (described as inter-brand distances) was used to determine the market share of each brand given the prices of all brands considered.

In the first generation of these models, the marketing practitioners specified the contexts (social, self-rewarding, functional, *etc.*) and the characteristic ideals, tolerances and criticality of each brand attribute in each context. They also specified their estimates of the proportion of demand accounted for by consumers in each context. The model incorporating these judgements and estimates was then run over a subset of the data available on prices and sales of each brand. Usually, the data was obtained from supermarket scanners for a geographical region such as the UK or metropolitan areas of the United States. A binary search algorithm was used to obtain the best fit in terms of smallest root mean squared errors (RMSEs) or minimum absolute percentage errors (MAPEs). The search algorithm changed the specified sensitivities of consumers to prices, to relative distances among brands and to the relative market strengths implied by the brand attributes relative to the CDAP functions. It then changed the proportions of demands accounted for by consumption in each context and, finally, it changed the ideal values of the various attributes in each context. The result was a set of modifications to the qualitative judgements of the domain experts together with statistical measures of the consistency of those judgements with the numerical data. The RMSEs and MAPEs obtained with these models was in every case far better at tracking market shares over the holdout set (the data not used in parameterizing the models) than were the best ordinary least-squares models.

A second generation of these market models reported by Edmonds and Moss [13] incorporated only the practitioner judgements of the important brand attributes in different markets and used a genetic programming algorithm to identify contexts, the relative importance of each context and corresponding CDAP function parameters to minimize RMSEs. The contexts were not given mnemonic names by the model but they provided an important input to the development by marketing practitioners of their own understanding of the markets that had been modelled.

Clearly, the CDAP functions are entirely procedural and there is no explicit representation of agent cognition in the model. In a model which aggregates context-dependent demands rather than agents, there is no immediate scope for representing individual agents, much less their cognitive processes. However, to extend these models to the development of new markets arising from new product introductions such as the so-called "alcopops" or the development of new classes of consumers in the developing or emerging-market economies, some representation of agent cognition would be essential to model emerging tastes and, so, demands for brand attributes in various social contexts. In such extensions to the models described here, the behaviour emerging from populations of software agents will also yield numerical simulation outputs amenable to statistical comparisons with the empirical record. In such cases, not only will we have well validated representations of cognition but also the models themselves, including their representations of qualitative phenomena, will be as well verified as statistical technique allows.

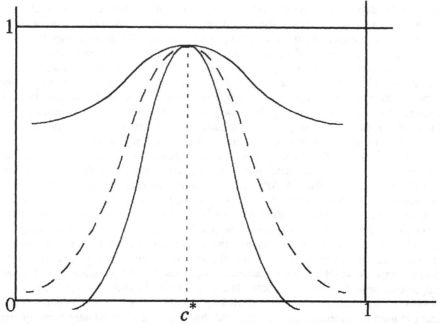

Fig. 1. The three functions (*upper*, *middle* and *lower*) relate the contribution to demand strength for the same ideal value of the brand attribute but are critical to different degrees. Because the values of the functions for each attribute of the brand are multiplied together in determining brand strength, the shallowest function is the least critical because deviations from the ideal reduce the contribution to strength by the smallest amount. The "variance is an index of how tolerant consumers in this social context will be to deviations of actual characteristic intensity from the ideal at c^*

4 Relating Domain Expertise to "Statistical Signatures": Modelling the Management of Critical Incidents

The model described in this section, and reported in detail by Moss *et. al.* [1], was devised to investigate the extent to which improved communication within an organization can prevent critical incidents from becoming full-scale crises. for these purposes, a critical incident is one which threatens to disrupt or actually disrupts normal operations but which is contained and resolved using the existing assets and procedures of the organization. A crisis is an interruption of the activities of the organization sufficiently extensive as to threaten its survival and which cannot be resolved with the existing assets and procedures of the organization.

This notion of the "statistical signature" as used (though not defined) by Arthur *et. al.* [14] seems to be a statement about the visual appearance of a line chart. Though a useful notion, it is not sufficiently well defined to provide as clear a verification of a model as was obtained in the models of the previous section. In wave theory, the statistical signature is a defined on the parameters of the Fourier transform[2]. There is no reason in social simulation to rely on the Fourier transform in particular. The determination of appropriate transforms to evaluate the realism of numerical outputs from social simulation models is not an issue which has yet been addressed by the community. It should surely be on the agenda.

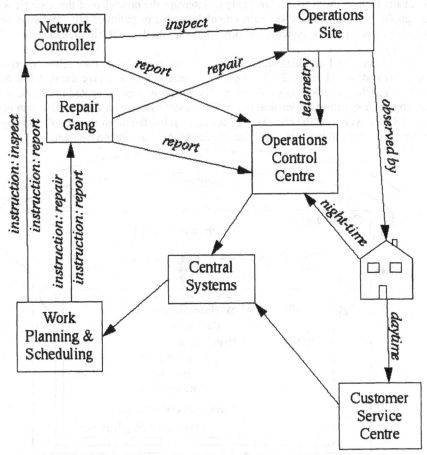

Fig. 2. The labels on the arrows describe the flows of information or actions among the various sources and repositories of information. The operations sites are not staffed and communicate by telemetry with the operations control centre. *Central Systems* and *Work Planning & Scheduling* are computer systems. The rest are of the boxes represent people or the persons grouped as departments or sections

In this section, a model is reported in which the output is characterised by a plausible series of outcomes conforming to the sorts of statistical outputs (though on a much shorter time scale) and qualitative phenomena associated with empirical observations

---

[2]Kathleen Carley acquainted me with this definition.

of the relevant activities of the company being modelled. The model also contains an explicit and well validated representation of agent cognition together with an accurate description of the relevant information systems and organizational structure of an actual company. The model is concerned with the systems and procedures for responding to critical incidents in the water and sewage services industry. Critical incidents include those which are likely to interrupt the provision of these services to the public or which will cause environmental damage or pollution but are containable with the existing assets, systems and procedures normally available to managers of the company.

The systems and organizational structure of the company as they relate to critical incidents is depicted in fig. 2. The cognitive agents in the model are the network controllers and the operations control centre. The model was implemented in SDML with the container structure depicted in fig. 3. The model cycles over days and, within each day, 18 task cycles. At the end of every six task cycles, the network controller changes although the same three controllers are active in the same rotation each day.

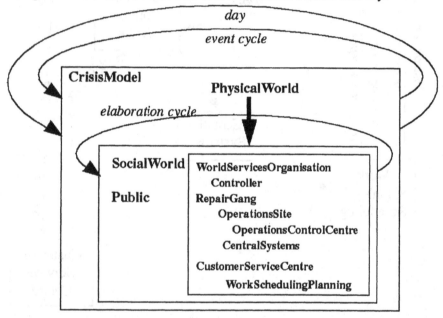

Fig. 3. The agent of type PhysicalWorld decides which, if any, primary events will occur spontaneously according to the specified probabilities and, if any such event does occur, assigns it to an operating site at random. If there are already events occurring at an operating site, the PhysicalWorld propagates consequential events at random from the specified probabilities and assigns them to the appropriate operations site. After the PhysicalWorld determines the state of the world, all of the agents in the social world fire their rules in parallel. They cycle over the time period *elaborationCycle* which is a step in elaborating mental models. After each cognitive of artificially intelligent agent determines any mental models it requires and takes such actions as are implied by those mental models, if is finished for that task cycle

The causes of specific events are not in practice known to the individuals involved in critical incident management until the manifestations of the incident have been observed and the situation analysed. Even then, they might make the wrong diagnosis. For these reasons, it would not be appropriate to post the causes of a particular incident to a database accessible by all agents. Consequently, the relevant clauses are asserted privately by the PhysicalWorld to its own databases and the fact of the occurrence of the event is asserted to the database of the operation site at which the event is to occur. This assertion is achieved by the explicit addressing of the clause *eventOccuring event* where *event* is actually *fire*, *pumpFailure*, *contaminationIncident*, or the like. Once one such event has been allocated to the operating site, then with the appropriate probability all of the consequential events and their consequential events, *etc.* are also allocated at random to that site. In subsequent time frames, secondary consequences are allocated to that site with the specified probabilities in every event cycle while events with those secondary consequences continue. Events, once allocated, remain a feature of the site until they are remedied, if there are remedies, and the events which gave rise to them have been eliminated.

The operating sites (in practice mystified) recognize two kinds of event: telemetric and publicly observable events. When a site has had a telemetered event asserted to its databases, it sends a message stating that it has that event to the OperationsControl-Centre. When a site has a publicly observable event asserted to its databases, it selects at random a percentage of households and asserts the occurrence of that event to their databases. In the simulations reported here, each household of 100 had a 10 per cent probability of being selected to receive such a message. Because the information contained in those assertions refers to actual information which is available selectively, once again explicit addressing of the assertions is appropriate.

The OperationsControlCentre agent forwards the telemetry and public reports to the CentralSystems agent who decides on the actions to be taken. The instructions to take these actions are addressed explicitly to the WorkPlanningAndScheduling agent who allocates the work by addressing the instructions of an agent of type RepairGang or Controller as appropriate. The reports by the repair gangs or controllers are addressed to OperationsControlCentre agent. Repairs take the form of actions asserted by the repair gang to the operating site and then read from the operating site's databases by the PhysicalWorld instance.

The cognitive behaviour in this model is by the instances of type Controller, and the workPlanningAndfScheduling, OperationControl and CentralSystems instances. These agents learn by specifying and testing models which are held on their respective databases as private clauses — *i.e.* clauses which can be asserted by an agent only to its own database and read only by that agent.

Agent cognition: learning as modelling

Agent cognition is represented as a process of model generation and testing within a means-ends framework [15]. This approach has its origins in the cognitive science literature, classically Soar and, in a slightly different vein, Anderson's ACT-R [16]. Both rely on problem-space architectures which are in effect relationships between goals and the sub-goals needed to achieve those goals.

In the critical-incident model, the controllers build models relating remediable causes to consequences. They are assumed to know which individual events are causes of which other individual events but not the associated probabilities. Because of the differing probabilities of some events occurring as direct and immediate results of other events and some occurring as an indirect consequence and at subsequent times, it is not always clear which causal events are the most important to remedy first. The procedure they follow to formulate models is, in the absence of any applicable model, to generate a new model which postulates as a single cause the kind of event which is a cause of the largest number of the other observed events at the same site. For example, early in one simulation run, two events occurred spontaneously at one of the operating sites: an intruder forced entry and the water pressure dropped. As a result, virtually everything else that could happen did happen. These events included a fire, a chlorine leak, a power supply failure, discoloured water, contamination and pollution, low water levels, no water to customers and a water taste or odour. The controller sent to inspect the site concluded that the key event to resolve was the presence of the intruder because among the observed events, more of them had intrusion as a possible cause than they had for any other causal event. The runner-up as the key event was fire which came second to intrusion only because one possible cause of a fire is an intrusion but fires do not cause intrusion.

Table 1. Controllers' endorsements

token	value
noEffect	-1
NewModel	0
ReducedEvents	1
EliminatedAllEffects	2
ReporterdModel	2
specializedModel	3

. The models were used by the controllers to identify and report to central systems the primary cause or causes of an incident. If, as a result of that report, the remedy applied on the instruction of central systems eliminated at least one of the events identified by the model, then the model was endorsed as having reduced the severity of the incident. If the result of applying the model was to eliminate all of the events covered by the model (*i.e.* all of the causes and all of the effects), then there was a further endorsement to that effect.

Endorsements are tokens that have associated numerical values. The agents of type Controller, for example, could endorse their own mental models with any or all of the endorsements in table 1.

Whenever a new model was formulated by a controller, it was endorsed as "new-Model". If the model was used to generate recommend an action or set of actions and, that action having been taken, fewer critical events were reported in the next period, then the model was endorsed has having reduced the number of events. If the incident were ended, then the model would be endorsed as having eliminated all events.

Whenever there was a choice of models to invoke during a critical incident, the best endorsed model was used. The best endorsed model was the one with the highest endorsement value. the endorsement value was calculated as

$$E = \sum_{e_i \geq 0} b^{e_i} - \sum_{e_i < 0} b^{e_i} \qquad (1)$$

where b is an arbitrary number base not less than 1. Each term on the right of equation (1) is the decimal value of sum of the values of the endorsements in number base b. So if the number base is 2, then an endorsement of the third level of importance (such as specializedModel in Table 1) will be twice as important as an endorsement of the second level of importance (such as eliminatedAllEffects Table 1). An endorsement of any level of importance will always be b times as important as an endorsement of the next lower level of importance.

Negative endorsement values are interesting for their magnitude and their negativity so the second term on the left in equation (1) is the sum of the magnitudes of the negative endorsement value in number base b. The magnitude of the negative endorsement values is subtracted from the magnitude of the positive endorsement values to obtain the total endorsement value of the model or other endorsed object.

In the North West Water model, the endorsement base was 1.2. In other models, where a coarser distinction is to be made among endorsement levels, the number base might be (say) 2 or 3.

5 Results

The results of the simulations indicated that communication reduces the time required to resolve critical incidents but that events which are too complex to be resolved by the usual procedures are not affected by improving normal communications. In terms of outputs which correspond to observable statistics, the number of event cycles elapsing from the onset of an incident at an operating site until the absence of any events at the same site was recorded for every incident over the various simulation runs. When network controllers shared their successful mental models, the percentage of incidents resolved within two event cycles increased from some 50 percent to about 60 percent. The proportion that took more more than four event cycles increased from 5.9 to 7.65 per cent on average (with a confidence interval of 0.99). However, model sharing made no significant difference to the percentage of events that took more than two but not more than eight event cycles to resolve.

Now the model was set up to yield very large numbers of incidents of greater and lesser complexity. The relative probabilities of the occurrence of each type of event were obtained from the company concerned. The absolute probabilities were much higher so that statistically meaningful results could be obtained relatively quickly with the available computational resources. By "much higher" here is meant a level which, if realized by the company concerned, would involve loss of licenses, jail terms for the directors and public enquiries. However, we did obtain a "statistical signature" derived from a well validated representation of agent cognition and an empirically accurate specification of company structure, systems and procedures.

Is this statistical signature in some sense accurate? We have no criteria by which to give an answer. The statistical signature, like the stylized fact, is clearly a useful notion but, for the sake of clarity and to give us confidence in the implications of our models, we should pin down what we mean by it in some formal or consistent way. One possibility is to show that models representing the time scales involved more realistically can be parameterized to yield low RMSEs and MAPEs or similar measures of simulation accuracy and that condensing the time scales and either aggregating or reducing the numbers of agents have predictable effects.

6 Relating Emergent Behaviour to Non-Statistical Data: Modelling the Transition Economy of the Russian Federation

Using the same representation of cognition as in the critical-incident model, another statistical signature was sought in a project to capture qualitatively described events in the Russian Federation. In general, it is well known that enterprises are not paying their workers wages and inter-enterprise debt is growing very fast and inflation is substantial. There is an interesting question here in how agents learn to cope in such an unstable social environment. However, one problem with modelling such environments is that we do not find reliable data series emanating from them due, in large measure, precisely to their instability.

The particular period considered was that of the "arrears crisis" of 1992. The time pattern of the growth of inter-enterprise arrears is shown in fig. 4.

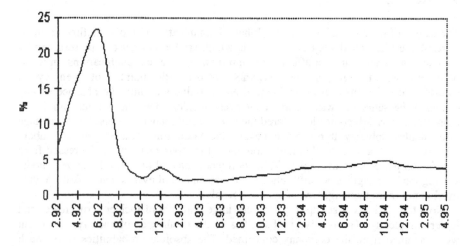

Fig. 4. The percentage monthly growth rate of inter-enterprise debt arrears in the Russian Federation from February, 1992 to April, 1995. Source: The Monthly Bulletin of the Working Centre on Economic Reform of the Government of the Russian Federation, no.1, June 1995, p.2

The evolution of the arrears crisis provides a clear example of how enterprises cope with situations characterised by significant uncertainty. In the Russian case, enterprises were forced to adopt a survival strategy giving priority to existing, recognized constraints. There was no possibility to maximize anything in the framework of those constraints [17]. Indeed, the scale of the accumulated debt and its persistence suggest that enterprises that debt reduction was not a high priority. For one thing, both the liquid assets of enterprises and their debts have been growing simultaneously. The debt became an element of their survival strategy being instrumental in prolonging the existence of a business environment they were accustomed to, i.e., the one governed by soft budget constraints. Because the accumulated bad debt grew out of proportion on the national scale and became commonplace in all industrial sectors, this important business indicator ceased to be seen as a symptom of poor management efficiency.

There were three production sectors: factories producing outputs for both the mining and agricultural sectors, mines producing outputs for the manufacturing sector and farms producing outputs for the agricultural sector itself and for consumption by households. the model cycled over dates and within each date the agents in the economy cycled over communication cycles during which they made offers to buy and agreements to sell products

With this model, it was by no means difficult to generate rapidly growing inter-enterprise debt arrears. In fact, all models had these arrears but the early models had flat price, employment and output series. It was clear that some important aspect of the cognitive processes of enterprise managers was being missed. The mental models of the agents were generated initially by random combinations of actions and implied consequences for the goals of the enterprises which included sales volumes and cash holdings. Because of the extent to which the modelled economy captured the instability of the actual Russian Federation economy, there were no signals from this generate-and-test approach to developing mental models to identify a small set of models which would inform goal-enhancing behaviour. Noise but no signals were being provided by the economy itself.

We then looked for other sources of information which we found in the transactions process itself. The information available to enterprises included the prices it was being charged by its suppliers as well as the supplier's record of filling orders for their outputs. They also knew which of their own customers were paying for the goods they acquired and the prices they charged. A natural hypothesis was that enterprises would imitate the behaviour of the most successful enterprises known to them. The instability and limited information sources and general lack of reliability of information in the economy indicated that the best source of information was observation and the observations were of the suppliers and customers of the enterprise. Paying bills without holdings of cash was not a possibility even if this were a mark of success in customers. But raising prices was always possible and this was the behaviour that emerged. A result of assuming that mental models were informed by direct observation, the simulation model generated a volatile price inflation series with a strong upward trend. It turned out, though we did not have the published inflation figures at the time, that the official price series is indeed marked by the sort of volatility we found. Once again, and acknowledging its defects, the notion of the statistical signature provided a useful target for social simulation modelling.

7 Conclusion

All of the models described here represented agents or their behaviour in ways which were validated independently of the models. The behaviour of consumers in the intelligent market modelling system conforms to the independent views of marketing practitioners. The representations of cognition in the critical-incident and transition-economy models conformed to important, common aspects of the main software

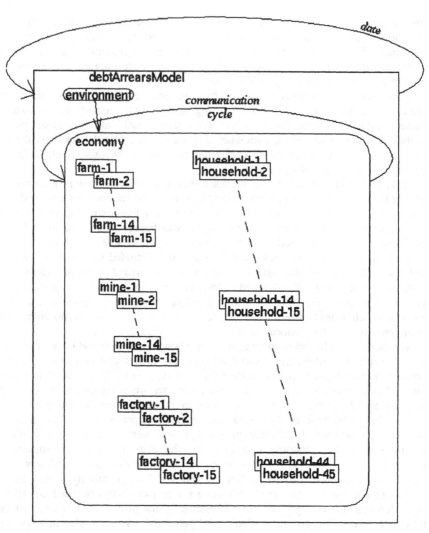

Fig. 5. The structure of the model of inflation and inter-enterprise debt arrears for the economy of the Russian Federation.

architectures corresponding to experimentally verified theories of cognition. In all cases, the models captured empirically observed characteristics of the agents and their environments. The differences in the verification of each model was that we had exceptionally good statistical data with which to verify the market models by means of standard statistical measures whereas the other two models relied on stylized facts and statistical signatures which do not, as yet, entail any clear formal criteria. The reasons were different in each case. In the critical-incidents model, the condensation of time gave us more useful results even though, with some expense, it would have been possible to obtain data about the actual duration of critical incidents. This would be a good case in which to develop techniques for mapping numerical social simulation output into actual statistical data. In the case of the arrears model, there is no reliable statistical evidence so that all we have to rely on are stylized facts. Validation of the model by appeal to domain experts and perhaps survey evidence concerning sources of information and the extent to which enterprise managers rely on different sources of information will doubtless help to validate our representations and verify qualitative model outputs.

Clearly the models discussed in this paper are distinguished by their role as representations of actual systems: markets for given sets of competing brands, a set of functions of a particular company, specified empirical problems facing a much-studied if little-understood economy. There a many models in this vein, though not all are concerned with management and economic issues. Anthropological simulations by Doran and his colleagues or models of emergent behaviour undertaken by Cress at Surrey, or the simulations of the emergence of altruistic behaviour by Pedone and Parisi are examples of relatively abstract social simulation models concerned with empirical phenomena not directly related to either economics or management issues.

Social simulation frequently entails emulation of real phenomena. The point of this paper has been partly to suggest some means of making the links between the models and their empirical referents clear and, where possible, measurable; but more importantly to put a case for the importance of relating social simulation models explicitly to the empirical phenomena. If this case were accepted, then the development of procedures for making those links in ways that avoid mere handwaving and unsupported assertions of relevance is by implication an important thread in the continuing development of the social simulation literature.

8   References

[1] Moss, Gaylard, Wallis and Edmonds (1998), "SDML: A multi-agent language for organisational modelling", *Computational and Mathematical Organization Theory*, in press.

[2] Konolige, K. (1988), "On the relation between default and autoepistemic logic", *Artificial Intelligence*, v. 35, pp. 343-382.

[3] Armstrong, J.S. (1978) Forecasting with econometric methods: Folklore *versus* fact", Journal of Business, v. 51, pp.

[4] Bunn, D. and Wright, G. 1991 "Interaction of judgmental and statistical forecasting methods: issues and analysis", *Management Science*, v.37, pp.501-518

[5] Turner, D.S. (1990), "The role of judgment in macroeconomic forecasting", *Journal of Forecasting*, v. 9, pp.315-345.

[6] Collopy, F. and Armstrong, J.S. (1992), "Rule-based forecasting: Development and validation of an expert-systems approach to combining time-series extrapolations", *Management Science*, v.38, pp.1394-1414.

[7] Moss, S., M. Artis and P. Ormerod (1994), A Smart Macroeconomic Forecasting System. *Journal of Forecasting* 13 (3), 299-312.

[8] Newell, A.(1990), *Unified Theories of Cognition*, (Cambridge MA: Harvard University Press).

[9] Laird, J.E., A. Newell and P.S. Rosenbloom (1987), "Soar: An architecture for general intelligence", *Artificial Intelligence*, v. 33, pp. 1-64.

[10] Cooper, R., J. Fox, J. Farringdon and T. Shallice (1996), "A systematic methodology for cognitive modelling", *Artificial Intelligence*, v. 85, pp. 3-44.

[11] Ye, M. and K.E. Carley (1995), "Radar Soar: Towards an Artificial Organization Composed of Intelligent Agents", *Journal of Mathematical Sociology*, v. 20, pp. 219-246.

[12] Moss, Scott and Bruce Edmonds (1997), A Knowledge-based Model of Context-Dependent Attribute Preferences for Fast Moving Consumer Goods, *Omega*, 25, 155-169.

[13] Edmonds, Bruce and Moss, Scott (1997), "Artificially Intelligent Specification and Analysis of Context-Dependent Attribute Preferences", Centre for Policy Modelling Technical Report 97-28

[14] Arthur, W.B., J. Holland, B. LeBaron, R. Palmer and P. Tayler (1996), "Asset Pricing under Endogenous Expectations in an Artificial Stock Market", University of Wisconsin-Madison, Social Systems Research Institute 9625.

[15] Moss, Scott and Bruce Edmonds (1997), "Modelling economic learning as modelling", Cybernetics and Systems.

[16] Anderson, J.R. (1993), *Rules of the Mind* (Hillsdale NJ: Lawrence Erlbaum Associates).

[17] Aukutsionek, S. (1995) "The Market Reform and Transitional Crisis", *The Russian Economic Barometer*,vol.4, no.1, pp.22-41.

Economic Theory of Renewable Resource Management: A Multi-agent System Approach

M. Antona, F. Bousquet, C. LePage, J. Weber, A. Karsenty and P. Guizol

Cirad, Campus de Baillarguet, BP 5035, 34032 Montpellier cedex, France
{antona,bousquet,lepage,weber,karsenty,guizol}@cirad.fr

Abstract. Multi-agent methodology is used for various purposes, such as distributed solving problem, network management, etc. Multi-agent systems are also used for simulation. Usually, the emergence of macroscopic properties is studied by simulating the behavior of agents and their interactions at a microscopic level. It is a bottom-up approach. Recently emphasis has been placed on the links between the macroscopic and the microscopic levels combining the bottom-up and top down directions. We are currently developing a multi-agent simulator to illustrate and discuss the principles of the economic theory of renewable resource management. The management of renewable resources, from an economic point of view, may be based on public interventions at the macroscopic level or on regulation at the microscopic level. The simulator uses the Cormas environment (Bousquet *et al.*, 1998). First, a renewable resource dynamics is simulated on a theoretical grid. Second, economic agents are represented. Different agents, belonging to different stages of an industry, are represented. Agents collect the resources and others use this resource as an input for transformation. The agents' behavior and objectives are heterogeneous. Economic exchanges are simulated. We reproduce the market-oriented approach (Cheng & Wellman, 1996) which assumes that a general equilibrium sets a global price. We also simulate the trade rules proposed by Epstein and Axtell (1996) in which there is no global price. The aim is to evaluate the differences between these two approaches from the ecological and economic points of view. Third, when an industry is established we simulate various actions at the macroscopic level. Economic theory proposes various interventions such as taxes, quotas, trade and market organization. We test these actions and observe their effects on the society of agents. We observe the quantity of resources, the benefits to the agents, the rent obtained from the macroscopic interventions and how it is shared. This simulator provides a didactic framework to explain economic theory for resource management. Later, we will use it for field study by importing field data. From the computer science point of view, this simulator will be used to test various algorithms for agent coordination. From an economic point of view, it introduces the notion of space and a time frame in the scope of resource management.

1   Introduction

Multi-agent methodology is used for various purposes, such as distributed solving problem, network management, etc. Multi-agent systems are also used for simulation. Usually, the emergence of macroscopic properties is studied by simulating the behavior of agents and their interactions at a microscopic level. It is a bottom-up approach. Recently emphasis has been placed on the links between the macroscopic and the microscopic levels combining the bottom-up and top down directions.

We are currently developing a multi-agent simulator to illustrate and discuss the principles of the economic theory of renewable resource management. The exploitation of renewable resources is a field in which numerous economic analyses have been performed, mainly based on neoclassical theory. This theory considers various categories of decision-making units or economic agents (producers, consumers) whose behavior is characterized by individual decisions directly governed by the scarcity of available resources. Economic agents' preferences are predetermined. This theory was first used to study the way changes in resource scarcity modify the behavior of agents.

Then, using established maximization postulates regarding the behavior of decision-making units[1], proponents of this theory have developed analytical tools to define the conditions of "optimal" resource allocation on the collective level. The decision-making units transmit information regarding their preferences (case of the consumer) or their production (case of the producer) via a system of market prices. Under certain hypotheses, the behavior of decision-making units with specific objectives provides a means to achieve efficient allocation of resources at the collective level. "Market exchanges (...) can, in a certain set of abstract circumstances, lead to a situation of equilibrium in which no further arbitration or reallocation of goods can profit an individual without detriment to another. For all cases of initial resource distribution between the various economic agents, there is a single equilibrium (...) in which all possible gains of the exchange are obtained" (Meuriot, 1987). Economic agents' decisions are then coordinated by the price system mechanism, although there is no direct interactions between agents.

In the case of renewable resources, the same framework is used, integrating an ecological dynamic. In the case of free access of agents to the stock of renewable resources, the stock is too limited to maximize economic net benefits. The analysis examines the difference between the optimal situation, defined on the basis of the same postulates of economic agent behavior, and the situation of free access. A part of the economic literature on resource management is based on a normative approach, which involves determining the measures to be taken to cause the behavior of the producer or harvester of the resource to reach the optimal solution for resource harvesting. This approach calls for the existence of

---

[1] Postulates which are: (i) for the consumer, the maximization of the utility of a basket of goods subject to the constraint of income; (ii) for the producer, maximization of a profit subject to the constraint of production cost.

a system of supervision and control imposed by a central entity (Sutinen, 1993). The measures to be taken comprise a set of management tools, restricting access to resources or increasing the total cost of production.

Using multi-agent simulation models, we study the management of renewable resource and simulate on a spatial frame, two rules of interaction between agents: interaction through a price system and centralized exchanges (i.e. no direct interactions between agents) as described above and direct interaction through local trade (Epstein & Axtell, 1996). Individual agent trade behaviour is based on neo-classical microeconomic theory[2]. Our aim is to observe how the society of agents and the renewable resource react within the two rules of interaction, while implementing tools of management such as quotas and taxes.

The multi-agent model provides a new approach to these questions by making it possible to simulate local interactions between agents and with the environment.

2 Materials and methods

2.1 The industry and the management tools

In the literature on resource management, the most common representation is based on an ecosystem which resource(s) is/are represented globally and on human activities of harvesting the resource, represented in the aggregated form of a cost function. Ecological variables (renewability of the resource and response of the resource to a pressure) and socioeconomic variables such as demand, intensity of resource harvesting[3] and its cost for the different agents are thus synthesized. One can see that in this representation, harvesting of the primary renewable resource is the agents' sole objective. Exchange is secondary and its rules are not specified. Exchange is necessary only to set an equilibrium price upon which the agents' consumption and production patterns will depend. The scale of observation is the ecosystem. The scale of public intervention for the management is the stage of harvesting characterized by uniform agents.

There is a second representation of renewable resource allocation which covers more than the simple primary harvesting of the resource. It considers that the resource is subject to derived demand behaviours of final users and not of its primary harvester. The pertinent observation scale is the industry as a whole. Exchange thus becomes the social behavior to be studied. This representation takes account of the heterogeneity of agents. It also allows to introduce two concepts rarely considered in the first approach : the space of production and the agent location, i.e., the proximity with respect to each other and with respect to the resource to be exploited.

---

[2] i.e. an internal computation of welfare associated with exchanges.

[3] The intensity of harvesting, characteristic of each agent, is expressed in a standardized, summated manner, in terms of harvesting days or level of investment for example.

We chose to represent resource exploitation in the form of an industry, i.e., of agents with various functions ranging from harvesting and transformation of the resource, through to consumption. Representation in the form of an industry makes it possible to formalize exchanges between each of these stages. This type of representation is rarely found in the literature on renewable resources, which most often aggregates all levels in the form of a cost function of the whole industry (Charles, 1988).

Two methods for coordination of resource utilization are considered. In the first, exchange is centralized at each stage, i.e., overall supply and demand for a commodity (resource or transformed one) are aggregated and compared via a central balancing mechanism which establishes a single price applicable to all agents supplying or demanding the commodity.

In the second, exchange is decentralized and the price results from bilateral interactions between suppliers and consumers. The mechanism proceeds according to rules of negotiation between agents from different stages of the industry. There is no single price for the commodity at each stage of the industry. We are moving towards a representation model in which the economy is perceived as a network of agents (Kirman, 1997)(Steiglitz *et al.*, 1996).

The proposed model is relevant to the discussion of management instruments as a set of collective rules, in the case where the viability of a society is dependent upon resources. The economics of resource management describes the way to regulate resource harvesting to ensure optimal allocation, i.e. that which maximizes net benefits and to avoid overexploitation of the resource. It shows that the optimal economic allocation is also optimal according to the ecological point of view . To this end, the behaviour of agents must be modified to achieve this desirable outcome. This is the role attributed to the management tools. There are two main categories of management tools: tools which reduce harvesting intensity or inputs (number of harvesters, harvesting technology, input costs) and those which directly limit the quantities harvested (outputs). Inputs are reduced by imposing a limit on the number of harvesters (licenses) or via taxation of inputs. Outputs are reduced by setting harvesting quotas. The conditions of use and the effects of the various management tools are widely discussed in the case of renewable resource (fishery, forest and water resources).

We will discuss the use of two types of management instrument, taxation and the setting of harvesting quotas in the industry. We will compare how management instruments, specific to a centralized system, can be applied in the case of decentralized one.

2.2 Cormas

The Cormas tool was built using VisualWorks. It uses and proposes Smalltalk as a development language. Cormas is used to develop multi-agent simulation models (Bousquet *et al.*, 1998). Different types of program are available to the modeller.

The first set of programs concerns the agents. The interactions between agents are defined in space or through communication. The environment is represented by a spatial grid. The dynamics of the environment is simulated like a cellular automaton. The principles of the tool are similar to the Sugarscape principles (Epstein & Axtell, 1996). Different types of agent are defined: situated agents, communicating agents and group agents. The situated agent possesses a spatial reference and has a perception range. A communicating agent possesses a mailbox. The group agent is defined as a communicating agent which is composed of other agents or cells of the environment. There are two modes of interaction. The first concerns the way in which space is taken into account. We created a spatial environment containing the situated agents. By space, we mean physical space (territory, zone, region). The space is divided into cells or patches linked by relations of proximity. The cell is the smallest referenced spatial unit[4]. The second type of interaction involves the notions of message and transmission channel. Communicating agents can send each other messages through a channel. The channel models a communication path between agents who are not necessarily neighbors. The channel implements message transmission primitives between connected agents.

The second set of programs concerns overall control of the dynamics. To perform a simulation, it is first necessary to create an artificial world in a given configuration. A space must be created and its dimensions defined, along with the number of agents required and the state in which they exist. The time dynamics of interactions between agents must then be specified. This poses scheduling problems. For this reason, in the case of simulations, we isolate the control part of the dynamics. It is as important for the modeller to define the control as it is to define the behavior of agents. Indeed, the different types of control determine the sensitivity of simulations.

The third set seeks to define an observation of the simulated system. We introduce the concept of viewpoint. Hence, a portion of space or an agent will be observed from different viewpoints. The Cormas user is thus both a modeller and an observer. He must therefore define his observation and implement it, in the same way as he programs agents and the control of dynamics. Three interfaces are proposed: scientific graphs, a grid to visualize all the cells and situated agents. The third layer is a link observer which is used to observe the communicating agents and communication graphs which structure the networks.

3   Experiment : industry model and management tools

3.1   Principles of the model

Two models are developed to handle the question of exchanges within an industry and management tools. These models share common features i.e., a common mode of operation and assumptions regarding agents' behavior. They differs on the exchanges mechanism between stages of the industry.

---

[4] To play its role as a medium, as an intermediary between agents, the patch possesses a list of its occupants and implements primitives which enable communication to take place. It also provides primitives for access to its vicinity (immediate or extended).

A common mode of operation. We draw on a spatially-explicit industry comprising agents at different stages of the industry and whose dynamics we are seeking to represent. So the model includes:

- a space containing a renewable resource,

- agents which have different positions in the industry - from the collector who moves in the space and harvests the resources to the final transformer who is in contact with the world outside the system. Four stages are considered.

- a resource exchanged at various stages of the industry. The renewable resource is exchanged between the harvester and a first transformer, that is to say, on the market between stage 1 of the industry and stage 2. The transformed resource is exchanged on the two others markets.

Common assumptions regarding agents' behavior. The basic assumption regarding the agents' behavior, is based on the individual maximization of a satisfaction function. The agent is a rational agent which tries to improve its welfare. To define how much product an agent will buy or sell, an agent will compute the internal valuations of the commodities it wants to exchange. This valuation is given by the marginal rate of substitution (MRS) of one commodity by another.

As expressed in Epstein and Axtell (1996), the MRS is the ratio of two relative internal scarcities, linked to the need of the resource (called by Epstein and Axtell metabolic cost). In our model, it is assumed that $Money$ is a good exchanged with the resource or the transformed resource, Wm being the willingness to have money. So the MRS is, for each agent, the ratio of money scarcity and resource scarcity. The relative internal scarcity of money, $Money/Wm$, may be explained as the amount of time until death if there is no resource gathering. But it is less clear for the resource. Why does an agent need the resource ? The relative internal scarcity of the resource relies on a capacity concept. For the seller it may be the need to have products to sell in the future. For the buyer it may be the need to have products to make the firm work or to satisfy final consumer's needs.

The differences between the two models. Exchange are represented within the industry via two mechanisms: one centralized and one decentralized, which involve different price setting mechanisms. The first model considers a centralized system of exchange in the form of a price-setting mechanism which simultaneously balances total supply and total demand at each level of the industry. The central mechanism is described by an auctioneer, that sets a price for the commodity available on each stage of the industry. Buyer or seller agents make supply and demand proposals at these prices. The auctioneer compares aggregated supply and demand for each product and revises the proposed prices until supply and demand are matched (Cheng & Wellman, 1996). Through a process of trial and error, a price system is obtained which establishes a balance between global supply and demand for each product on the market.

The second model assumes that prices are established as a consequence of inter-individual relations between agents of each stages. The exchanges are de-centralized and solely dependent on the individual characteristics of the agents.

3.2   Implementation of the industry model

Space, resource and agents.

Space. The agents move on a spatial grid specified by its:
· dimensions. We chose a squared grid comprising 2500 patches.
· boundary conditions. We chose periodic conditions, i.e. a toroidal space.
· spatial connectivity. In our model, each patch has eight neighbors.

Resource. At every point on the lattice there is an amount of resource, denoted R. The resource capacity (denoted K), defined as the maximum value the resource amount can take at this point, and the growth rate (denoted α) is used to establish a rule for resource regeneration after harvesting by the agents (see Eq. 1).

$$R_{t+1} = \min((R_t + \alpha), K) \tag{1}$$

Therefore the *Patch* class has three attributes, their initial values are given in table 1.

Table 1. Patch's attributes

α	K	R Initial value	Equation
0.05	1	0.5	1

Agents. Each agent belongs to a stage of the industry, collects or buys the resource, transforms the resource and sells the transformed resource (see figure 1). In the model four stages are considered. The first stage is the harvester agent which collects the resource. At this stage there is no transformation. At the second stage the agent buys the resource from first stage agents then transforms it and sells it to third stage agents. The third stage agent buys the resource from a second stage agent then transforms it and sells it to a fourth stage agent. The fourth stage is the last stage of the industry. The fourth stage agent buys the resource but does not sell it. This fourth stage agent receives an imposed quantity of money. It represents the exogenous quantity of money introduced into the industry.

Each agent has three variable attributes (state variables):
· *EndIn*, that represents the amount of resource bought by the agent.
· *EndOut*, the amount of resource transformed to be sold.

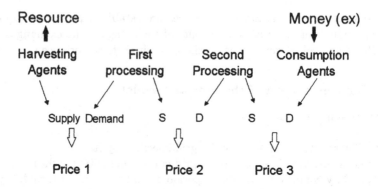

Fig. 1. The stages of the industry

· *Money*, that represents the money possessed by the agent.

The initial values used for all the experiments, and the numbers of the equations defining the update functions of these three attributes are given in table 2.

Table 2. Agent's State Variables

		Agent1	Agent2	Agent3	Agent4
Money	Initial value	2	20	100	180
	Equation	5	6	6	6
EndIn	Initial value	0	5	25	50
	Equation		2	2	
EndOut	Initial value	1	5	25	0
	Equation		3	3	

Each agent has also four constant attributes (parameters):

· The production cost (denoted PC) represents an expense made by the agent at each step. For the first stage agents it represents a kind of movement cost to reach the resource site. For the other stages of the industry, it represents the transforming costs. This cost is a coefficient which will be multiplied by the harvested resource for the first stage agents and the quantity bought for the other stages.

· Wm represents the willingness to have money.

· Wr represents the willingness to have the resource or transformed resource, depending on the stage of the industry.

· The margin, denoted M. This attribute fixes the quantity of money a buyer will keep from a transaction. The value of the margin depends on the stage of the industry.

The initial values of these parameters used for all the experiments are given in table 3.

Table 3. Agent's parameters

	Agent1	Agent2	Agent3	Agent4
PC	0.5	0.4	0.6	0.8
M	1	2	3	4
Wm	2	2	2	2
Wr	2	2	2	2

The agents are given a set of rules. Some rules are shared by the two models, mainly movement rules for the first stage agents, transformation rules and internal valuation rules.

· The movement rule is a kind of gradient search algorithm for the first stage agent : from all the neighboring positions of the patch, find the unoccupied site having the most resource, move to this site and collect all the resource at this new position. At this point the agent's accumulated resource ($EndOut$ attribute) is incremented by the resource collected. We consider that there is no transformation at this stage of the industry. The first stage agent pays a sum equal to the product of its production cost by the harvested resource.

· For the simulation of local trade we assume that there is a transport cost between the localized agents. This transport cost is paid by the seller.

· The transformation rule differs with the stage attribute. The first stage and fourth stage agents do not transform: the quantity sold is therefore the quantity collected (stage1). For the second and third stages, 3/4 of the resource bought is transformed (1/4 is lost, see equation 2). The transformation rate is 2/3, therefore the amount of resource transformed to be sold represents the half of the amount bought (see equation 3).

$$EndIn_{t+1} = qtBought + 0.25EndIn_t \qquad (2)$$

$$EndOut_{t+1} = 0.5EndIn_t - qteSold \qquad (3)$$

· The marginal rate of substitution, which is a characteristic of the agent, gives the agent's internal valuation of the resource. In order to define how much quantities an agent will buy or sell, each agent will compute the marginal rate of substitution (MRS) of commodity for money. An agent's MRS of resource or transformed resource for money is the amount of resource the agent considers to be as valuable as one unit of money. Thus the MRS is computed for each agent, when he is going to sell and when he is going to buy (equation 4).

$$MRS_{\text{seller}} = \frac{\frac{Money}{Wm}}{\frac{EndOut}{Wr}}, \qquad MRS_{\text{buyer}} = \frac{\frac{Money}{Wm}}{\frac{EndIn}{Wr}} \qquad (4)$$

· The fourth stage agent is given a fixed quantity of money at each time step. This quantity of money is calculated to ensure that the industry is in approximately financial equilibrium. Excluding the results of trade, the equations are :

For first stage agents:

$$Money_{t+1} = Money_t - PC.EndIn \qquad (5)$$

For higher stages agents:

$$Money_{t+1} = Money_t + M - PC.EndIn \qquad (6)$$

At this point the resource has been described, the agents and their internal computations have been defined.

How can the prices be computed at each stage ? Two models have already been presented for multi-agent systems: the centralized market and local trade (Cheng & Wellman, 1996) (Epstein & Axtell, 1996) (Kirman, 1997).

The two exchanges protocol.

Centralized exchanges and global equilibrium prices. The principle is an iterative search for a price that leads to a balance between total supply and total demand at each stage of the industry. To do this we represent a new agent, the Auctioneer, who represents the centralizing mechanism. This agent will propose a set of prices to the agents (P_1, P_2, P_3). P_1 represents the exchange price between the first and the second stages, P_2 the exchange price between the second and the third stages, P_3 the price between the third and the fourth stages. Each agent receives the message from the auctioneer and computes its marginal rate of substitution[5] (see equation 4).

The seller, who offers an amount of resource from the *EndOut* attribute, will compare the price proposed by the auctioneer and its marginal rate of substitution. If the price exceeds its MRS the seller offers its amount of resource (*EndOut*).

---

[5] In this implementation of the model, we move away from the strict Walrasian model which assumes that the agent's supply function is a continuous one, as shown in the Cheng and Wellman model (Cheng & Wellman, 1996).

The buyer, who demands an amount of resource, will also compare the price proposed by the auctioneer (denoted PPa) and its marginal rate of substitution. If its MRS exceeds the price, the buyer demands a quantity defined by the ratio $(Money / (PPa + PC))$.

Both the buyer and the seller send a message to the auctioneer with their supply and demand proposals. The auctioneer compares the sum of the supplies and the sum of the demands. As the total demand will never be exactly equal to the total supply, a threshold is defined (total supply/10). As soon as the difference between supply and demand falls below the threshold, the price is fixed and the market is considered as cleared for this price.

Thus the auctioneer agent has three main attributes :

Price, which is a set of three prices, P_1, P_2, P_3.

Threshold, defined as Total supply/10

ClearedMarket, which is a set of three Boolean values that records the already cleared markets and the non-cleared markets.

Local trade. The principle is that each agent is placed in the environment. Even the agents from stage 2, 3 and 4 are situated on the spatial grid. At each time step, the following rules will be computed. The first stage agents harvest the resource. Then the stage3 agents find a buyer and sell their resource, then the stage2 agents find a buyer and sell their resource, then the stage1 agents find a buyer and sell their resource.

To find a buyer, each agent compares the offers from all the agents belonging to the stage next to him. The agent compares its MRS to each buyer's MRS. The price is computed as the geometric mean of the two MRS's. Once this trade price has been defined, the agent computes the expected gain, taking into account the money of the buyer which defines the quantity that can be bought and also the spatial position of the buyer. A transport cost is deducted from the expected gain. Once the best buyer has been defined, the trade occurs, money and resource are exchanged.

Implementation of management tools. Two types of management tools are compared, quotas and taxes. Both assume that a global controller is able to define measures unforceable to the entire society of agents.

Quotas. The global quota is a management instrument which directly affects the environment (the stock of resource). It does not affect the allocations and characteristics of each agent. It provides a means to control the quantities of resource harvested in a given zone and over a given period. When the quantities harvested exceed the global quota, harvesting is stopped.

Here, quotas are simply the definition of a maximum amount of resources harvested by the society of agents. The quota is a global quantity, not redistributed as individual quotas for each agent. In the simulation, resource collection is stopped as soon as the quota is reached. Certain agents may be prevented from harvesting, since the other agents have already reached the global quota. In the simulation, the agents are randomly ordered. It is therefore realistic to believe that the effects of the quotas will not always concern the same agents.

Taxes. The tax has an incentive value as it directly affects the individual behavior of agents. Here, a share of the gain from the sale of product is taken from the seller. This share is proportional to the quantity sold. Each agent thus has a new attribute (*tax*). This tax is levied cumulatively from all agents and it is possible to examine, through simulation, the effects of redistributing the product of this tax at different stages of the industry.

4 Experiments and results

4.1 Experiments

This article presents an initial approach to the use of the simulator. Here, several scenarios are tested. The aim is to compare simulations presenting different management tools[6]. The simulator was calibrated to produce realistic results. For example, we check that the price increases with the different stages of the industry. The initial parameters were chosen very carefully. The initialization of an industry from a resource harvested at the first stage of the industry and from an exogenous quantity of money given at the fourth stage (the final consumer) raises a number of problems. Flows of money and resource will gradually spread within the industry before coherent prices are established.

The default parameter values for all simulations are indicated in tables 1, 2, and 3. There are fifty first stage agents, ten second stage agents, three third stage agents and one four stage agent. At the start of each simulation, each patch has a resource equal to 0.5. The situation is one where resource regeneration is practically equivalent to resource harvesting by agents. We will test the management tools under conditions of limited resources, with eight different scenarios:

1. Local trade without tax nor quotas
2. Local trade and Global quota = 25 resource units
3. Local trade and Tax = 0.2 applied to stage1
4. Local trade and tax = 0.2 applied to stage1 and distribution of the tax on the stage 2
5. Global equilibrium without tax and quotas
6. Global equilibrium and Global quota = 25 resource unit
7. Global equilibrium and Tax =0.2 applied to stage1
8. Global equilibrium and tax = 0.2 applied to stage 1 and distribution of the tax on the stage 2

---

[6] It is not to analyze sensitivity to different parameters.

4.2 Results

S1 Local trade simulation without regulation tools. For local trade simulations, we obtain as many different prices as there are exchanges. The prices gradually converge. On average, after 100 time steps, we obtain $P_1 = 15$, $P_2 = 22$ and $P_3 = 33$. P_3 is highly variable.

On average, 12 units of resource are exchanged between the first and the second stages.

S2 Local trade simulation and global quota. The quotas have a major impact on the first two average prices. $P_1 = 20$, $P_2 = 27$ and P_3 fluctuates around 33. P_3 is very variable. On average, 10 units of resource are exchanged between stage1 and stage2. The global quota reduced the average quantities exchanged at the first stage but the price are higher for stage 1 and 2.

S3 Local trade simulation and individual taxes applied to stage 1. The tax levied remains practically constant around a value of 5. $P_1 = 16$, $P_2 = 23$ and P_3 fluctuates around 33. On average, 10 units of resource are exchanged between stage1 and stage2. The level of average price1 and price2 is reduced with a decrease in the quantities exchanged.

S4 Local trade simulation and redistribution of taxes to stage 2. The values are lower, especially between the stage 1 (harvest) and stage 2 (first transformation). $P_1 = 12$, $P_2 = 18$ and P_3 fluctuates between 35 and 43. On average, 12 units of resource are exchanged between stage1 and stage2.

S5 Global equilibrium without taxes and quota. Here, three prices are fixed, reflecting total supply and total demand at each stage.

In this case, $P_1 = 12.5$, P_2 fluctuates between 15 and 22 and P_3 fluctuates between 22 and 32. The quantities exchanged between the first two stages fluctuate between 12 and 16.

S6 Global equilibrium and global quota. The quotas have an effect on the price structure. $P_1 = 15$, P_2 fluctuates between 17 and 27, P_3 fluctuates between 27 and 38. The quantities exchanged fluctuate between 12 and 14.

S7 Global equilibrium and individual taxes applied to stage 1. The taxes have very little effect on price structure. $P_1 = 12$, P_2 fluctuates between 15 and 22 and P_3 between 22 and 32. The quantities exchanged between levels 1 and 2 fluctuate between 12 and 17.

S8 Global equilibrium and redistribution to stage 2. Redistribution does not change the results.

These results are the first ones of an on-going research. They are consistent with the expected effects of management tools, although some results are to be described more precisely (in term of cost of production and earnings at each stage). But one can make two remarks related to the comparison between the two models and the two management tools.

The first remark concerns the differences between centralized and decentralized systems. The prices are higher in a decentralized system, though the quantities exchanged are larger in a centralized system. This may be due to the introduction of higher production costs in the decentralized system : transports costs are added at each stage of the industry, though they remain very low. More probably, it is due to the pattern of exchanges in a decentralized system, because here, exchange does not necessarily occur at each time step. For example, an agent may not be interested in a price, or a buyer may be short of money. Money or commodities thus may be accumulated by agents not involved in exchange during several time steps.

This is observed most often between stages 3 and 4. We note that the stage4 agent rarely buys from the three seller agents at each time step. Synchronization occurs. A stage3 agent sells its products, thus acquiring money, then proceeds to buy until its turn to sell comes round again. The flows of money and products are irregular. It then sells. This system of rotation, which has repercussions on the earlier stages, takes time to become synchronized, a fact which probably partly explains the considerable variability of price 3. In the decentralized system, local histories of accumulation and past exchanges are very important and we rapidly observe that agents differ from each other.

As regards the effects of the management tools, there is little difference between the two types of model (centralized and decentralized systems). We note that the quotas have a major impact, in the form of increased prices, in both types of simulation (see figure 2 and 3). Taxes play a very minor role. In other experiments, we will attempt to increase the amount of taxes or we will vary the stages at which the tax is imposed, for example between stages 3 and 4, at the downstream end of the industry. Tax redistribution has no effect on a centralized system. On the other hand, we observe an effect on the decentralized system, i.e., a decrease in prices P_1 and P_2. Stage1 agents accumulate less money if the tax is redistributed. Conversely, the agents of the two other stages have a much higher income. In next simulations, we will also test different redistribution scenarios.

5 Discussion

In economics, this experiments provide an interesting means to understand how macroscopic (global) interventions, i.e., management tools, are able to affect simulated interactions at the microscopic (individual level). We are interested in simulating how observable changes in the opportunities and constraints char-

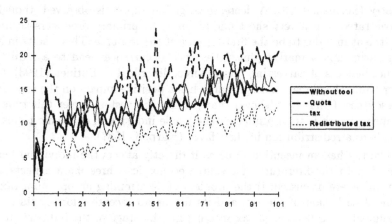

Fig. 2. Local Trade. Evolution of the mean prices between stage1 and stage2 agents

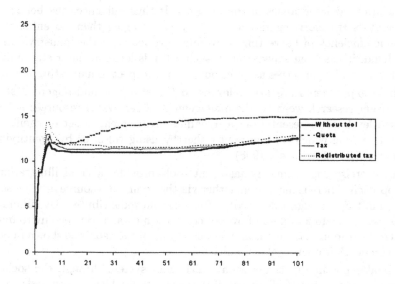

Fig. 3. Global equilibrium. Evolution of the global price between stage1 and stage2 agents

acterizing the environment of the decision-making units (consumers, producers) modify the behavior of these units.

The effects of quota are documented in the literature concerning fishing and forestry (Sutinen, 1993). A decrease in global supply is observed, though it is concentrated over a very short period since the primary producers accumulate investment in order to be the first to harvest the resource. This results in a price irregularity and a market glut. These two occurrences lead to a reduction in the net benefits of harvesting the resource, described by Sutinen (1993). On the other hand, the global quota probably has a positive impact on the conservation of resources. It has been shown that primary harvesters prefer this type of instrument, which is sub-optimal for the whole industry in economic terms, since it leads to a redistribution in their favor (Karpoff, 1987).

The tax has an incentive value as it directly affects the individual behavior of agents. In the literature of resource economics, three main aspects of this instrument are discussed: i) the problem of determining an optimum tax level; ii) the distribution of the tax and its use as an incentive for agents or as an instrument for collection of tax income; iii) the stage of the industry at which the tax has the best incentive effect.

The payment of a tax at the first stage of the industry is recommended by the World Bank in the field of forestry (Grut et al., 1990). Whether it concerns the area harvested or the quantity of resource, it increases the cost of access to the resource and hence reduces the income received by the harvester while raising prices at later stages in the industry. It thus influences the behavior of all operators transforming the resource by encouraging them to enhance the economic efficiency of harvesting or to minimize losses in the industry. On the other hand, it has been shown that if such a tax is levied at later stages in the industry, its no longer serves as an incentive with respect to harvesting practices.

These experiments are also relevant to the study of multi-agent systems. Our current research work on the management of renewable resources is based on three levels of representation: a dynamic environment, a set of agents and a collective level which we represent either by using rules, or by agentifying a group level (Rouchier et al., 1998).

The exercise concerning management tools provides a good illustration of this approach. There is mediation, either via the common resource or via a social system built up through the activity of agents and redistributed. By simulating quotas, we simulate a system of overall control which acts via the environment. Through its response, the environment acts upon all the agents as shown in other experiments (Bousquet et al., submitted).

It is also possible to structure a multi-agent system through the social or economic organization of all agents. Taxes are a tool which corresponds to this approach. The product of all agents is globalized and then redistributed. Some authors, such as Parisi (1997), have already begun to study the redistribution relation. We have already seen that the types of environmental responses are important; likewise the types of response of the collective entity (forms of redistribution) also appear to be of major significance.

In both cases, with quotas or taxes, there is a circular relation between the agents and either the environment or a collective entity which, in this case, manages a quantity of money. This simulator opens up numerous avenues of research. One aspect which may be relevant to the multi-agent systems and also to environmental economics is the study of how agents act in response to their perception of the collective entity. How will an agent react if it knows it is to be taxed and if it knows the modes of redistribution of the product of the tax ? How will this affect the agent's action? If the agent modifies its action by behaving differently (more or less harvesting, more or less transformation) this will transform the micro-macroscopic relation. A second aspect relevant to environmental economics and management is the identification of what circumstances are necessary in order management tools are more likely efficient both in economical and ecological terms. What is the role played by the structure of the industry, the location of the industry, the nature of exchange relationships ?

We may assume that in reality, systems are not so decentralized or so centralized. A seller agent knows approximately how much its neighbors sell, a buyer adjusts and compares the sellers' prices. However, the spatialization and heterogeneity of agents of the industry will introduce a certain degree of diversity.

References

Bousquet, F., Bakam, I., Proton, H., & LePage, C. 1998. Cormas: Cmmon-Pool Resources and Multi-Agent Systems. *Lecture Notes in Artificial Intelligence*, **1416**, 826–837.

Bousquet, F., Duthoit, Y., Proton, H., LePage, C., & Weber, J. submitted. Tragedy of the commons, co-viability of the environment and the society. *Adaptive Behavior*.

Charles, A.T. 1988. Fishery socioeconomics : a survey. *Land economics*, **64**, 276–295.

Cheng, J.Q., & Wellman, M.P. 1996. *A convergent distributed implementation of General Equilibrium*. Tech. rept. Santa-Fe Institute.

Epstein, J., & Axtell, R. 1996. *Growing Artificial Societies : Social Science from the bottom up*. Complex Adaptive Systems Series. Cambridge and London: MIT Press.

Grut, M., Gray, J.A., & Egli, N. 1990. *Forest pricing and concession policies: managing the high forests of West and Central Africa*. Tech. rept. 143. World Bank.

Karpoff, J. 1987. Suboptimal controls in common resource mangement, the case of Fishery. *J. Polit. Econ.*, **95(1)**, 179–184.

Kirman, A. 1997. The economy as an evolving network. *Journal of Evolutionnary economics*, **7**, 339–353.

Meuriot, E. 1987. *Les modèles bio-économiques d'exploitation des pêcheries, démarches et enseignements.* Rapports économiques et juridiques 4. IFRE-MER.

Parisi. 1997. What do to with a surplus. *Lecture Notes in Economics and Mathematical Systems,* **456**.

Rouchier, J., Barreteau, O., Bousquet, F., & Proton, H. 1998. Evolution and co-evolution of individuals and groups in environment. *In: Proceedings of the Third International Conference on Multi-Agent Systems.* AAAI Press.

Steiglitz, K, Honig, M., & Cohen, L. 1996. A Computational Market Model Based on Individual Auction. *In:* Clearwater, S. (ed), *Market-Based Control. A Paradigm for Distributed Resource Allocation.* World Scientific.

Sutinen, J. 1993. *Cadre d'étude sur la gestion efficiente des ressources biologiques de la mer.* AGR/FI/EG 93 (3). OCDE.

ABCDE: Agent Based Chaotic Dynamic Emergence[*]

Pietro Terna

Università di Torino, Dipartimento di scienze economiche e finanziarie G.Prato, corso
Unione Sovietica 218bis, 10134 Torino, Italia
terna@econ.unito.it

Abstract. This paper concerns agent based experiments in the field of
negotiation and exchange simulation. A computer simulation environment is
built, showing the emergence of chaotic price sequences in a simple model of
interacting consumers and vendors, both equipped with minimal rules.
"Swarm" is the framework of the model (www.santafe.edu/projects/swarm), a
simulation tool with a strong object oriented structure, also very useful to
separate in a clear way the model level from the level of the observer. Swarm
if fully programmable in Objective C, with many powerful libraries, aimed at
modeling the objects and the schedules of our experiments, with lists and
arrays where necessary. Finally we introduce a tool (Cross Target method:
CT), useful in building artificial laboratories, for experiments with learning,
self-developed consistency and interaction of agents in artificial worlds, in
order to observe the emergence of complexity without *a priori* behavioral
rules: The perspective of our work is that of developing CT within the Swarm
framework to replicate the ABCDE experiment in this light-rules or no-rules
context.

1 Introduction

This paper starts with the definition of agent based models and then introduces the
main problems arising in their construction, mainly focusing on software problems.
Section 2 "Agent based models" underlines the usefulness of agent based models in
the social science perspective, also focusing on the main computational problems
(memory management and time management in simulation); Section 3, "The Agent
Based Chaotic Dynamic Emergence (ABCDE)", introduces a small specific
application of those techniques, modeling a consumer-vendor interaction experiment
where chaos emerges as a side effect of the agents' behavior, in a spontaneous way,
i.e. avoiding the use of equations to produce apparently non-deterministic data series
when parameters lie in a particular range; Section 4, "The Self-development of
Consistency in Agents' Behavior" introduces artificially intelligent agents founded

---

[*] This research has been supported by grants from the Italian Ministero dell'Università e della Ricerca scientifica e tecnologica, inside the project
"Intermediazione finanziaria, funzionamento dei mercati ed economia reale".

upon algorithms that can be modified by a trial and error process without *a priori* behavioral rules.

The project is that of developing, in a parallel way, models built upon simple agents interacting in the Swarm context with light rules (without the CT technique) and with soft rules (mainly, the quest for consistency in the agent's behavior) always in the Swarm context with the CT technique.

2 Agent based models

The starting point is the choice on model foundations: If we choose the agent based model paradigm we enter a wide unexplored world where methodology and techniques are largely "under construction."

2.1 An Overview

An interesting overview comes from the following Web sites: Syllabus of Readings for Artificial Life and Agent-Based Economics[1]; Web Site for Agent-Based Computational Economics[2]; Agent-Based Economics and Artificial Life: A Brief Intro[3]; Complex Systems at the University of Buenos Aires[4]; Computational Economic Modeling[5]; Individual-Based Models[6]. With respect to social simulation we refer also to Conte et al. [1] and, in economics, to Beltratti et al. [2]; also of interest is The Complexity Research Project[7] of the London School of Economics and Political Science.

At present, the best plain introduction to agent based modeling techniques is in Epstein and Axtell [3]. For a thoughtful review of the book, see Gessler [4]. As Epstein and Axtell (Cap. 1) note:

"Herbert Simon is fond of arguing that the social sciences are, in fact, the hard sciences. For one, many crucially important social processes are complex. They are not neatly decomposable into separate subprocesses--economic, demographic, cultural, spatial--whose isolated analyses can be aggregated to give an adequate analysis of the social process as a whole. And yet, this is exactly how social science is organized, into more or less insular departments and journals of economics, demography, political science, and so forth (...)"

"The social sciences are also hard because certain kinds of controlled experimentation are hard. In particular, it is difficult to test hypotheses concerning

---

[1] http://www.econ.iastate.edu/tesfatsi/sylalife.htm

[2] http://www.econ.iastate.edu/tesfatsi/ace.htm

[3] http://www.econ.iastate.edu/tesfatsi/getalife.htm

[4] http://www.cea.uba.ar/aschu/complex.html

[5] http://zia.hss.cmu.edu/econ/

[6] http://hmt.com/cwr/ibm.html

[7] http://www.lse.ac.uk/lse/complex/

the relationship of individual behaviors to macroscopic regularities, hypotheses of the form: If individuals behave in thus and such a way--that is, follow certain specific rules--then society as a whole will exhibit some particular property. How does the heterogeneous micro-world of individual behaviors generate the global macroscopic regularities of the society?"

"Another fundamental concern of most social scientists is that the rational actor--a perfectly informed individual with infinite computing capacity who maximizes a fixed (nonevolving) exogenous utility function--bears little relation to a human being. Yet, there has been no natural methodology for relaxing these assumptions about the individual."

"Relatedly, it is standard practice in the social sciences to suppress real-world agent heterogeneity in model-building. This is done either explicitly, as in representative agent models in macroeconomics (Kirman, [5]), or implicitly, as when highly aggregate models are used to represent social processes. While such models can offer powerful insights, they "filter out" all consequences of heterogeneity. Few social scientists would deny that these consequences can be crucially important, but there has been no natural methodology for systematically studying highly heterogeneous populations."

"Finally, it is fair to say that, by and large, social science, especially game theory and general equilibrium theory, has been preoccupied with static equilibria, and has essentially ignored time dynamics. Again, while granting the point, many social scientists would claim that there has been no natural methodology for studying nonequilibrium dynamics in social systems."

The response to this long, but exemplary, quotation, is social simulation and agent based artificial experiments. According to the Swarm documentation[8] we introduce a general sketch about how one might implement an experiment in the agent based modeling field.

2.2 Tools useful in Social Sciences: Design and Characteristics

An idealized experiment requires, first, the definition of: (i) the computer based experimental procedure and (ii) the software implementation of the problem.

The first step is that of translating the real base (the physical system) of our problem into a set of agents and events. From a computational point of view, agents become objects and events become steps activated by loops in our program. In addition, in a full object oriented environment, time steps are also organized as objects.

We can now consider three different levels of completeness in the structure of our software tools.

– At the lowest level (i.e., using plain C) we have to manage both the agent memory structures (commonly with a lot of arrays) and the time steps, with loops (such as

---

[8] http://www.santafe.edu/projects/swarm/

"for" structures) driving the events; this is obviously feasible, but it is costly (a lot of software has to be written; many "bugs" have to be discovered);
- At a more sophisticated level, employing object oriented techniques (C++, Objective C, etc.), we avoid the memory management problem, but we have nevertheless to run time steps via the activation of loops;
- Finally, using a high level tool such as Swarm, we can dismiss both the memory management problems and the time simulation ones; in high level tools, also the events are treated as objects, scheduling them in time-sensitive widgets (such as action-groups). The ABCDE model (see Sec. 3) introduced below is built according to these design techniques.

Obviously, there are many alternatives to a C or Objective C environment. More generally, we have to consider the multiplicity of tools aimed at developing agent based software applications. For an idea of these tools, visit the following "no name" Web sites: www.ececs.uc.edu/~abaker/JAFMAS/compare.html and the highly interesting Linux AI/Alife mini-HOWTO[9].

For a more complete discussion of this subject and for a discussion about agent based models and intelligent agents, see Terna [6].

In Appendix we report a direct reference to the Swarm environment, used in this work for the ABCDE experiment; the CT technique also (see Sec. 4) is introduced here in the perspective of rewriting it with Swarm.

3 The Agent Based Chaotic Dynamic Emergence (ABCDE)

This example concerns an agent based experiment in the field of negotiation and exchange simulation. One can replicate or modify the experiment applying Swarm (1.0.5 or above) to "make" an executable file from the content of the archive compressed file abcde-#_of_experiment_version-#_of_Swarm_version.tgz[10].

3.1 Chaos from Agents

The experiment shows the emergence of chaotic price sequences in a simple model of interacting consumers and vendors, both equipped with minimal rules.

Mainstream chaos supporters look for sets of equations that produce apparently non-deterministic data series when parameters lie in a particular range. But what about the plausibility of these synthetic constructions? In the ABCDE model we are not seeking to produce chaos: it emerges as a side effect of the agents' behavior.

---

[9] http://www.ai.uga.edu/~jae/ai.html
[10] This archive file can be obtained via email form the author or downloaded from the link contained in Ref. [6]; finally, in the future, may be from the "anarchy" archive in the Swarm site.

3.2 ABCDE Structure

There are ten consumers and ten vendors; in other words, we have twenty agents of two types. Each agent is built upon an object, i.e. a small Objective C program, capable of reacting to messages, for example deciding whether it should buy at a specific offer price. Both agents-objects-consumers and agents-objects-vendors are included in lists; the simulation environment runs the time, applying at each step the actions included in a temporal object (an action-group) and operates with the agents sending messages to their lists. There is a shuffler mechanism to change the order in which the agents operate and to establish random meetings of the members of the two populations.

At every simulation step (i.e., a tick of the simulation clock), artificial consumers look for a vendor; all the consumers and vendors are randomly matched at each step. An exchange occurs if the price asked by the vendor is lower than the level fixed by the consumer. If a consumer has not been buying for one or more than one step, it raises its price level by a fixed amount according to the counter rule and the sensitivity parameter introduced below. It acts in the opposite way if it has been buying and its inventory is greater than one unit.

A simulated vendor behaves in a symmetric way (but without a sensitivity parameter): it chooses the offer price randomly within a fixed range. If the number of steps for which it has not been selling is greater than one, it decreases the minimum and maximum boundaries of this range, and vice versa if it has been selling.

In detail, we have the following steps:
- At each time step t, each artificial consumer (an agent) meets an artificial vendor (another agent), randomly chosen.
- The vendor fixes its selling price, randomly chosen within a small range.
- The consumer accepts the offer only if the selling price falls below its buying price level.
- At each time step t each agent (consumer or vendor) increases its transaction counter by 1 unit, if it makes a transaction; it decreases it by 1 unit in the opposite case.
- When their counters are less than -1 (sensitivity = 0) or less equal than -1 (sensitivity = 1), *consumers* change their internal status: they raise their buying price by a fixed amount.
- When their counters are greater than 1 (sensitivity = 0) or greater equal than 1 (sensitivity = 1), *consumers* change their internal status in the opposite direction: they reduce their buying price by a fixed amount.
- When their counters are less than -1, *vendors* change their internal status: they reduce, by a random amount (from 0 to a fixed value) both the limits of the range within which they choose the selling price.
- When their counters are greater than 1, *vendors* change their internal status in the opposite direction: they raise, by a random amount (from 0 to a fixed value) both the limits of the range within which they choose the selling price.

3.3 Running the ABCDE Experiment

In all the experiments, the result is that the mean price behavior emerges as cyclical, with chaotic transitions from one cyclical phase to another. From a methodological point of view there are two kinds of emergence.

- Unforeseen emergence: While building the simulation experiment, we were only looking for the simulated time required to obtain an equilibrium state of the model with all the agents exchanging nearly at each time: The appearance of a sort of cyclical behavior was unexpected;
- Unpredictable emergence: Chaos is obviously observable in true social science phenomena, but it is not easy to make a reverse engineering process leading to it as a result of an agent based simulation.

We have now to define the parameters used in the eight experiments reported in the Figures of this paragraph. Parameters: "theLevel" is the initial price below which consumers buy (it changes independently for each consumer while the simulation evolves); "agentNumber" is the number of consumers and vendors; "minStartPrice" and "maxStartPrice" are the initial limits within which vendors choose their selling price (they change independently for each vendor while the simulation evolves); "use_printf" is a technical parameter to print internal values; the "reactivityFactor" is a multiplying factor that enhances the fixed values used by consumers and vendors to modify their prices or range of prices; "sensitivity" is zero or one, with the meanings introduced above.

In Table 1 we introduce the parameters used in the experiments presented in the following Figures.

Parameters and Experiments	Fig. 1	Fig. 2	Fig. 3	Fig. 4	Fig. 5	Fig. 6	Fig. 7	Fig. 8
theLevel	50	50	50	50	25	25	25	25
agentNumber	10	10	10	10	10	10	10	10
minStartPrice	45	45	45	45	70	70	70	70
maxStartPrice	55	55	55	55	90	90	90	90
use_printf	0	0	0	0	0	0	0	0
reactivityFactor	1	1	3	3	1	1	3	3
sensitivity	0	1	0	1	0	1	0	1
standard Swam random seed	yes	yes	yes	yes	yes	yes	yes	yes

Table 1. Parameters of the experiments reported in Fig. 1 to 8.

In the experiments reported in Fig.1 to Fig.4, the starting points are a buying price level of 50 (on a scale from 0 to 100) and a selling price range from 45 to 55 on the same scale. Initially, all the consumers and vendors have the same parameters, but during the simulation, they evolve on an individual basis. One could say that the memory of the system lies in the consumers/vendors random interaction.

The series reported in the Figures are the mean of global prices (all prices offered in each day or cycle) or the min. or max. within global prices. (The "alternative way" of the title is related to an internal calculus problem) [11].

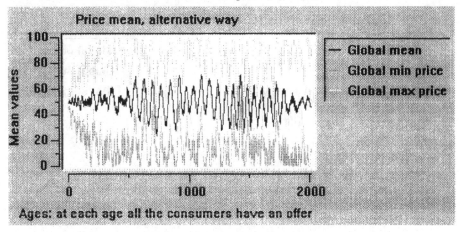

Fig. 1. Starting with a balanced situation, low reactivity and low sensitivity.

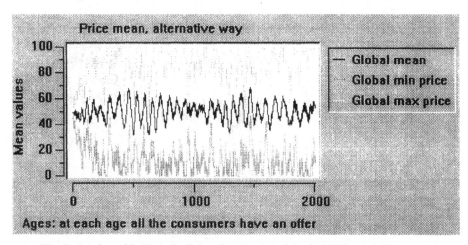

Fig. 2. Starting with a balanced situation, low reactivity and high sensitivity.

The experiments reported in Fig.1 and Fig.2 start form the balanced situation described at the beginning of the paragraph. With a low reactivity factor, the presence or the absence of the sensitivity parameter in the behavioral choices of the consumers only changes the amplitude of the fluctuations, but has no effect on the chaotic appearance of the global mean of the prices offered in each cycle.

Technically: the FFT[12] of the series of data shows only one peak, related to the constant value; Lyapunov exponents are in the range 0.6-0.7 and both capacity and

[11] Technical note, to replicate the experiment use abcde-1_0_1-1_1 or abcde-1_0_2-1_2.

correlation dimensions are less than 5. In Fig. 2 data, in the range 501-1000, a strange attractor emerges in the singular value decomposition space. For a discussion concerning the meaning of chaos in these experiments, see Sec. 3.4.

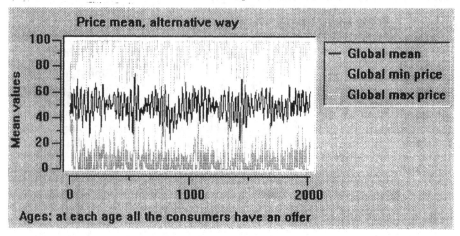

Fig. 3. Starting with a balanced situation, high reactivity and low sensitivity.

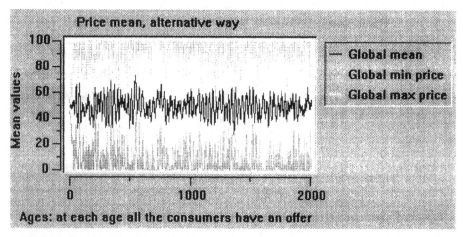

Fig. 4. Starting with a balanced situation, high reactivity and high sensitivity.

Also the experiments reported in Fig.3 and Fig.4 start form the balanced situation described at the beginning of the paragraph, but with a high reactivity factor, which improves the cyclical effect; the presence (Fig. 4) of the sensitivity parameter reduces the amplitude of the fluctuations; anyway, chaos appears.

---

[12] Fast Fourier Transformation.

The FFT shows the same results as above; Lyapunov exponents are in the range 0.5-0.8 and both capacity and correlation dimensions are less than 5. Data in Fig. 4 shows decidedly a strange attractor in the singular value decomposition space.

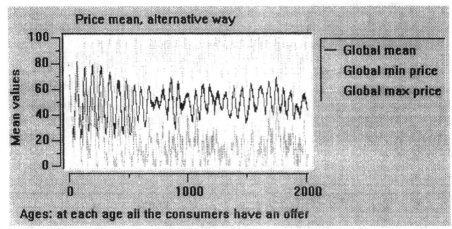

Fig. 5. Starting with an unbalanced situation, low reactivity and low sensitivity.

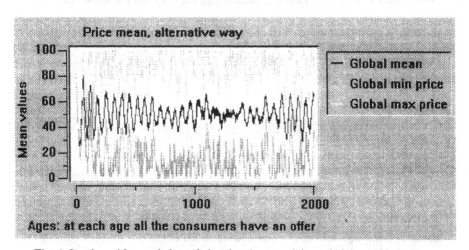

Fig. 6. Starting with an unbalanced situation, low reactivity and high sensitivity.

In the experiments reported in Fig.5 to Fig.8, the starting points are a buying price level of 25 (on a scale from 0 to 100) and a selling price range from 70 to 90 on the same scale; so we are in an unbalanced situation. With a low reactivity factor, in Fig.5 and Fig.6, chaos emergence is evident and the effect of the sensitivity parameter reinforces it.

The FFT shows the same results as above; Lyapunov exponents are in the range 0.4-0.5 and both capacity and correlation dimensions are less than 5.

With a high reactivity factor, in Fig.7 and Fig.8, cyclical effects appear to be more strong than the chaos emergence; anyway, introducing the sensitivity parameter, in Fig.8, chaos appears again, showing also a strange attractor (Fig. 8) in the singular value decomposition space.

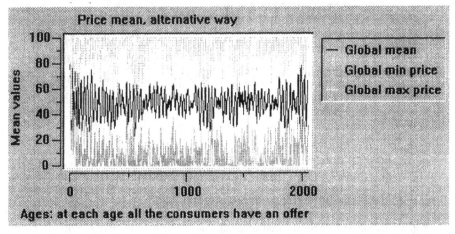

Fig. 7. Starting with an unbalanced situation, high reactivity and low sensitivity.

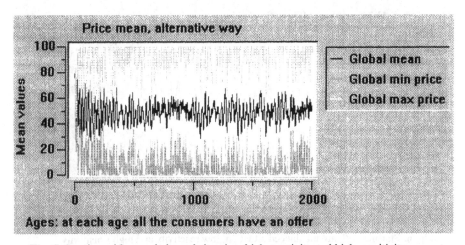

Fig. 8. Starting with an unbalanced situation, high reactivity and high sensitivity.

The FFT shows the same results as above; Lyapunov exponents are in the range 0.4-0.5 and both capacity and correlation dimensions are less than 5.

3.4 A general comment about chaos

A general comment about chaos in these experiments: we are here in presence of endogenous chaos, emerging from agent interaction. The price memory is diffused in the agents, having a collective effect of synchronization or heterogeneous behavior in the agents' reaction to the exchange prices. Our model is not considering spatial coordinates, so an agent can bargain with another; with that the introduction of spatial distances and, as a consequence, of behavioral habitudes in agents' matches, the complexity of our structure can increase.

Chaos is here considered as random appearance of deterministic data; the measures reported above proof that our series are also technically chaotic; we know, by construction, that here chaos - or randomness - is not related to a well specified structure, but to collective behavior, which we are not able to describe ex ante in an analytical form. This is a form of chaos interesting for social sciences: the agent based chaotic dynamic emergence, or ABCDE.

4 The Self-development of Consistency in Agents' Behavior

With the purpose of generalizing the result obtained above, reducing the role of the user defined rules and, more generally, as a future perspective of work both in the agent based and in the Swarm contexts, in this Section we introduce the use of intelligent agents founded upon algorithms that can be modified by a trial and error process without *a priori* behavioral rules.

We remind that the project is that of developing, in a parallel way, models built upon simple agents interacting in the Swarm context with light rules (without the CT technique, as in Section 3) and with soft rules (mainly, the quest for consistency in the agent behavior) always in the Swarm context with CT technique.

In a soft rule context it is highly interesting also to replicate classical experiments built upon human agents, such as Chamberlin [7] and Smith [8], [9].

4.1 The Cross-Target (CT) Idea

We introduce the following general hypothesis (GH): an agent, acting in an economic environment, must develop and adapt her capability of evaluating, in a coherent way, (1) what she has to do in order to obtain a specific result and (2) how to foresee the consequences of her actions. The same is true if the agent is interacting with other agents. Beyond this kind of internal consistency (IC), agents can develop other characteristics, for example the capability of adopting actions (following external proposals, EPs) or evaluations of effects (following external objectives, EOs) suggested from the environment (for examples, following rules) or from other agents (for examples, imitating them). Those additional characteristics are useful for a better tuning of the agents in making experiments.

To apply the GH, we are at present using a tool employing artificial neural networks; the original program is developed in C language and will be transferred in the Swarm context. We observe, anyway, that the GH can be applied using other algorithms and tools, reproducing the experience-learning-consistency-behavior cycle with or without neural networks.

A general remark: in all the cases to which we have applied our GH, the preliminary choice of classifying agents' output in actions and effects has been useful (1) to clarify the role of the agents, (2) to develop model plausibility and results, (3) to avoid the necessity of *a priori* statements about economic rational optimizing behavior (see, for some examples, Beltratti et al. [2] and Terna [10]).

Economic behavior, simple or complex, can appear directly as a by-product of IC, EPs and EOs. To an external observer, our CT agents are apparently operating with goals and plans. Obviously, they have no such symbolic entities, which are inventions of the observer. The similarity that we recall here is that the observations and analyses about real world agents' behavior can suffer from the same bias. Moreover, always to an external observer, CT agents can appear to apply the rationality paradigm, with maximizing behavior.

Following the GH, the main characteristic of these CT agents is that of developing internal consistency between what to do and the related consequences. Always according to the GH, in many (economic) situations, the behavior of agents produces evaluations that can be split in two parts: data quantifying actions (what to do) and forecasts of the outcomes of the actions.

4.2 The Cross-Target Method

Choosing the artificial neural network tool to develop CT technique, we specify two types of outputs of the artificial neural network and, identically, of the CT agent: (1) actions to be performed and (2) guesses about the effects of those actions.

Both the targets necessary to train the network from the point of view of the actions and those connected with the effects are built in a crossed way, originating the name Cross Targets. The former are built in a consistent way with the outputs of the network concerning the guesses on the effects, in order to develop the capability to decide actions close to the expected results. The latter are similarly built with the outputs of the network concerning the guesses of the actions, in order to improve the agent's capability of estimating the effects emerging from the actions that the agent herself is deciding[13].

CTs, as a fulfillment of the GH, can reproduce economic subjects' behavior, often in internal "ingenuous" ways, but externally with apparently complex results.

The method of CTs, introduced to develop economic subjects' autonomous behavior, can also be interpreted as a general algorithm useful for building behavioral models without using constrained or unconstrained optimization techniques. The kernel of the method, conveniently based upon artificial neural networks, is learning by guessing and doing: control capabilities of the subject can be developed without defining either goals or maximizing objectives.

Fig.9 describes a CT agent learning and behaving in a CT scheme. The agent has

---

[13] Guesses about actions are so always internally generated; at the beginning of the acting and learning phase, they are near random; then they are determined by the learning process, in a consistent way with effects guesses or estimations. External points of view can be superimposed to internal guesses (see EPs in Sec. 4.1).

to produce guesses about its own actions and related effects, on the basis of an information set (the input elements are $I_1, ..., I_k$). Remembering the requirement of IC, targets in learning process are: (1) on one side, the actual effects - measured through accounting rules - of the actions made by the simulated subject; (2) on the other side, the actions needed to match guessed effects. In the last case we have to use inverse rules, even though some problems arise when the inverse function is undetermined.

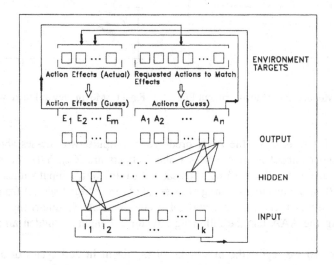

Fig. 9. The cross-target construction.

We think that it would be useful to develop the GH also in other ways, in case employing neither neural networks nor CT, to verify the reproducibility of our results in other contexts.

The flexibility in software structure necessary to perform this kind of methodological parallel experiment is the final reason for migrating, in the perspective of our future work, from a self developed tool as the present CT program, to a more standardized platform, such as Swarm.

4.3 CT: An example without Swarm

We introduce here an example of our CT experiments, related to our previous work, without the Swarm introduction. The presentation is aimed to facilitate the reader in considering the possible interest of our technique.

This first experiment is about motion of agents foraging for food (see Terna [10]). We apply the following scheme. On a plain with (x,y) coordinates, the subject is initially in (10,10) while the food is fixed in (0,0). The ANN (Artificial Neural Network) simulating the subject has the following inputs: X(t-1), position in the x direction at the time t-1; Y(t-1), position in the y direction at the time t-1; dX(t-1), step in the directions x, at time t-1 (bounded in the range ±1); dY(t-1), step in the directions y, at time t-1 (bounded in the range ±1).

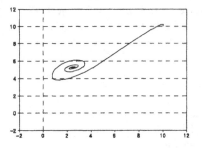
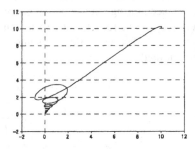

Fig.10. Moving toward food, without EO. **Fig.11.** Moving toward food, with EO.

Using CT terminology, the ANN produces as outputs two guesses about effects and two guesses about actions. Guesses about effects are X(t), Y(t). Guesses about actions are dX(t) and dY(t), all with the same meaning of the input values. Positions X(t) and Y(t) have also the meaning of distance of the artificial subject from the food (distance evaluated employing rectangular coordinates). Summarising, the ANN representing the AAA has the following structure: 4 input, 6 hidden and 4 output nodes.

In Figure 10 we report the movement of the agent in 200 cycles of acting and learning. The agent goes toward the food on the basis of a simple implicit mechanism, which explains also the situation of locking in the middle of the path. The mechanism works in the following way: at the beginning of the experiment, the ANN produces random outputs, in a small interval around the central value between minimum and maximum. This effect is always present and is easily explained by considering the consequence of the initial random choice of the weights, that gives on average a null sum of the inputs of the sigmoidal transformation. In the case of the logistic functions, that input gives an output of about 0.5, corresponding to the mean between minimum and maximum values. As a consequence, the initial guesses about the effects of the movement give estimated positions around the central point where food is placed, with some variability.

In other term, the initial guess is that of being near the food. CTs immediately correct this wrong estimate, but they also correct the guesses about actions (the movements), to develop their consistency with the (wrong, but positively optimistic) guesses of effects. So, the artificial agent moves in the correct direction, but the process rapidly goes in a locking situation, with mutual consistency between effects and actions.

Now, imposing an EO on the side of the effects, that is the target of reducing in each cycle the distance from food to the 75% of the distance of the previous cycle, the food is easily gained, as reported in Figure 11. We underline that no suggestion is introduced about the direction of the movement.

Appendix: The Swarm Environment

In this Appendix we are turning more properly our attention to the Swarm world. The term "world" is appropriate, because Swarm is a system of software libraries, but also a vigorous interactive community working with them, as we can observe by taking part to the Swarm mailing lists[14].

In the Swarm context, we use the Object-Oriented Programming language Objective-C. According to the Swarm documentation, computation in a Swarm application takes place by instructing objects to send messages to each other. The basic message syntax is:

```
[targetObject message Arg1: var1 Arg2: var2]
```

where `targetObject` is the recipient of the message, `messageArg1:Arg2:` is the message to send to that object, and `var1` and `var2` are arguments to pass along with the message.

According to the Swarm documents: "The idea of Swarm is to provide an execution context within which a large number of objects can *live their lives* and interact with one another in a distributed, concurrent manner."

In the context of the Swarm simulation system, the generic outline of an experimental procedure takes the following form.

– Create an artificial universe replete with space, time, and objects that can be located, within reason, to certain "points" in the overall structure of space and time within the universe and allow these objects to determine their own behavior according to their own rules and internal state in concert with sampling the state of the world, usually only sparsely.

– Create a number of objects which will serve to observe, record, and analyze data produced by the behavior of the objects in the artificial universe implemented in the previous steps.

– Run the universe, moving both the simulation and observation objects forward in time under some explicit model of concurrency.

– Interact with the experiment via the data produced by the instrumentation objects to perform a series of controlled experimental runs of the system.

A remark about the consequences of publishing the result of a simulation: Only if we are using a high level structured programming tool, it is possible to publish simulation results in a useful way. Quoting again from Swarm documentation:

"The important part (. . .) is that the published paper includes enough detail about the experimental setup and how it was run so that other labs with access to the same equipment can recreate the experiment and test the repeatability of the results. This is hardly ever done (or even possible) in the context of experiments run in computers, and the crucial process of independent verification via replication of results is almost unheard of in computer simulation. One goal of Swarm is to bring simulation writing up to a higher level of expression, writing applications with reference to a standard set of simulation tools."

---

[14] http://www.santafe.edu/projects/swarm/mailing-lists.html#support

For this, the fact that the Swarm structure has two different levels is very useful. There is the model level (and we can have nested models of models, or swarms of swarms) and the observer level which considers the model (or the nested models) as a unique object to interact with, in order to obtain the results and to send them to various display tools and widgets.

Finally, the diffusion effect is a cumulative one, both for the production of reusable pieces of programs and for the standardization of techniques to allow experiments to be replicated easily.

Obtaining and Using Swarm: Swarm is developed at the Santa Fe Institute[15] and it is freely available[16], under the terms of the GNU[17] license. Swarm runs under Unix / Linux operating system and, more recently, under Windows 95 and Windows NT, using the "GNU-Win32: Unix for Win32[18]."

References

1. Conte, R., Hegselmann, R., Terna, P. (eds.): Simulating Social Phenomena. Springer, Berlin (1997).
2. Beltratti, A., Margarita S., Terna P.: Neural Networks for Economic and Financial Modelling. ITCP, London (1996).
3. Epstein, M.E. and Axtell, R.: Growing Artificial Societies - Social Science from the Bottom Up. Brookings Institution Press, Washington. MIT Press, Cambridge, MA(1996).
4. Gessler, N.: Growing Artificial Societies - Social Science from the Bottom Up. Artificial Life 3 (1997) 237-242.
5. Kirman, A.: Whom or What Does the Representative Agent Represent. Journal of Economic Perspectives 6 (1992) 126-39.
6. Terna, P: Simulation Tools for Social Scientists: Building Agent Based Models with SWARM. Journal of Artificial Societies and Social Simulation 2 (1998) <http://www.soc.surrey.ac.uk/JASSS/1/2/4.html>.
7. Chamberlin, E.: An Experimental Imperfect Market. Journal of Political Economy, April (1948) 95-108.
8. Smith, V.: An Experimental Study of Competitive Market Behavior. Journal of Political Economy, April (1962) 111-137.
9. Smith, V.: Microeconomic Systems as Experimental Science. American Economic Review 5 (1982) 923-955.
10. Terna, P.: A Laboratory for Agent Based Computational Economics: The Self-development of Consistency in Agents' Behaviour. In Conte, R., Hegselmann, R., Terna, P. (eds.): Simulating Social Phenomena. Springer, Berlin (1997).

---

[15] http://www.santafe.edu

[16] http://www.santafe.edu/projects/swarm/

[17] http://www.fsf.org/

[18] http://www.cygnus.com/misc/gnu-win32/

Formalising the Link between Worker and Society in Honey Bee Colonies

David J.T. Sumpter and D. S. Broomhead

University of Manchester Institute of Science and Technology, P.O. Box 88, Manchester, M60 1QD, UK

Abstract. Honey bee colonies consist of tens of thousands of interacting bees. The colony has only limited centralised control and many of its functions arise from the self-organised actions of individual bees. We use an example from nectar foraging to illustrate how process algebras may be used to describe formally the behaviour of bees as communicating agents. Logical properties of a 'colony' of these agents are then established and a computer simulation is described which adds dynamics to the process algebra description.

1 Introduction

Simple communication mechanisms between individuals, such as pheromone and dance signals, allow social insect colonies to complete complex tasks, often without centralised control. Models of the interactions inside the colony, usually in the form of cellular automata or 'Artificial Life' models, are becoming more and more popular for investigating how colonies efficiently co-ordinate their work in a dynamic environment [13, 14, 15]. These models usually aim to demonstrate, through simulation, an abstract principle about activity or communication and do not focus on specific examples of insect behaviour. There is often no formal specification of behaviour which stands independent of implementation. Without this specification it is difficult for other modelers to reproduce a simulation's results or to analyse the colony level dynamics of a model abstracted from its implementation.

Formal specification of the behaviour of communicating agents is possible through process algebras such as the Calculus of Communicating Systems (CCS) [6]. By ascertaining the rules by which a worker honey bee communicates with other workers and her environment, we can construct CCS models describing individual bee behaviour. By allowing that bees communicate concurrently, we create a multi-agent model of a real honey bee colony. General properties of bee agents in such a model can be established using temporal logics. These properties can be tested against the behaviour we set out to model, both giving us insight into that behaviour and allowing us to correct deficiencies in our model. In the current paper we investigate how an individual bee forages for nectar. We show that a number of bee agents, who are able to perform a *waggle dance* to communicate the location of nectar sources, can work together to exploit sources which they would have been unable to locate on their own. We also show that this communication is limited in that it cannot efficiently identify when a source is exhausted.

For simple CCS models, the insight into the colony's workings provided by logical analysis of the individual bees is limited. However, the addition of temporal properties to our model allows us to address questions such as how a colony can best distribute its workers between foraging sites. To this end, the CCS is used as a specification of a computer simulation. The simulation has temporal features specific to its implementation but preserves all the CCS rules, allowing us to understand which behaviours arise from implementation and which from the underlying model.

2 Colony Organisation

Honey bee colonies performs a variety of complex tasks, such as nest building and foraging for food, which are well beyond the capabilities of an individual bee. However, it is believed that the colony behaviour is not centrally controlled. The information and instructions which an individual bee receives come from the other workers she comes in to contact with. The colony structure is such that the decision of individuals to work on a certain task can be made through local information without reference to a complete overall picture of the colony's situation. In this way, the work of individuals to achieve a cluster's global goal is said to be *self organised* [3].

Self-organisation of tasks in a colony requires *positive feedback* from those bees performing useful tasks to those who are unemployed or performing unnecessary tasks. For example, if one bee locates nectar she can inform unemployed bees in the hive of its location via the waggle dance. Self-organisation also requires *negative feedback* where a bee can sense that continuing her task is pointless. For example, a foraging bee who flys to an exhausted nectar source will not return to that source. Feedback between individual bees allows the colony to adopt a strategy which is not only suitable in its current environment but adaptable to changes in environmental conditions. Many of the feedback mechanisms for the organisation of honey bee foraging have been documented in 'The Wisdom of the Hive' by T. Seeley [7]. The current paper takes part of his description of nectar foraging, formalises it in CCS to establish its logical properties then describes a computer simulation of it dynamical properties.

3 Formal Description of Foraging

Process algebras are a set of formal rules which are used to specify computer algorithms [5, 6]. Once a specification is created in the language of the process algebra it can be manipulated to permit logical reasoning about the algorithm it represents. One such process algebra is the Calculus of Communicating Systems (CCS) [6]. CCS gives specifications in terms of communicating agents. This is useful when considering a number of algorithms which execute concurrently, linked together by communication channels.

3.1 Calculus of Communicating Systems

CCS deals with *agents*, which can be thought of as the possible state of a bee or a collection of bees; and *actions* which are the means by which agents become other agents. Our colony may be represented as a connected graph where each vertex corresponds to an agent and each edge to an action. For example, the agent

$$\text{Scout}_b = good_b(s).\text{Search}_b(s) + bad_b.\text{Unemployed}_b$$

is a bee, labeled b, which is scouting for a site containing nectar. Either bad_b could occur in which case she will become Unemployed_b or $good_b(s)$ would cause the bee to $\text{Search}_b(s)$ for some site s. We will compose single bee agents in parallel to give a colony agent. So,

$$\text{Scout}_1 | \text{Scout}_2$$

represents two bees searching for nectar in parallel. The main language constructs of CCS are as follows,

sequential composition	$a.C$	after action a the agent becomes agent C.
parallel composition	$C|D$	the agent behaves as two agents, C and D, proceeding in parallel.
choice	$a.C + b.D$	the agent becomes either C or D dependent on whether action a or b occurs first.
restriction	$C \setminus A$	this agent is like C except that no action in A can be performed on it or any agent derived from it.

We write $C \overset{a}{\rightarrow} D$ to denote that D is derivable from C by action a.

Each input action, a, occurs in conjunction with a complementary output action, $\overline{a}$. So an agent with two parallel components both waiting to perform complementary actions, $a.C|\overline{a}.D$, may perform an internal action to become $C|D$. Input and output actions will be used in our foraging example to represent the waggle dance performed by the bees.

Since we will be dealing with bee agents which pass information to each other, we use an extension of basic CCS known as value passing CCS. This allows parameterised agents and actions (e.g. $good_b(s)$ is passed parameter s and $\overline{dance}(b, s)$ passes parameters b and s). Full details of the syntax of value passing CCS can be found in Bruns [4].

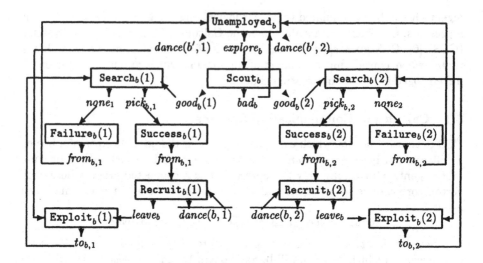

Fig. 1. A graphical representation of a single CCS bee in the Concurrency Workbench (CWB) [12]. The vertices represent agents and the edges are labeled with the action which causes transitions between agents.

3.2 A CCS Model of Foraging

In nature, an unemployed bee will wait in the hive until she receives a signal from a returning forager bee, in the form of a waggle dance, describing the location of nectar. If she receives such a signal she will fly to the source. Otherwise, she may leave the hive and scout for a source herself. Once she is at the source she will pick up some nectar and return it to the hive, possibly performing the dance to recruit more foragers. The following CCS describes the structure of this process.

$$\text{Exploit}_b(s) = to_{b,s}.\text{Search}_b(s)$$
$$\text{Search}_b(s) = pick_{b,s}.\text{Success}_b(s) + none_s.\text{Failure}_b(s)$$
$$\text{Success}_b(s) = from_{b,s}.\text{Recruit}_b(s)$$
$$\text{Failure}_b(s) = from_{b,s}.\text{Unemployed}_b$$
$$\text{Recruit}_b(s) = \overline{dance(b,s)}.\text{Recruit}_b(s) + leave_b.\text{Exploit}_b(s)$$
$$\text{Unemployed}_b = dance(b',s).\text{Exploit}_b(s) + explore_b.\text{Scout}_b$$
$$\text{Scout}_b = good_b(s).\text{Search}_b(s) + bad_b.\text{Unemployed}_b$$

The variable b gives the bee a unique identity, b' is the identity of another bee and s specifies a site containing nectar.

The bee receives mostly input (rather than output) actions which come from non-bee agents (e.g. flowers, distance to nectar locations). The exception being the $\overline{dance(b,s)}$ output action which a bee will perform as input to another bee which is awaiting a $dance(b,s)$. Figure 1 gives a graphical representation of a CCS bee with access to two food sources. The bee can be one of 12 agents, each agent the result of a single action. If we create an agent consisting of two unemployed bees acting in parallel,

$$\text{Unemployed}_1|\text{Unemployed}_2,$$

the number of possible agents increases to 145. For three bees there are 1729 agents. It quickly becomes intractable to write down all the possible agents made up of more than a few bees acting in parallel.

4   Logical Properties of Foraging

The above CCS description of foraging is non-deterministic, describing the order in which actions occur but not the time or probability of their occurrence. However, the description is sufficient to reason logically about how our agents behave as individuals and in parallel. To do this we need a logic which can express properties of the various agents derivable from a finite or infinite series of actions on the starting agent. We should be able to ask questions such as "Can an Unemployed_1 agent take nectar from source 1 (perform $pick_1(1)$) without finding the source herself (performing $good_1(1)$)?". The logic we use is an extension of Hennessy-Milner logic allowing us to define fixed point equations on logical expressions. Although we avoid a rigorous description, it is based on the modal μ-calculus [8]. A good description can be found in Bruns [4].

4.1   Logical Fixed Point Equations

Hennessy-Milner (H-M) logic formulas have the following syntax:

$$\phi ::= \mathcal{T} \mid \mathcal{F} \mid \phi_1 \wedge \phi_2 \mid \phi_1 \vee \phi_2 \mid [A]\phi_1 \mid \langle A \rangle \phi_1$$

These formulas are truth functions which we will evaluate on the set of subsets of agents. $\mathcal{T}$ and $\mathcal{F}$ hold respectively true and false. The formula $[A]\phi_1$ holds if all members of the set A of actions lead to an agent where ϕ_1 is true. The formula $\langle A \rangle \phi_1$ holds if some action in the set A leads to an agent where ϕ_1 is true. The $\phi_1 \wedge \phi_2$ holds if ϕ_1 and ϕ_2 both hold and $\phi_1 \vee \phi_2$ holds if one of ϕ_1 or ϕ_2 holds.

The set A denotes the set of actions which it is possible for the agents to make. For example, in the CCS agents of a single bee in figure 1, $from_{1,2} \in \mathcal{A}$ but $jump_1 \notin \mathcal{A}$. The symbol '$-$' acts as an abbreviation for all actions in $\mathcal{A}$ except those following the $-$. Therefore, $\langle - \rangle \mathcal{T}$ holds if there exists any action which leads to an agent and $[-]\mathcal{F}$ holds if there is no action which leads to an agent. We often omit the set braces when describing sets of actions so $\langle -a, b \rangle \phi = \langle \mathcal{A} \setminus \{a, b\} \rangle \phi$. Note that since $\mathcal{A}$ is the set of actions applicable to the agents, $[A]\mathcal{T}$ is true and $\langle A \rangle \mathcal{F}$ is false for all $A \subseteq \mathcal{A}$.

Let $\mathcal{G}$ be the set of all agents. The set $\|\phi\| \subseteq \mathcal{G}$ is the set of agents which satisfy ϕ. For example, in figure 1 ,

$$\|\langle - \rangle\mathcal{T} \wedge [-to_{1,s} : s \in S]\mathcal{F}\| = \|\langle - \rangle\mathcal{T}\| \quad \cap \quad \|[-to_{1,s} : s \in S]\mathcal{F}\|$$
$$= \{\text{Exploit}_1(s) : s \in S\},$$

(where is $S = \{1, 2\}$ is the set of all sites) is the set of all agents which can only do action $to_{1,1}$ or $to_{1,2}$.

Usually, we wish to express properties of agents with recursive behaviour. These cannot be expressed in terms of H-M logic but we can express them as solutions to a *fixed point equation*. For example,

$$P = \phi \wedge [-]P \qquad (1)$$

where ϕ is an H-M logical formula. P is an arbitrary proposition which we will evaluate by assuming a set of agents $G_P = \|P\|$. Therefore

$$G_P = \|\phi \wedge [-]P\|$$
$$= \|\phi\| \cap \{C| \text{ if } C \xrightarrow{a} D \text{ then } D \in G_P \quad \forall a \in \mathcal{A}, \forall D \in \mathcal{G}\}. \qquad (2)$$

So G_P is a set of agents for which ϕ holds immediately and all sets of actions out of an agent in G_P lead to agents which are in G_P. If $\phi = \langle - \rangle\mathcal{T}$ then we are testing for deadlock or, more precisely, lack of it (i.e. if the agent can perform some action and every action from that agent leads to an agent which can also perform an action). In general, there is no unique solution to equation 2 or any other fixed point equation.

The fixed points which give us useful information about sets of agents are the *maximum* and *minimum* fixed points. Both of these evaluate as a unique set of agents. Given a fixed point equation, $P = \psi(P)$ where $\psi(P)$ is a logical formula parameterised on an arbitrary proposition P (For example, in equation 1, $\psi(P) = \phi \wedge [-]P$). We write the maximum fixed point equation as,

$$\psi^0 \wedge \psi^1 \wedge \psi^2 \wedge \psi^3 \wedge \psi^4 \wedge \ldots \qquad (3)$$

where

$$\psi^0 = \mathcal{T}$$
$$\psi^{i+1} = \psi(\psi^i)$$

where $\psi(\psi^i)$ is obtained by replacing all the occurrences of P with ψ^i. As shorthand, equation 3 is written $\max(P = \psi(P))$.

$G_{\text{max}} = \|\max(P = \psi(P))\|$ is the largest possible set with every agent which does not satisfy $\psi(P)$ excluded and is unique for any given $\psi(P)$. For example, the maximum fixed point of equation 1 is,

$$max(P = \phi \wedge [-]P) \qquad (4)$$

which evaluates as the set

$$G_{max} = \|\mathcal{T}\| \quad \cap \quad \|\phi \wedge [-]\mathcal{T}\| \quad \cap \quad \|\phi \wedge [-](\phi \wedge [-]\mathcal{T})\| \quad \cap \quad \ldots \quad (5)$$

This gives us a practical method of obtaining G_{max}. Starting with the set $G = \|\mathcal{T}\|$ we can iteratively update G by intersecting it with each successive term of the right hand side of equation 5. Once further intersections do not decrease the size G then $G_{max} = G$. The maximum fixed point is most often used to find when a property of an agent is always true or must become true through a series of actions.

The minimum fixed point equation is similarly defined as

$$\min(P = \psi(P)) = \psi^0 \vee \psi^1 \vee \psi^2 \vee \psi^3 \vee \psi^4 \vee \ldots$$

where,

$$\psi^0 = \emptyset$$
$$\psi^{i+1} = \psi(\psi^i)$$

$G_{min} = \|\min(P = \psi(P))\|$ is then the smallest possible set including every agent which satisfies $\psi(P)$. For example,

$$min(P = \phi \vee \langle - \rangle P), \quad (6)$$

gives the smallest set of agents such that each agent satisfies ϕ or could possibly satisfy ϕ after a number of actions. In practice, G_{min} for equation 6 is obtained by starting with an empty set $G = \|\mathcal{F}\|$ and performing successive unions of each term from

$$\|\mathcal{F}\| \quad \cup \quad \|\phi \vee \langle - \rangle \mathcal{F}\| \quad \cup \quad \|\phi \vee \langle - \rangle(\phi \vee \langle - \rangle \mathcal{F})\| \quad \cup \quad \ldots \quad (7)$$

Once further unions do not increase the size G then $G_{min} = G$. Minimum fixed point equations are used to find if a series of actions from a given agent may eventually lead to a property being true.

4.2 Locating Nectar Sources

We can now apply our logical fixed point equations to reason about our earlier definition of foraging behaviour. For example, can a solitary unemployed bee who never attempts to explore for a nectar source ever successfully 'pick' some nectar? In nature we would expect the answer to this question to be 'no'. We restrict our set of agents in figure 1 so they cannot make or receive external dance signals,

$$\texttt{Solitary} = \texttt{Unemployed}_1 \setminus \{dance(b, s) : b \in B, s \in S\}$$

where $B = \{1, ..., n\}$ is the set of all bees. We will test if

Fixed Point Equation 4.1

$$\min(P = \langle pick_{1,s} : s \in S \rangle \mathcal{T} \vee \langle -explore_1 \rangle P)$$

which gives the set of agents which may eventually perform $pick_{1,1}$ or $pick_{1,2}$ without first doing $explore_1$

satisfies `Solitary`. As in equation 7, we evaluate the minimum fixed point by starting with $\|P_0\| = \emptyset$ and taking unions of successive relabelings of P,

$\|P_1\| = \{\text{Search}_1(s) : s \in S\}$

$\|P_2\| = \{\text{Search}_1(s), \text{Exploit}_1(s), \text{Scout}_1 : s \in S\}$

$\|P_2\| = \{\text{Search}_1(s), \text{Exploit}_1(s), \text{Scout}_1, \text{Recruit}_1(s) : s \in S\}$

$\|P_3\| = \{\text{Search}_1(s), \text{Exploit}_1(s), \text{Scout}_1, \text{Recruit}_1(s), \text{Success}_1(s) : s \in S\}$

$\|P_4\| = \{\text{Search}_1(s), \text{Exploit}_1(s), \text{Scout}_1, \text{Recruit}_1(s), \text{Success}_1(s) : s \in S\}$

$\quad\quad = \|P_3\|.$

So $\|P\|$ does not contain the `Solitary` agent and the bee must find the nectar source herself. The model is consistent with what we expect from nature.

The agent,

$$\text{Couple} = (\text{Unemployed}_1 | \text{Exploit}_2(2)) \setminus \{dance(b, s) : b \in B, s \in S\}$$

is two bees, of which the second is exploiting nectar source 2. Can the `Unemployed`$_1$ bee now 'pick' some nectar? There are 145 agents which can be derived from actions on `Couple` so we use an automated proposition checker (The Concurrency Workbench [12]) to check equation 4.1 and find it is indeed satisfied. Only through the dance of another bee can unemployed foragers who are unwilling to explore find a nectar source.

In nature, only a small number of bees will scout for nectar sites [7], with most waiting in the hive to be recruited. Consider the agent

$$\text{Colony}_n = (\text{Unemployed}_1 | .... | \text{Unemployed}_n) \setminus \{dance(b, s) : b \in B, s \in S\}.$$

The CWB can be used to check that

Fixed Point Equation 4.2

$$\max \big(P = [good_{b,1} : b \in B] \min(Q = \langle pick_{1,1} \rangle ... \langle pick_{n,1} \rangle \mathcal{T}$$
$$\vee \langle -good_{b,1} : b \in B \rangle Q) \wedge \langle - \rangle P\big)$$

which gives the set of agents which after a single $good_{b,1}$ action may do actions $pick_{1,1}$, then $pick_{2,1}$ up to $pick_{n,1}$ without another $good_{b,1}$ action is satisfied by $\texttt{Colony}_n$. Unfortunately, since the process of checking satisfaction is automated, we have not *proved* that equation 4.2 holds for an arbitrary size of n. Instead we have tested it with the CWB for n up to 4. Extending our test to a proof would require some inductive reasoning about the effects of adding each $\texttt{Unemployed}_{n+1}$ agent. This is a serious limitation in our current usage of CCS.

This limitation aside, it is clear that our model captures the notion of positive feedback through the waggle dance. If one bee discovers a foraging site it is possible for her to inform all other bees of its location. In reality, it is unlikely that a single forager will inform all other bees of the location of a source of nectar - rather the feedback will result in a n increasing number of foragers able to recruit others to exploit the source.

4.3 Detecting Exhaustion of a Nectar Source

Although bees are known to communicate when a certain site contains nectar supplies there is no evidence that they report when a site is no longer profitable. This is reflected in our model, with *dance$_s$* being the only action which is performed internally between bees in $\texttt{Colony}_n$. Consider the agent,

$$\texttt{Forage}_n = (\texttt{Exploit}_1(1)|....|\texttt{Exploit}_n(1)) \setminus \{dance(b,s) : b \in B, s \in S\}$$

and

Fixed Point Equation 4.3

$$\max \left(P = \overbrace{[none_1]...[none_1]}^{f\,times} \min \left(Q = \langle to_{b,1} : b \in B\rangle \mathcal{T} \vee \right.\right.$$
$$\left.\left. \langle -good_{b,1} : b \in B\rangle Q\right) \wedge [-none_1]P\right).$$

which gives the set of agents such that if an agent performs f none$_1$ actions without having ever previously performed none$_1$ then without a good$_{b,1}$ action it will still be able to perform to$_{b,1}$.

We use the CWB to show that $\texttt{Forage}_n$ satisfies 4.3 for $f < n$. In an environment where sites of profitable nectar foraging are constantly changing it is not energy efficient for every individual in the colony to discover for herself that nectar supplies are exhausted. This contrasts with foraging ants who leave pheromone trails to indicate a short path to a food source, but will not leave a trail when this path turns out to be too long [1]. In the absence of such a feedback mechanism we suggest that a fraction of returning foragers can become unemployed. We change our CCS description to reflect this:

$$\texttt{Success}_b(s) = from_{b,s}.\texttt{Decide}_b(s)$$
$$\texttt{Decide}_b(s) = recruit_b.\texttt{Recruit}_b(s) + giveup_b.\texttt{Unemployed}_b$$

While the site is profitable this effect is balanced by the recruitment pressure of the rest of the successful foragers. When the site becomes unprofitable, however, this mechanism produces an exponential decay of foragers returning to the site. In order to demonstrate this effect we must specify the probability of either *recruit$_b$* or *giveup$_b$* occurring within a simulation.

5   Simulating Dynamic Properties of Foraging

Process algebras which include temporal and probabilistic notations do exist and have been used to 'prove' properties of social insect societies [10, 11]. For now, we concentrate on using our CCS description as a specification of a computer simulation of foraging behaviour. We ensure that all properties which hold for the CCS description will also hold for the simulation. The addition of temporal and stochastic properties will allow us to investigate how an individual bee balances her own recruitment and voluntary redundancy to maximise the colony's nectar intake under variable conditions.

5.1   The Simulation Model

We specify a multi-agent computer simulation with each agent from our CCS for a single bee as a possible state of a simulated bee. The simulation was written using Swarm, details of which can be found in another article within this conference proceedings [9]. Most of the actions which the bee performs are driven by external output actions (e.g. flowers, distance etc.). Without rewriting the semantics of CCS to introduce synchrony it is very difficult to specify external entities which will force output actions to occur in a way which models the environment of a real bee. Instead, we specify $T(a)$ to be the number of simulation steps between a bee starting to wait to perform some action, a, and actually performing it. For example, $T(good_b(s))$ gives the time it takes a bee to find site s. If the site contains no nectar then this is infinite, if the site does contain nectar then $T(good_b(s))$ is a random sample taken from a Geometric distribution with parameter p_S, the probability of finding a site in a single time step (see table 1).

action	$T(action)$	action	$T(action)$	action	$T(action)$
$to_{b,s}$	$d_s + T_n$	$recruit_b$	0	$dance(b', s)$	$-$
$pick_{b,s}$	0 or ∞	$giveup_b$	0	$explore_b$	T_e
$none_s$	1	$dance(b, s)$	0	$good_b(s)$	T_S or ∞
$from_{b,s}$	d_s	$leave_b$	0	bad_b	T_b

Table 1. The number of simulation steps, $T(action)$, between a bee starting to wait to perform some action, *action*, and actually performing it. d_s is a constant defined by the distance from the hive to site s. The values T_e, T_b, T_S and T_n are random variables from a Geometric distribution with parameters p_e, p_b, p_S and p_n respectively.

When an agent has a choice between actions, $a_1.C + a_2.D$ then the action, a_i, with the smallest $T(a_i)$ will occur. For example, the agent Scout$_b$ will perform bad_b if $T_b < T_S$ for all s otherwise it will perform $good_b(s)$ for the site, s with the smallest T_S. In general, if $T(a_i) = T(a_j)$ for two actions then we choose to perform a_i or a_j by 'tossing a fair coin'. An exception to this rule arises for the agent Decide$_b$. We choose $giveup_b$ with probability p and $recruit_b$ with probability $1 - p$. Similarly, we specify that a bee will $\overline{dance(b, s)}$ a number of times selected uniformly at random between 1 and $d_{\max}$ before performing $leave_b$. Note that $T(\overline{dance(b', s)})$ depends entirely on the arrival of another bee performing $\overline{dance(b, s)}$. These observations combined with our original CCS model give the specification of our simulation. This is by no means a formal specification but, if implemented properly, the simulation is consistent with all the properties proved in section 4.

5.2   Changes in Strength of Recruitment

Consider again the agent Decide$_b(s)$. We now look at agents which will never perform a recruitment dance,

$$\text{NeverDance}_n = \text{Colony}_n \setminus \{recruit_b : b \in B\}$$

Using the Concurrency Workbench, we can show that fixed point equation 4.2 is not satisfied by NeverDance$_n$. In terms of our simulation, this means that if, the probability of a worker becoming unemployed is unity, then the time taken until the colony can fully exploit a source, s, depends on how frequently it performs $good_{b,s}$ (i.e. how long it takes an individual bee to find the source). Since, in real honey bees, this frequency is relatively low we should expect any simulation of NeverDance$_n$ will seldom show high exploitation of a source.

CCS allows us to look at the cases when $p = 1$ and $p = 0$. We are more interested in what happens between these values. This is where we put our simulation to use. A successful forager returning to the hive will either become unemployed with probability, p, or will recruit an average of $d = (1 + d_{\max})/2$ unemployed bees (assuming they are available to be recruited) with probability, $1 - p$. Assuming d and p are constant for all bees, if $d(1 - p) > p$ then the number of foragers will increase as more foragers fly out and return from the site. If the site remains profitable then eventually nearly all bees will become employed there. The time it takes until 90% employment is achieved at a profitable site increases with p. When $p > d/(d + 1)$ there will be insufficient recruitment to increase the number of employed bees. We see in figure 2 that as p approaches $d/(d + 1)$ the time until 90% employment is achieved appears to diverge. Similarly, the time until the colony detects that a site is exhausted decreases as p approaches $d/(d + 1)$.

It is not surprising that stronger recruitment by the bees will lead to quicker employment at a site but slower awareness of a site's exhaustion. This would suggest that a constant rate of recruitment is not particularly useful to the colony

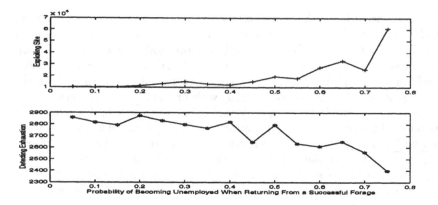

Fig. 2. Total number of bee time steps lost before a colony is fully exploiting a newly discovered site and until it has fully detected a sites exhaustion plotted against p. For detection of a new site we integrate over the number of bees wh are unemployed from a site's detection until 90% of the bees are employed at the site. For detection of exhaustion, we integrate over the site becoming exhausted until all bees are aware that the site is exhausted (i.e. are not employed at the site). $d = 4$ for all simulations.

as a whole, since it must respond slowly to either a new site becoming profitable or a current site becoming unprofitable. In order that the colony functions efficiently, individual foragers must adjust their recruitment rate as employment at a site changes. In nature the strength of the waggle dance depends on factors such as nectar quality and the time taken to unload to the bees who store the nectar in the hive [7]. So d and p are different not only for different bees but on different foraging trips by the same bee.

5.3 Distinguishing Between Two Equal Sites

If there are two profitable sites with equal quality nectar at equal distance from the hive how does the colony distribute its bees between the two sites? We assume that $d_s(1-p_s) > p_s$ for both sites $s \in \{1, 2\}$. Furthermore, $p = p_1 = p_2$ and $d = d_1 = d_2$ since both sites are equal. We set up the simulation with 200 bees and two foraging sites such that $T(to_{b,1}) = T(to_{b,2})$. We begin the simulation with site 1 profitable for the bees ($T(pick_{b,1}) = 0$) and site 2 unprofitable. After a short period of recruitment, most bees are employed at site 1. Once near full employment is achieved, we let site 2 become profitable. Random fluctuations allow a few bees to become scouts and find site 2. Bees returning from a successful scout attempt to recruit from the small pool of unemployed bees.

Figure 3 shows a time series of number of bees employed at sites 1 and 2 when $p = 0.75$ and $d = 4$. The results show a marked tendency for the majority

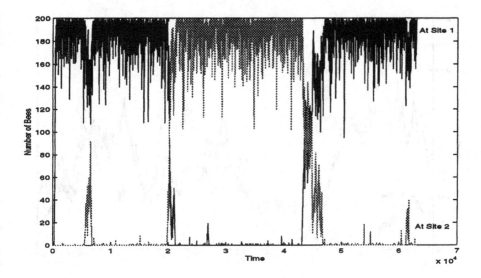

Fig. 3. Number of bees employed (from a colony of 200) at sites 1 and 2 over time when $p = 0.75$ and $d = 4$.

of the colony to exploit a single site at any given time. Occasionally random fluctuations will cause the foragers to switch from one site to the other. As we increase d the switching between sites becomes less frequent since fewer bees are scouting. These results are inconsistent with the behaviour of real bees. Seeley used two sugar solution feeders in a nectar scarce environment to show that a colony will balance its assignment of workers to sites in proportion to their profitability [7]. The results are consistent, however, with experiments where ants offered two equal paths to a food source will eventually all take the same path [1]. Ants lay pheromone trails for recruitment while the bees use the waggle dance. Both these mechanisms lead to reinforcement and positive feedback.

As d tends toward $p/(1 - p)$ the proportion of unemployed bees increases. Unemployment in foragers is a commonly observed feature of real bee colonies. Although not contributing toward the task of gathering nectar unemployed bees use very little energy. When $d = p/(1-p)$, instead of the bees continually switching between the two sites, both sites are foraged at. Averaged over 40000 time steps, the mean number of bees foraging at sites 1 and 2 are similar (40.52 and 43.9 respectively). The corresponding standard deviations are 44.7 and 48.2, indicating large fluctuations in attendance at each site. Furthermore, the correlation coefficient between the two sites, -0.332, is significant at a 1% level. This indicates that the simulated colony fails to keep a proportional balance of workers at the two sites. Since there is a limited supply of foragers, when one

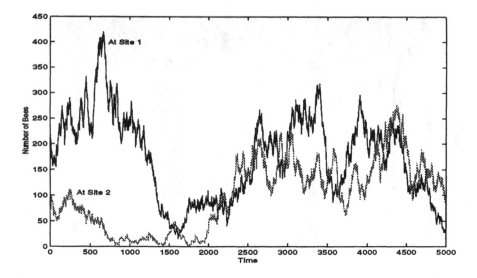

Fig. 4. Number of bees (from a colony of 500) employed at sites 1 and 2 over time when $p = 0.75$ and $d = 3$.

site is busy the other is likely to be quiet.

All the simulations described so far have colonies of only 200 bees. Real colonies contain thousands of foraging bees. It is possible that a natural colony's ability to assign foragers to sites in proportion to their profitability is due to the large number of foragers it has at its disposal. The previous simulation was repeated with 500 bees. The number of bees foraging at each site over 5000 time steps can be seen in figure 4. In the first 1000 time steps most of the foraging is done at site 1. This is followed by a period of proportional foraging at both sites. For larger simulations, the number of bees at the two sites evolve independently of each other when there are many unemployed bees. However, with fewer unemployed bees, the number at each site is again negatively correlated. Although the simulated behaviour is closer to that of a real colony, it does not explain how proportional foraging can be maintained over long periods of time. One explanation is that some individual bees have a strong preference for specific sites [7]. This would prevent the number of foragers at single site reaching extremes.

Honey bees live in large colonies and the waggle dance recruits only a few bees to a site at a time. Experiments where ants have been seen to follow a single trail to a food source usually examine small colonies. Furthermore, pheromone trails may be a stronger recruitment mechanism than the waggle dance. The simulation presented here can be parameterised to produce the recruitment behaviour seen in various species of social insects. For the honey bee, it is beneficial for the colony to 'know' about all profitable sites, since when one becomes exhausted it can quickly swap to exploiting another. The simulation shows that by keeping positive feedback in recruitment at low levels the hive maintains a number of unemployed bees who can respond quickly to changes in the sites available for foraging.

6   Discussion

Social insects can be studied at either the individual level or the colony level. The problem for theoretical biologists is to tie together the data available at these two levels into coherent theories about the nature of colony organisation. CCS allows a colony agent to be a parallel composition of concurrent individual agents. The behavioural properties of individual insects can be established from the data and built into a CCS model. We can then use temporal logics to check if these properties imply the behaviour we see in the colony. In section 4, we used this technique to reveal a possible weakness in a simple model of bee foraging. This led not only to an improved model but to a better understanding of what bee communications cannot achieve. However, the actual features of bee foraging which we proved remain simple. Furthermore, we were unable to produce proofs about arbitrary numbers of agents. If CCS and temporal logics are to be used to formalise multi-agent simulations then it must first be demonstrated that they can prove interesting properties of more complex systems than the one described here.

CCS does not allow a dynamical description of behaviour. It states the order in which actions are possible but not the times at which they occur. In section 5 we described a simulation of our foraging model. The simulation preserves the properties established in section 4 but added certain temporal and probabilistic features. It aided our investigation of how individual foragers might set the rate at which they recruit other bees so as to maximise their own and the colony's energy intake. Future work will develop the simulation to give us a clearer picture of how this is achieved. It is possible to implement an infinite number of simulations based on any given CCS. Indeed, we have implemented a spatial simulation of scouting and exploiting nectar, based on the same CCS as the simulation described in this paper [15]. The CCS allows us to separate properties of a simulation from those of the underlying description.

This paper clearly illustrates the width of the gap between formalisation of multi-agent models and the simulations which implement them. The simulations provide more useful results about recruitment in social insects than the CCS work which proceeds it. However, it is not possible to prove that the results of the simulation are correct or to fully investigate its parameter space. An extension of CCS known as Weighted Synchronous CCS (WSCCS) allows the expression of temporal and probabilistic properties of behaviours [11]. A model in WSCCS may be used to derive equations describing the rate at which populations of agents change. By grouping agents into those performing a certain task we can investigate patterns in colony level behaviour. For example, grouping agents by the site, s, at which they are foraging gives difference equations describing how a colony assigns its bees between sites. These equations can then be compared to experimental data and other colony level models. It is hoped that we will be able to use WSCCS, or some similar process algebra, to prove not only logical but temporal properties of theories of self-organisation.

Acknowledgments - This work was funded jointly by EPSRC and DERA, Malvern. Early work on the simulation was helped along enthusiastically by Christopher Booth and Richard Penney. Thanks to Graham Birtwistle for introducing us to temporal logics and providing his lecture notes. Thanks also to members of the Swarm hive and user community for technical advice. Iain Couzin, Carl Anderson and Francis Ratnieks provided useful discussion and references on social insect foraging. Finally, thanks to the anonymous reviewers for taking such an active interest in the paper.

References

1. Beckers R., Deneubourg J.L. and Goss S. : Trails and U-turns in the selection of the shortest path by the ant Lasius niger. *Journal of Theoretical Biology* (1992) 159: 397-415
2. Bonabeau, E. W. & Theraulaz, G. : Why Do We Need Artificial Life? In *Artificial Life: An Overview* (Langton C. G. ed.) MIT Press. (1995) 303–325
3. Bonabeau, E. W., Theraulaz G., Deneubourg, J-L., Aron, S. & Camazine, S.: Self-Organization in Social Insects, *Trends in Ecology and Evolution* (1997) 12: 188-193
4. Bruns, G. : Systems Engineering with CCS, Prentice Hall. (1997)
5. Hoare, C. A. R. : Communicating Sequential Processes, Prentice Hall. (1985)
6. Milner, R. : Communication and Concurrency, Prentice Hall. (1989)
7. Seeley, T. D. : The Wisdom of the Hive Harvard University Press, London. (1995)
8. Stirling, C. : Modal and Temporal Logics for Processes, *LFCS report ECS-LFCS-92-221* Department of Computer Science, Edinburgh. (1992)
9. Terna, P. : ABCDE: Agent Based Chaotic Dynamic Emergence, *In this book*
10. Tofts, C. : Describing Social Insect Behaviour Using Process Algebra, *Transactions of the Society for Computer Simulation* (1992) 227-283
11. Tofts, C. : Processes with Probabilities, Priority and Time, *Formal Aspects of Computing* (1993) 3 536-564
12. The Concurrency Workbench *http://www.dcs.ed.ac.uk/home/cwb/*
13. The Swarm Simulation System *http://www.santafe.edu/swarm/*
14. StarLogo Models of Biological Superstructures. *http://www.psu.edu/dept/beehive/starlogo/starlogo.htm.*
15. Honey Bee Simulation Homepage. *http://www.ma.umist.ac.uk/dsumpter/beesim/index.html.*

Non-merchant Economy and Multi-agent System: An Analysis of Structuring Exchanges

J. Rouchier, F.Bousquet

CIRAD-TERA, Campus de Baillarguet, BP 5035, 34032 Montpellier, France
rouchier@cirad.fr, bousquet@cirad.fr

Abstract. The hypothesis is that the exchanges of goods structure the society, and especially the non-merchant exchanges. Their aim is to express unselfishness, but also to generate a moral debt that builds strong reciprocal links. A multi-agent system was built with 100 agents and a resource, the interactions being only gifts. For the simulations, the agents have different rules to perform gifts and to organize their memory. The results are analyzed by the agent as well as by the modeller, with different points of view: either local or global and with different time length.

The aim of the work described in this paper is to explore the correlation that exists between the way goods circulate and the structure of power in a society. Ideally, to study this question, it would be interesting to observe a society where all the relations between people could be depicted in terms of good exchanges. However, such a society does not exist and since it is not possible to isolate the effect of one dynamic while excluding the others in real societies, it seemed accurate to build an artificial world.

Several kinds of exchanges can be identified among human societies. The most common one has been often analyzed by anthropologists, appearing in any societies, but mostly in the ones based on non-merchant economies: the gift (Godelier, 1996). The focus here was put on one special society, the kwakiutl one, since the system was based on the description of the potlatch. We will describe the organization of the exchanges in this economy of gifts, and explain its special properties. Then we will describe the artificial world created, the simulations and the results we got, and conclude on the new understanding this work implied.

1 Why potlatch was chosen as an example

A differentiation can be made for economics relations between the merchant and non-merchant ones. Both are present in each society, but their importance vary (Godelier, 1996). In our society, merchant exchanges are regarded as the only important ones, while in most societies, those classically observed by the anthropologists, the non-merchant exchange, the gift, is the base of economic and social life (Mauss, 1968). Two main differences in the points of view and in the logics underlying the systems can be seen.

Firstly the ways possession is considered are almost in opposition. In the societies where a gift is the main way of exchanging, the possession of goods is not what matters. Contrary, what is important is to express that one is not worried about material questions. The contempt for possessions is expressed through distribution or destruction of goods, having great feasts or in the everyday life. Only the rich can spend a lot, and giving is necessary to acquire a predominant status, whereas the poor one is the one that receives without being able to give[1].

In that context, to receive a gift is equivalent to being helped, and then to be dependent of the giver. To be recognized as able to spend, one has to perform counter-gifts, even if it is not necessarily an immediate action. What differs with a debt in a merchant society is that the link is not suppressed when the counter-gift is made, even if the values are at equilibrium, the memory of the dependency stays[2]. The debt created by the gift is not only material but also moral, and is not erased: one can see a succession of asymmetrical links but with no necessary end to the relation. So, depending on the kind of exchange, there exists different logic and dynamics within the group, between the people, for several time scales.

One example of a gift and counter-gift behavior has been well documented: it is the potlatch. Described by Boas at the beginning of the century(Boas, 1966), it is a system of gifts and counter-gifts that also has a very aggressive dimension. The power relations are established principally during great feast. Giving is there only as a way for the individuals and groups to express their opposition, not to share. They dominate each other by giving as well as destroying great quantities of objects like furs or grease or "coppers" (copper statues). There, the counter-gift, that is made usually after a year, and it is not just the same object that is given back, but at least twice what had been received. The descriptions that were made of this agonistic practice show that the whole society (or at least all those that were neither women nor slaves) was involved in interdependent fights, renewed regularly. This global dimension, along with the fact that the exchanges were explicitly analyzed by the actors as the bases of the power relations, made us use the description of Franz Boas to implement the model.

2 From interindividual exchanges to a model

2.1 two main themes treated

emergence The main question that made us build the model is "how is the society and the power relations within it influenced by the way the exchanges are performed ?" An underlying assumption is that the shape of the global

---

[1] One can note that in a merchant context, the power is expressed by accumulation more than spending.

[2] Another important point that makes this gift and counter-gift dynamics different from the debt is that one has not the choice to receive it. One cannot refuse a gift, but one has to give it back any way (this being a tacit rule in the interindividual relations).

organization is defined, at least partly, by some interindividual relations. The repetition of the exchanges would make an organization, that would not exist before these actions were performed, appear. That structure cannot be predicted from the definition of an individual agent and of the local dynamics, but does appear when a lot of individuals interact: it is called an emergence.

local and global observation Another underlying assumption is that any individual bases his actions on a representation of his environment, that he acquired through observation. His point of view usually differs from the one of the other individuals and from a global interpretation as well. A difference also appears when the analysis is made at a given moment or considering a certain length of time. Several points of view thus cohabit in the observation of the same object, depending on the scale of the observation and the involvement in the action.

In the kwakiutl society, what is important for an individual is to have as little debt as possible. A gift is made to show an imbalance in power: being a debtor means that one is dependent and is seen as a humiliating position. Hence, the first aim of a man who is given something is to pay it back as soon as possible.

What the sociologist sees when he observes the society is that nobody is free from debts or debtors among the whole kwakiutl group. Even more, the situation is never settled, always moving, since at any feast, a lot of counter-gifts are made: the humiliating feeling is the base of the dynamics, it is not the end of it. Even a powerful actor needs the others (to pay back so that he can get rid his own current dependencies) and the hierarchy appearing through a certain equilibrium is never fixed. This implies that all men are linked to many others, being involved in a lot of those never-ending challenging relations. In this society there is no insurance or official guaranty and this mutual and general interdependency is what is important for the dynamics and the individual survival in the group.

a shared questioning The MAS research community, and not only social sciences, is interested in these two topics(Ferber, 1994).

Firstly MAS relies principally on the emergence phenomenon: it is from local actions that the system is defined. Once the agents and their interactions have been defined, the use of simulations permits us to see the new phenomena appear. There are two uses for this principle. One needs to see certain types of collective actions being perform and then search for the minimal definition of an agent behavior to get to a certain result (Drogoul, 1994) (Doran, 1994). On the other hand, one can implement agents that have a certain behavior so as to see what kind of collective actions it will lead to (Bousquet *et al.*, 1998),(Epstein & Axtell, 1996).

In that situation, one can see that the one who is in charge of building the model and the one who wants to observe it are not in the same position(Ferber, 1996). The one who creates the system has to define the perception, motivation and logic for the action for each agent. Once this dynamics has been set up and the simulations go, the observation has to be organized. As the world is virtual, there is not a single information that can come to the observer that he does not define or look at in a rigorous way. Any information that should be perceived has to be clearly expressed (for example in terms of links, or number of occurrences), and the specific tools for these points of view created (with the use of statistics).

2.2 the hypothesis of the model

To build the MAS model, we define the agents' individual dynamics, including its aims and needs, and the way it is in interaction with its environment (with the objects and the other agents surrounding it). A few assumptions were made about these relations, based on the representation we had after reading the Boas description.

resources In the descriptions of the kwakiutl society, it is explicitly said that the appropriation of goods to circulate was never a problem. The natural environment was apparently very rich and there was no scarcity of any resource. The main point about production is that the ones that were spending the goods were not the ones who would work to get them. The free men, to have feasts, had a lot of slaves to accumulate what was needed.

The interaction with the environment in the model is built on these ideas: we consider that agents have slaves, whose number changes since it is possible to buy some more. Then, each slave produces the same value, that does not change from one year to another.

goods Actually, the goods that circulate in the society described were of different kinds, like copper statues or furs, but the relative value of the object were well known by the kwakiutl, and there were some equivalence between the quantities exchanged. This is why all that circulates in the virtual world is represented by one unique good and expressed by an amount.

What we also considered is that there were two kinds of goods produced, those that were used in everyday life and those that were to be exchanged. Each object that was to circulate would then belong to one of the two groups as soon as it was built, and the domains would not interfere. This is why in the model the agent does not need the units it has to survive in any way, it only deals with surplus.

interactions between agents We are interested by the influence of the form of the exchanges on the society, so all the relations between individuals in this artificial world are based on exchanges of goods. There is no other kind of relation, no global knowledge on the others, no communication.

Since there is no explicit exchange of information, it could be seen like the agents do not communicate. In the description of the real society it is clear that performing a gift is a way to show disinterest as well as to challenge the other to do at least the same. Hence whenever an object is given, it is as if a message was sent at the same time. It is the same in the model, since the agent will integrate the action of the other as an information to constitute their knowledge of society.

representation of the others The agent constitutes its knowledge thanks to the meaning that is to be read in actions. The aim of all the agents is the same, since they are forced to receive and give back and then are dependent until then, is to shorten the time he owes to another (like in the kwakiutl society where the position of a debtor is the one that is uncomfortable). In the model an agent evaluates another only by observing their interactions (the exchanges) and by comparing the time each one takes to give back. We will see these rules in the description. What is interesting is that the knowledge induced by these information depends entirely of the point of view and may change from one agent to another.

3 The implemented model

3.1 description

The model has been implemented using Smalltalk, an object-oriented language, on the Visualwork platform.

definition of an agent An agent is defined by its name. It knows the name of all the others, and can get in touch with any of them. It has possessions, expressed by a number of "units" that represents goods. It has slaves, and their number defines how many units it gets at each time step. It has a memory that is empty at the beginning and built along the simulation, made of two lists. In the first one are the current debts stocked, being remembered as a couple [name of agent that gave - amount]. The other list in the memory contains the names of the "relations", all the agents met since the beginning of the simulation[3]. For each relation the five last exchanges that took place are stocked, represented as [date - amount - circulation direction], as well as the opinion the agent has of this relation.

a universe for simulation In the universe built, there are 100 agents. The simulations performed are successions of 500 time steps. In the initial state, all the agents are identical. They have no possessions, they have five slaves, they have no debts and the list of relations is empty. Any agent can get in touch with any other one in the society, even if it has never met it, at any moment. There are three different protocols to define a simulation, but the succession of actions during each time step is the same for all.

actions of the agents The agent firstly adds to its possessions what it gets proportionally to its number of slaves (10 unities for one slave). When it has enough units, 200, it buys a slave that costs 50. Then it makes its plans: the counter-gifts and gifts it is going to make. Considering the number of units it has it first selects the maximum number of debts it can pay back. Then it decides of three

---

[3] About the difference between interaction and relation, several authors define it in their analysis of group dynamics (Hinde, n.d.), (Wellman, 1996).

gifts of equal value made to agents with whom it is not involved with at that moment (none is in debt with the other). There are different kind of choices, which determine the kind of simulation. All the agents make their plan before any good circulates, so that a gift made at a time step cannot be given back at the same period, and then the goods circulate. For each counter-gift the debts is erased in the agent list. For each gift performed, a new debt is added to the list of the one who receives it. The exchange is added in the memory: a debt is added and new informations about the relation.

agents' criterion Once all the goods have been given and received for all the agents, each one evaluates those it met at this turn. This evaluation exists only in two kinds of simulations, as we will see. It is based on the memory of the 5 last exchanges performed. In that case, between A and B, the five last exchanges define four series of {gift ; counter-gift}:

$$A \rightarrow s_{ab}^1 \rightarrow B$$
$$\text{(a gift)}$$

(t^1)

$$B \rightarrow 2 * s_{ab}^1 + s_{ba}^1 \rightarrow A$$
$$\text{(a counter-gift and a gift)}$$

$(t^{1'})$

$$A \rightarrow 2 * s_{ba}^1 + s_{ab}^2 \rightarrow B$$
$$\text{(a counter-gift and a gift)}$$

$(...)$

If A gives the amount s_{ab}^1 to B, and B gives back after t^1 time steps, we note r_{ab}^1 the ratio of time taken for one unit: $r = \frac{t}{s}$. Conversely, if B gives to A we get r_{ba}^1, which is the ratio of time taken for A to give back. Then B has an evaluation of A, that is based on two series of (see Eq. 1), from which can be deduced that $mark_b = - mark_a$.

$$mark_a = \log \frac{r_{ab}^1 + r_{ab}^2}{r_{ba}^1 + r_{ba}^2} \tag{1}$$

The final evaluation of the other is an average of the ancient evaluation and the mark attributed at this turn, the past evaluation influencing less than the new one(see Eq. 2),, the evaluation being 0 before enough exchanges have been performed. At each time the evaluation is made, only the last series of {gift ; counter-gift} is kept in memory and the other erased.

$$eval_a(t) = \frac{eval_a(t-1) * 25 + mark_a(t) * 75}{100} \tag{2}$$

The higher the evaluation, the more powerful the other is thought to be, because the quicker it gives back the gifts. The agent also has a representation of its own position in the social group: either it calculates an average of all the marks it knows[4], or it knows how many weaker and more powerful there are in the group.

simulation protocols There are three kinds of simulation defined: a difference is made in the elaboration of plans, with different criteria for the choice of the counter-gifts and the gifts that are to be made.

o The first simulation represent the "no memory" way to plan. To do a counter-gift, the agents give back double the amount received. The counter-gifts are made beginning with the highest amount. When it is not possible to give back anymore, the agent makes gifts randomly, since there is no memory kept of the other. With that first kind of rule, the agent gets rid of its debt, but does not necessarily make a gift to the same agent at the same time: the first gift received doesn't put the agent in a repeated relation.

There is a variation for this type of simulation, with "limited memory": two of the three gifts made have to concern one of the relations of the agents.

o In the second simulation the counter-gift is made with the "redistribution" process. The agent has to give again immediately to the one it is giving back to. The amount sent is randomly chosen, between 0.5 and 2 times the one received. Again, the agents choose as many counter-gifts as it can do, beginning with the one with the highest amount, and chooses randomly the amount of the gift it makes to the agents it is giving back to. After doing all these counter-gifts and gifts in a row, it makes three choices of gifts to do.

An evaluation of the others takes place in this context, but it is not used yet as a base for the action. The evaluations are all expressed with a number between -10 and 10: the "weak" ones are those with an evaluation under -7.

o The last simulation protocol is the "redistribution-elimination" one. For this protocol, the agent recognizes its "weak" relations. Then it makes the counter-gifts that concern those relations, but doesn't give to them again, and even more, it forbids itself to get in touch with it anymore. Once these first counter-gifts have been made, the plans are completed with the same methods as in the previous simulations.

sum up We recapitulate the different parameters for the agent and the actions it can perform in Table 1. As a brief sum up, we can say that all that the agents want to do is to have as little debt as possible and then to have other agents indebted. They have no choice so that to do an action or an other and all respect the same rule for each simulation.

---

[4] And since, in the relation between A and B, $eval_a = - eval_b$, A knows the image that B has of it and conversely.

Table 1. Agent's parameters

it has		at the beginning	it knows how to
goods		0	accumulates
			receive gifts
slaves		5	buy
debts		none	give back
representations	of the others	none	evaluate another
	of itself	none	evaluate itself

3.2 observation

As seen before, what the sociologist interprets as important in the society within which the potlatch takes place is the creation of interpersonal links and of a global dependency based on reciprocity. That is why different criteria are observed during the simulations, that try to take into account not only the idea of power but also of integration. What is observed for each agent is, at each turn:

dependency/power criteria: the number of debts, of debtors,
   integration criteria: regular relations (met during the ten preceding time steps),
   economic criteria: the number of units possessed, the number of slaves.

It is possible to know how each agent evaluates each of its relations. It also has a representation of its own position in the group, which is the "image" of itself : it is a synthesis of all the evaluations of the others[5].

There is thus an interesting difference of point of view for the observer and the agent itself. The agent only has a local knowledge, based on a time comparison, and knows the society by aggregating its individual appreciations. The observer can only look at all the criteria defined before and compare all of them between all the agents, making correlations between their apparition: it is only by knowing the whole group that it is possible to understand an individual.

3.3 results

The simulations were performed with the different protocols, as described in the previous section. It is only after 150 time steps that the differences are very clear and after 400 that the situation is stable[6].

the "no memory" simulation The first simulation is when the agents do not have to make a new gift after they get rid of their debt, two groups can be identified. There is a very strong difference that appears when one observes the first three criteria (number of debts, of debtors and of meetings), that are

---

[5] We can visualize it as an average, or as a graphic showing the number of relations for each evaluation attributed (translated between -10 and 10).

[6] And this is why the simulation where eventually chosen to be 500 time steps long.

strongly correlated. In the first group the "powerful" agents have a lot of debtors (at least 95), have less than 8 debts and meet less than 20 other agents in 10 time steps. Some of them even have less than one debt as an average (when a debt is made it is paid back at the following step). It does not take the same time for all the powerful agents to have these characteristics, the minimum being about 150 and the maximum 350 time steps. They are anyway about 20 in the society at the end of each simulation. The others, the "weak" agents have less than 40 debtors, meet about 50-60 other agents in ten steps and have at least 30 debts all the time. So the one with whom more agents are dependent are at the same time more lonely, who meet very few other agents.

Regarding the number of slaves that have been bought during the whole simulation: not all the agents can buy some, and actually only less than 15 do. But in that case they do buy a lot, and have at the end between 20 and 150 slaves. The link can be made only in one direction with the characterization we gave of power: all the agents that acquire more than 20 slaves are powerful, considering the previous criteria, but the rest of the powerful ones do not buy any during the simulation.

About the amount possessed, it is amazing to see how much it varies from one step to an other, and that its average is not a relevant indicator of power. It is impossible to predict between two agents which one is going to be regarded as powerful or as weak only by knowing what they possess; at the same time some powerful agents have few units.

In the case of the "limited memory" protocol, the differentiation is still very clear for these criteria. Only one change appears: the number of agents met in ten time steps is reduced a lot. The powerful agents are then characterized by the number of debts and of debtors, and the number of slaves, that are in the same proportion for each category as they were in the other simulation. The division in two categories concerns approximately the same number of agents, about 20/80.

the "redistribution" simulation When the agents have to make a gift as soon as they get rid of a debt, the differentiation between agents is not as clear as before. Actually they all have a number of debts that oscillates between 50 and 60 and a numbers of debtors that is between 40 and 50. The meetings are much less numerous: they just meet 15 other agents in 10 turns after a time. The only difference that can be identified between the agents is their number of slaves. In that case, all of them are able to buy at least one slave during the simulation, but the maximum of slaves bought is about 20. The possession of goods can still be linked to no other information.

Then it is possible to consider the image that the agents have of themselves. What is amazing is that there is no correlation between the only "objective" criterion that shows some differences and these results. The agents that bought a lot of slaves sometimes have a very bad image of themselves. What is regarded as a bad image is when the agent evaluates more agents as stronger than him, when the average of the evaluation is positive. During the same simulation, among the agents that bought only one or two slaves, half of them feel strong compared to their relations.

the "redistribution-elimination" simulation In this simulation, there is a change in the behavior after the 150th time step, beginning with "redistribution" one and then switching to elimination once the opinion already exists. This implies an important change in the results.

There is still no great difference appearing between the agents, the only one being the number of slaves possessed. The results themselves change: 20 time steps after they began selecting the ones with which they get in touch, the agents meet many more agents in 10 time steps (about 80). Their number of debts and debtors has still the same average but there are very important oscillations around the medium number. One point is then linked to the idea of power: the one that have more slaves than the others, have smaller oscillations, with an amplitude of 5 instead of 15.

The image of themselves in the society has a value that is much nearer 0 than in the other simulations, which means that they have a vision of a more homogenous society, and this is true for all the agents.

4 Discussion

4.1 What we saw

The observation was based on 6 criteria for each agents. Three of them had regular values, and it was possible to recognize the emergence of certain local behavior, and then to distinguish different classes for the agents. This global observation gave an analysis of the results considering each simulation separately but also comparing between the protocols, each one defining a specific behaviors for the agents. The differences between protocols that imply differences in the results concern various questions: the redistribution (that distinguish the two first simulation from the others), the use of memory in choices. What was quite predictable was the difference that appears between the different points of view in the observation, because the type of information and the time-scale are different.

redistribution A great difference between the protocols appears with the obligation to make a gift for any counter-gift performed. It has a huge influence on the results, and this is why we dare calling the structure appearing an emergence: different local behavior transforming the global one, even while the agents are not aware of any global effect of their actions. In the simulations where the link is stopped by giving back, there is a real differentiation between agents: some are not dependent, but are put out of the social net, with only few regular relations. In the other type of simulations the agents are all very well integrated and there is no real difference regarding the number of debts.

Actually this can be put in correlation with an observation that Godelier made in his last book (Godelier, 1996). He exhibits that the potlatch, as the expression of opposition, is specific among the non-merchant exchanges: the opportunity is let not to keep on exchanging. He remarks that in the societies where potlatch exists the hierarchy is not well-settled and is actually built by the repeated exchanges, whereas the gift and counter-gift classical dynamics are to be seen where hierarchies are already stable. The results in the artificial world are thus interesting: the social difference appears in the simulations where the redistribution is not forced, like in potlatch, an the society stays homogeneous when the agents have pursue with the link immediately by giving again. In any case, an important number of dependents is associated with an exclusion from the exchange dynamics.

accumulation and time There were two criteria that had something to do with the goods possessed: firstly the quantities of units and their average, and the number of slaves. The fact that an agent buys slaves means that it has the ability to have a lot of units at one given moment. It does not imply that it is regularly wealthy: the two criteria consider the same fact but not in the same time length. What we saw in the simulations is that the number of slaves was correlated with the situation of power in the first simulations, whereas the number of units were not.

What Weber shows is that the economic power in the societies observed is shown by the ability of getting the goods when needed, but not necessarily to accumulate in time. This punctual accumulation is possible because of the number of dependents: giving to someone is thus a real investment, in both economic and social dimension(Weber, 1985).

incoherence between points of view The two ways of observing the artificial world, from the local and global points of view, are based on the idea of dependency in the interaction (being a question of time for the agent and of number of relations for the observer). The results of these observations differ, with almost no correlation between the local and global points of view, and even sometimes contradiction. Anyway, it was used in the "elimination" protocol to influence the actions of the agents.

elimination In the simulation with redistribution, it is interesting to evaluate the impact of the elimination of a relation. It does not have an effect on the differentiation. There is only a small difference between the agents on an "objective" level: those regarded as weak have a less stable position regarding the debts. However, the effect is important on the image that the agents have of themselves. While acting all the agents stop the relations with the weakest ones: the effect is that their society seems more homogenous to them. By changing a behavior because of the image, it is principally the image that we changed.

4.2 to go further

a global point of view for the agent In this model we were trying to describe a model of some human actions. The fact is that in the real society, even if the sociologist and the actors have different points of view, it doesn't prevent the actor to look at his own society globally. The ethnomethodology developed this important point, saying that the main characteristic of man is to take in account the structures it belongs to, and, recognizing its rules, to act in the sense of its reproduction (Gilbert, 1993)(Lahire, 1992).

The agents in the model did not have the ability to get global information and their image of the society was a purely individual creation, based on local knowledge. It would be possible to put in another simulation a larger memory for the agents that would integrate some global remarks we made during the observation.

building a common point of view It would be even more interesting to allow the agent to identify the global vision they share with their own criteria. However, in most simulations the evaluations that the agent has of each of the others are very different. This implies directly that the evaluation the others have of it are also very variable. Hence, it is not possible for the moment to have an efficient global image of an agent that would be built with the agents' points of view. It would anyway be very interesting to find criteria on the group agreed by all the agents and motivating their actions.

What could be defined in this perspective could be called the reputation: a sort of common knowledge about each of the agents. It is possible to imagine such a knowledge, as being an average of the evaluations, or only what the majority believes, as soon as it would be possible to identify a stable opinion. Then this "official"representation could influence the building of the individual images: it would be a base for those that do not know the agent, could transform the opinion of those that did not agree before. This reputation could be thought to be reevaluated less often than the individual points of view, and hence would strongly influence the hierarchies to be stabilized (especially if, imitating humans, the agents have objectives regarding their own reputation).

5 Conclusion

This virtual world was built on a social issue: the role of specific interactions in the society, that the model was describing. Then some observation criteria were built in order to take into account the eco-anthropological analysis of the phenomenon. It was then possible to observe an differentiation, appearing between groups of agents, the structures clearly depending on the dynamics chosen for the simulations. At the same time the criteria had not the same importance for each simulations, some being useless to distinguish these appearing phenomenon.

The second questioning was about this criteria for observation within the system. Several points of view on the same object, the links created, were established and the agents' point of view used as a base for their choices. The coordination of these different observations and analysis was not very easy to use at that moment, but the building of individual representations is still studied.

References

Boas, F. 1966. *Kwakiutl Ethnography*. Chicago: The University of Chicago Press.

Bousquet, F., Proton, I.Bakam And. H., & Page, C. Le. 1998. Cormas : Common-Pool Resources and Multi-Agent Systems. *Lecture Notes in Artificial Intelligence*, **1416**, 826–837.

Doran, J. 1994. Collective memory and emergent human social complexity. *In: Mémoire Collective. Dialogue Entre Les SMA Artificiels (IAD) et Les Sciences Humaines et Biologiques*. Compiègne: Centre de recherche de Royallieu.

Drogoul, A. 1994. *La mémoire collective dans les SMA réactifs : l'exemple de Manta*.

Epstein, J.M., & Axtell, R. 1996. *Growing Artificial Societies. Social Science from the Bottom Up*. Washington DC, USA: The brookings institution.

Ferber, J. 1994. *La Kénétique : Des systèmes multi-agents à une science de l'interaction*. Vol. vol 8.

Ferber, J. 1996. *Coopération, intention et interaction. Une réponse à la "pelouse fourmilière" de Brassac et Pesty*. Hermès.

Gilbert, N. 1993. *'Emergence' in social simulation*.

Godelier, M. 1996. *L'énigme du don*. Fayard.

Hinde, R.A.

Lahire, B. 1992. *Précisions sur la manière sociologique de traiter du "sens" : quelques remarque concernant l'éthnométhodologie*. Vol. 59 - les enjeux de l'ethnométhodologie.

Mauss, M. 1968. *Sociologie et anthropologie*. PUF (4eme édition).

Weber, J. 1985. C=R-I, My God, My Gold ! (Réflexion sur la Porte Du Concept de Consumation). *revue du MAUSS*, **13**.

Wellman, B. 1996. *Are personal communities local ? A Dumptarian reconsideration*. Vol. 18. Elsevier science B.V.

Dynamics of Internal and Global Structure through Linguistic Interactions

Takashi Hashimoto

Lab. for Information Synthesis,
Brain Science Institute, RIKEN,
2-1, Hirosawa, Wako, Saitama, 351-0198, JAPAN
Tel: +81-48-467-9663   Fax: +81-48-467-9693
takashi@brain.riken.go.jp
http://www.bip.riken.go.jp/irl/takashi/

Abstract. Development of category structure in communication is studied by a constructive approach. Individuals having a word relation matrix as their internal structure communicate by uttering and accepting sentences. Words in sentences uttered are situated in relation with other words by each individual. Words make clusters according to their interrelationships. The structures and dynamics of clusters are studied. Coexisting commonality and individuality of clustering structure is observed in an ensemble of individuals.

1   Introduction

A Constructive Approach to Dynamically Complex Systems. Increasingly, biological, ecological, brain, language and social systems have been studied as complex systems. One of the characteristics of these systems is that they show various spatio-temporal dynamics, such as coexisting stability and adaptability, collective behavior, diversification, differentiation, hierarchical level formation, emergence or open-ended evolution. Chaotic behavior is also sometimes observed in these systems. It is thought that these characteristics arise from dynamical many-to-many interactions and high dimensionality (Kaneko and Tsuda, 1997). Some researchers have pointed out that considerations of self-referential features or internal observers are also crucial to understanding such dynamically complex systems (Tsuda, 1991; Gunji et al., 1997).

The conventional manner of studying these systems is to attempt to describe them objectively. However, structural instability or undecomposability between observers and observed systems, both of which typically occur in complex systems, can make such objective descriptions very difficult. In such cases, constructive approaches can be effective for studying the systems (Kaneko and Tsuda, 1994). One example of such an approach is to build models with elements having internal dynamics that interact with each other, and to then observe the emergence of global behavior. However, we assert that observation of the emergence of a global order is not enough in itself, since the phenomena shown in complex systems are usually not static but dynamic, and sometimes show open-ended evolution. Therefore, the constructed models must demonstrate not only emergence but dynamics of global behavior through the dynamics of elements.

Perhaps the key point in modeling complex systems is the introduction of the dynamics of elements. Elements can change their internal states and their relationship to other elements. By the individual dynamics, global and local levels are dynamically coupled, and this dynamical coupling drives the systems to be dynamic also at the global level (Kaneko and Tsuda, 1994).

Language as Dynamics. Language also should be studied as a dynamical complex system. Language can be viewed in two ways: structurally and dynamically. The structural view is a static one in which language structure, e.g. syntax (Chomsky, 1957) or pragmatic rules (Grice, 1975; Sperber and Wilson, 1986), offers idealized approaches to language. The alternative view is dynamic. It concentrates on the actual use of language rather than abstract notions of how language ought to be. Language is considered as a collection of dynamical processes based on the individual creative acts of speaking, hearing, writing, and reading.

Bakhtin has termed these two views abstract objectivism and individualistic subjectivism, respectively (Vološinov, 1986). He sketched out these two views as follows. In the former view, language is understood as "a stable, immutable system on normatively identical linguistic forms." In the latter view, in contrast, language is thought of as "activity, an unceasing process of creation realized in individual speech acts." Bakhtin stressed the importance of identifying language from the individualistic subjective standpoint, stating that "What is important for the speaker about a linguistic form is not that it is a stable and always self-equivalent signal, but that it is an always changeable and adaptable sign."

Clearly, the use of language is such a creative process, rather than the recognition of the "pre-established" forms. Words uttered are not connected with *a priori* and constant meanings. Words have fundamental polysemy. Language users are continually creating sense in fluctuating contexts by situating words in relation to other words (Fukaya and Tanaka, 1996).

Another way to understand the value of the dynamical view of language is by considering the notion of the metaphor. Metaphorical expressions are creative or dynamic precisely because they can "bend" conventionally structured language. By producing or understanding metaphorical expressions, especially creative metaphors, our internal structure should change. We cannot say that creative expressions are valid or not valid, since they are novel and cannot be understood by this distinction of a conventional language structure. Rather, we should consider whether or not we accept the expressions. If we accept them, our internal structure changes and our language structure might also come to be modified.

A constructive approach is also useful for studying language systems (Steels, 1997). The emergence of global order as a language-like behavior is observed by modeling individuals in terms of their linguistic interactions. This way of studying language constitutes a part of that of evolutionary linguistics. Evolutionary linguistics throws a bridge across the two viewpoints of language. The global structure, i.e. the structure common to individuals, described in the static view should emerged as a result of the dynamic processes of using language. It must be noted that the global structure in language should not be static. The change in internal structure resulting from the use of language induces the dynamics of the structure of language. In keeping with this point, we have previously studied a system of evolutionary grammars, which shows the emergence and dynamics of grammars common to communication networks (Hashimoto and Ikegami, 1996).

In this paper, we study the development of category structure from the viewpoint of language as a dynamical phenomenon. We have constructed a model of an ensemble of individuals communicating with each other. Individual agents understand sentences uttered by situating words in relation to other words. This results in an internal structure, the word relation matrix, peculiar to each individual. In this way, we continue to investigate our previously proposed usage-based viewpoint, in which the meaning of words is understood in terms of how language is actually used (Hashimoto, 1997). The usage of words in communication thus reflects the word relation matrix of each agent.

2 Algorithm for Calculating Word Relationships

We study the dynamics of categorization by observing how words in sentences are situated in relation to each other through communication between artificial agents. Each agent has its own word relationship matrix as its internal structure, which develops according to the agent's utterances and acceptances.

The algorithm for calculating the similarity between words in sentences is basically that of Karov and Edelman (Karov and Edelman, 1996) with a few modifications. They have presented an algorithm for word sense disambiguation based on similarity among words. A key concept in the algorithm is the mutual dependency between words and sentences. That is, similar words appear in similar sentences and similar sentences are composed of similar words. Similarities between words are calculated from similarities among sentences in which the words are used. The similarity between sentences is derived from that of words used in the sentences.

We make two modifications on their algorithm. One is that we consider the correlation of appearance between words in texts in deriving the relationship among words. A text is a set of sentences or, in the context of this paper, a conversation. If patterns of appearance of words in texts are similar, e.g., some words appear many times in a text but do not do so in the other texts, these words are considered to have high affinity. Conversely, different appearance patterns between words imply a disaffinity between them. The other revision is that the relationships are calculated immediately after uttering or accepting a sentence, since we are interested in the dynamics of word relationships in conversations.

The relationship between words and between sentences of an agent k are respectively defined by the following formulae:

$$R_{t,n}^k(w_i, w_j) = \begin{cases} \alpha^w \dfrac{\sum_{s \ni w_i} K_{t,n}^k(s) A_{t,n}^k(s, w_j)}{\sum_{s \ni w_i} K_{t,n}^k(s)} + \dfrac{1-\alpha^w}{2}\left(\dfrac{D_{t,n}^k(w_i, w_j)}{\sqrt{N_{t,n}^k(w_i) N_{t,n}^k(w_j)}} + 1\right) & \text{if } i \neq j , \\ 1.0 & \text{if } i = j , \end{cases}$$

$$\tag{1}$$

$$R_{t,n}^k(s_i, s_j) = \begin{cases} \alpha^s \dfrac{\sum_{w \in s_i} K_{t,n}^k(w) A_{t,n}^k(w, s_j)}{\sum_{w \in s_i} K_{t,n}^k(w)} + \dfrac{1-\alpha^s}{2}\left(\dfrac{D_{t,n}^k(s_i, s_j)}{\sqrt{N_{t,n}^k(s_i) N_{t,n}^k(s_j)}} + 1\right) & \text{if } i \neq j , \\ 1.0 & \text{if } i = j . \end{cases}$$

$$\tag{2}$$

Here, the subscripts n and t indicate a sentence and a text, respectively. A text is a conversation. The numbering system for sentences and texts is illustrated in Fig. 1. The binary relation $w \in s$ means that a word w is used in a sentence s, and $s \ni w$ means that a sentence s uses a word w. The first terms in (1) and (2) describe the usage similarity between words and between sentences, respectively, and the second terms the correlation between appearance of words and between that of sentences in texts, respectively. These two terms are combined with the coefficients α^w and α^s for words and sentences, respectively.

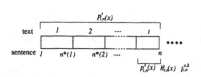

Fig. 1. The numbering system for texts and sentences; and the ranges of sentence for $P_{t,n}^k(x)$, $p_{t,n}^k(x)$, $h_{t,n}^k(x)$ and $l_{t,n}^{x,k}$.

The affinity of sentences to words and that of words to sentences are defined using the relationship between words and between sentences as follows:

$$A_{t,n}^k(s, w) = \frac{\sum_{s' \ni w} K_{t,n}^k(s') R_{t,n}^k(s, s')}{\sum_{s' \ni w} K_{t,n}^k(s')} ,$$

$$\tag{3}$$

and

$$A_{t,n}^k(w, s) = \frac{\sum_{w' \in s} K_{t,n}^k(w') R_{t,n-1}^k(w, w')}{\sum_{w' \in s} K_{t,n}^k(w')} ,$$

$$\tag{4}$$

respectively. In the four equations, (1) $\sim$ (4), weights for similarities and affinities define the contribution made by the appearance provability of each word and sentence and by the length of each sentence. The weight factors are defined as

$$K_{t,n}^k(s) = \frac{P_{t,n}^k(s)}{lg(s)} ,$$

$$\tag{5}$$

and

$$K_{t,n}^k(w) = \frac{1}{P_{t,n}^k(w)} ,$$

$$\tag{6}$$

where $lg(s)$ is the length of a sentence s, which is defined by the number of words included in the sentence; $P_{t,n}^k(w)$ and $P_{t,n}^k(s)$, to be defined later, are the appearance provability of a word w and that of a sentence s in all sentences from the first to the nth sentence, respectively. These weight factors mean that the more a word is used, the less informative it is; that the more a sentence is used, the greater its contribution is; and that a word in a longer sentence is less important than one in a shorter sentence.

Due to the symmetry of words and sentences in the functions $D_{t,n}^k$ and $N_{t,n}^k$, we can use a symbol x to denote a word (w) or a sentence (s) in the following equations. In order to consider the dynamics of internal structure through conversations, the correlation of words and sentences should be incrementally updated per each utterance and acceptance of sentences. The functions $D_{t,n}^k$ and $N_{t,n}^k$ are recursively defined as

$$D_{t,n}^k(x_i, x_j) = D_{t-1,n^*(t-1)}^k(x_i, x_j) + l_{t,n}^{x,k^2}(p_{t,n}^k(x_i) - P_{t,n}^k(x_i))(p_{t,n}^k(x_j) - P_{t,n}^k(x_j)) \,, \tag{7}$$

and

$$N_{t,n}^k(x_i) = N_{t-1,n^*(t-1)}^k(x_i) + l_{t,n}^{x,k^2}(p_{t,n}^k(x_i) - P_{t,n}^k(x_i))^2 \,, \tag{8}$$

where $n^*(t)$ is the last sentence in the tth text.

The appearance provability of x in all sentences from the first to the nth sentence $P_{t,n}^k(x)$ is defined as

$$P_{t,n}^k(x) = \frac{\sum_{t'=1}^{t-1} h_{t',n^*(t')}^k(x) + h_{t,n}^k(x)}{\sum_{t'=1}^{t-1} l_{t',n^*(t')}^{x,k} + l_{t,n}^{x,k}} \,, \tag{9}$$

and the appearance provability of x in a text t by the nth sentence is defined as

$$p_{t,n}^k(x) = \frac{h_{t,n}^k(x)}{l_{t,n}^{x,k}} \,, \tag{10}$$

where $h_{t,n}^k(x)$ is frequency, i.e., the number of appearances, of a word or a sentence, and $l_{t,n}^{x,k}$ is the length of a text counted by x, i.e., the number of all words or that of all sentences, in a text t by the nth sentence (see Fig. 1).

By uttering or accepting a sentence, the word-sentence affinity (4) is calculated from the word relation matrix at uttering/accepting the previous sentence; and the correlations among words and among sentences are updated. Then, these formulae are calculated in the order of (2) $\rightarrow$ (3) $\rightarrow$ (1). The relationship of a word with itself is set to be $R_{1,0}^k(w_i, w_j) = \delta_{i,j}$ for new words before the calculation. In the first text, $D_{1,n}^k(x_i, x_j)$ and $N_{1,n}^k(x)$ are 0, but the correlation of a word or a sentence with itself is always 1, i.e., $D_{1,n}^k(x_i, x_j)/\sqrt{N_{1,n}^k(x_i)N_{1,n}^k(x_j)} = \delta_{i,j}$.

3 Modeling for Conversations

In our model there are M topics $(0 \sim M)$, which are placed on a one dimensional space with the periodic boundary. A randomly selected topic with zero, one or two adjacent topics is presented to agents at the start of a conversation. The presented topics are collectively called a situation and a conversation is called a text.

In the initial state, agents do not know any words and do not have a name for any of the topics. At the beginning of each text, two agents are randomly selected to converse. A speaker agent randomly selects a topic from the presented situation and utters a sentence that includes the name for the topic. The speaker then updates its word relation matrix according to the uttered sentence. In the case that an agent has not had a name for the selected topic at the time of utterance, it creates a word by combining characters as the topic name.

A hearer agent accepts the uttered sentence if there are zero unknown words or one unknown word in the sentence. After acceptance, the hearer's word relation matrix is updated according to the accepted sentence, and then the agents take turns alternating their roles of speaker and hearer. The new speaker agent makes a sentence in reply to the accepted sentence. If the uttered sentence is not accepted by the hearer, the agents do not take turns and the speaker again selects a topic at random from the presented situation. When 5 sentences are not accepted or the number of sentences accepted by both agents becomes 100, the text is concluded, and then another pair of agents and a new situation are selected for a new text.

To make a sentence for utterance, a speaker arbitrary selects a focus word from the words in the accepted sentence. At the commencement of a text, the name for the selected topic serves as the focus word. The speaker adopts a sentence with the highest affinity to the focus word from the word-sentence affinity matrix (4) of the agent. If the adopted sentence is the same as the accepted sentence, the second highest affinity sentence is adopted. If the adopted sentence is the same as the sentence uttered by the speaker in the immediately previous conversation, then the third highest affinity sentence is adopted.

An agent modifies the adopted sentence to be uttered in proportion to the creativity rate c. There are three means of modification: addition, replacement, and deletion of a word. One of the three is selected depending on the sentence modification rates, m_{add}^s, m_{rep}^s, and m_{del}^s, respectively. A word for addition or replacement is selected from already known words. The word itself is also modified by addition, replacement, or deletion of a character depending on the word modification rates, m_{add}^w, m_{rep}^w, and m_{del}^w, respectively.

4 Simulation Results and Discussion

First, to demonstrate the internal dynamics of individuals, we will summarize the results of simulated conversations between two agents in §4.1 and §4.2, and then describe that of simulations in an ensemble of agents in §4.3. The simulations are made using in the following parameters. The maximum of topics M is 9. The set of characters is $\{a, e, i, o, u\}$. The creativity rate c is 0.1. The sentence modification rates are $m_{add}^s = 0.2$, $m_{rep}^s = 0.7$, and $m_{del}^s = 0.1$. The word modification rates are $m_{add}^w = 0.33$, $m_{rep}^w = 0.34$, and $m_{del}^w = 0.33$. The weight coefficients for similarity and correlation in (1) and (2) are $\alpha^w = \alpha^s = 0.4$ in the tw-agent simulations and 0.6 in the ensemble simulations. The results described here are for these specific parameter values; however nearly the same results can be observed using a wide range of parameter values.

An example of a conversation is as follows:

```
TEXT: 25 SITUATION: 0 1 2
TOPIC: 2
agent1.name[2]= ea          agent0.name[2]= i
   1: ea-i                      0: ea-eii-iii-iuuo-eii
   1: ea-eii-eii-eii            0: ea-i
   1: ea-eii-iii-iuuo-eii       0: iuuo
   1: eoi                       0: i-eoi
   1: i-eoi                     0: eoi
   1: i-ei-eoi                  0: i-eoi
   1: eoi                       0: i-ei-eoi
   1: i                         0: i-eii
   1: eii-eii-eii               0: eii-eii
   1: eii-eii                   0: eii-eii-ii-uuoe
   1: eii-eii-eii               0: eii-eii
   1: eii-eii                   0: eii-eii-ei
```

This example is the beginning part of text $t = 25$ of a simulation. The situation is composed of the topics 0, 1 and 2. The agent 1 selects the topic 2. The agent 1 has already named the topic 2 'ea' and the agent 0 has named it 'i.' As in this example, agents in a conversation can adopt different names for the same topic. The agent 1 utters a sentence "ea-i" based on the focus word 'ea,' which is the name for topic 2. The agent 0 accepts the sentence and replies with the sentence "ea-eii-iii-iuuo-eii" based on the focus word 'ea.'

4.1 Word Clusters

Flat and Gradual Clusters. Words make clusters according to their interrelationship. Figure 2(a) gives an example of a cluster structure. This figure is a scattered diagram drawn using the results of the principal coordinate analysis of the word relationship matrix $R(w_i, w_j)$ (1). We can see four clusters of words in the figure. There are roughly two types of clusters. The first is a cluster in which words are distributed over rather small regions, such as the words $1 \sim 4$ and $9 \sim 12$ in the figure. The other is a cluster in which words lie in a long and narrow region, such as the words $5 \sim 8$, here. The former type is called a flat cluster, for if we draw word relation matrix directly, as in Fig. 2(b), this type of cluster is seen as having a flat top. In the latter type, the word relationship gradually changes from one end of the cluster to the other. Since the relationship between words gradually decays, as shown in Fig. 2(b), we term this a gradual cluster.

Near the start of the simulations, a few flat clusters exist rather independently. Flat clusters extend their boundaries with new words and come to have gradual edges. Some sentences connect separated clusters. The structure of the word relationship is usually made up of a combination of the two types of clusters, as in Fig. 2.

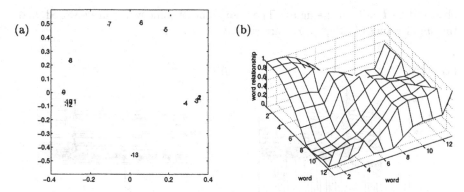

Fig. 2. (a) An example of scattered diagram of the word relation matrix $R(w_i, w_j)$ processed by the principal coordinate analysis. The X and Y axes are the first and second principal coordinates obtained by the analysis, respectively. Each number in the diagram indicates a word. (b) The word relationship matrix $R(w_i, w_j)$ shown in (a) is directly drawn in this graph. Words are listed in the X and Y axes. The number for each word corresponds to that of in (a). The Z axis is the value of $R(w_i, w_j)$.

Clustering as Categorization. Clustering can be regarded as a categorization of words by an agent through conversations, since words in a cluster have a stronger relation with each other and a weaker relation with words out of the cluster. The two major types of cluster structure, flat and gradual, correspond to two different concepts of a category. Because the boundaries of flat clusters are sharp, it is easy to distinguish whether or not an entity is a member of the cluster. This is a conventional concept of a category in which membership is rigidly determined by necessary and sufficient conditions. In contrast to the flat cluster, a gradual cluster shows a gradated change in relationship from large to small. This corresponds to a new concept of categorization. In the new concept, the degree to which words are included in a category is a matter of the gradient.

In actual simulations, these two types of clusters present in combination. That is, a cluster is likely to have a flat top and a graded boundary. In terms of categories, the flat top portion corresponds to central members of the category, and words having only a slight relation to the central words are peripheral members. This structure resembles that of a prototype category (Lakoff, 1987; Taylor, 1995).

4.2 Dynamics of Word Relationships and Clusters

Change of Word Relationships by New Usages. Word relationships change with conversations. We exemplify the transitions of the relationship of a word to other words in Fig. 3(a). This constitutes a portion of dynamics of the internal structure of an agent. Each line is sustained at a particular value with some fluctuations for some period of texts and with occasional large and abrupt changes. Simultaneous and large changes in relationships to many words are sometimes observed, as $t = 21$ in the figure. The high value of some words are lowered, and the small values of other words are rapidly increased.

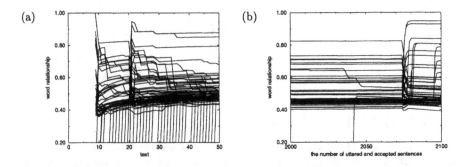

Fig. 3. (a) An example of a transition of word relationship per each text is depicted. The Y axis represents the relationship of the word **aa** to the other words $(R(\mathbf{aa}, w))$ of an agent at the end of each text. The X axis is the number of texts. Since the word **aa** appears at $t = 9$, the graph starts from that text. Lines arising from the X axis indicate the appearances of new words. (b) This is a transition of word relationship of the word **aa** to the other words per each uttered/accepted sentence in the text $t = 21$. The X axis is the number of uttered/accepted sentences (n) and the Y axis is the word relationship $R(\mathbf{aa}, w)$. Between $n = 2070$ and $n = 2080$, many words switch their relationships rapidly and simultaneously.

The simultaneous and large charges in word relation are induced by appearances of rare or new usages of words. Uttering or accepting a sentence in which a new word is used or a word is used in an unusual way may vary the word relationship largely and rapidly. We describe the dynamics of $R(\mathbf{aa}, w)$ per each utterance/acceptance of sentences in the text $t = 21$ in Fig. 3(b). A simultaneous and large change is observed between $n = 2070$ and $n = 2080$. The utterance of a sentence containing words in rare way of use at $n = 2074$ results in a large and rapid change in dynamics. Words used in this text $(t = 21)$ develop their relationship, and words that are not used in this text but that are used in other texts diminish their relationship. However, changes in the relationship to ubiquitously used words as a result of this appearance of rare usage are small.

Cluster Structure Dynamics. We next inquire how large changes in word relationships affect the cluster structure by observing word movement in scattered diagrams. The sentence-word affinity matrices $A(s_i, w_j)$ at before and after the large change ($n = 2074$ and $n = 2077$) are combined to form one matrix, and this matrix is processed using principal component analysis (PCA). The first and second principal components are used to draw the scattered diagram in Fig. 4. Corresponding words between before and after the large change are connected by arrows.

From this diagram, it can be seen that words in a cluster move in almost the same directions before and after this change; therefore, the whole structure of clusters does not change drastically. But the word aa, which is used in a rare way at $n = 2074$, moves in a different direction from words in the cluster at $n = 2074$. It changes the cluster to which it belongs. A large change in the word relationships between a particular word and others does not restructure the whole system of clusters, but this change effects the word relationship incrementally with each subsequent step. Thus the entire clustering structure may slowly transform.

Dynamical Stability and Adaptability. By uttering or accepting sentences in which usage of words are new or rare, some words change their positions in the clustering structure. But most words move coherently in the same direction, and thereby avoiding a sudden transformation of the whole structure. It can be said that the structures of clusters have the characteristics of stability and adaptability.

The dynamical stability and adaptability often seen in complex systems must be equipped for language systems. If a language is too rigid, its users will not be able to formulate new expressions to describe diverse experiences, and if it is too unstable, no structurization will be possible at either the individual of global level will be possible, and hence no communication will take place. Geeraerts explains this point as it pertains to categorization: "To prevent the categorical system from becoming chaotic, it should have a built-in tendency towards structural stability, but this stability should not become rigidity, lest the system stops being able to adapt itself to the

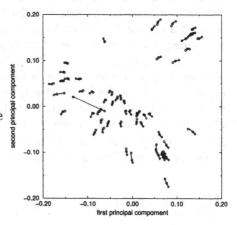

Fig. 4. This figure shows alterations of cluster structure before and after a large change in word relationship. It is the scattered diagram obtained from the principal component analysis of a matrix made by combining two sentence-word affinity matrices $A_{t,n}^k(s_i, w_j)$ at both before and after the change. The X and Y axes are the first and second principal components, respectively. Symbols o and ◇ mark words at before and at after the change, respectively, and the corresponding words are connected by solid arrows. The broken arrow means the move of the word aa.

ever-changing circumstances of the outside world (Geeraerts, 1985)."

4.3 Global Level

In the above sections, we have sketched out the development of the internal structure in individuals and its dynamics through conversations. In this section, we consider communication in an ensemble of agents. The focus issues are whether a structure common to the ensemble emerges and how individual dynamics effect the common structure, i.e., how commonality and individuality develop.

Definition of Distance Rate. Representing the disparity between agents numerically provides clues to understanding the degree to which the agents have a common internal structure and how the common structure behaves. We consider the Euclidean distance between word relation matrices of two agents as the distance between the agents. But since agents generally know different words, the matrices must be reconstructed for the words which either agent knows. In terms of a symbol $W_{t,n}^k$, denoting a set of words which an agent k knows at the nth sentence in a text t, a word relation matrix of an agent k is formally described as $R_{t,n}^k(w_i, w_j \mid w_i, w_j \in W_{t,n}^k)$. The reconstructed word relation matrix of an agent k to another agent k' is defined for words which either agent knows $(w_i \in W_{t,n}^k \cup W_{t,n}^{k'})$. For known words by the agent k $(w_i \in W_{t,n}^k)$, elements of a reconstructed matrix of an agent k are the same as those of the original matrix $R_{t,n}^k$. Those for words unknown by the agent k but known by the other agent k' $(\{w_i \mid w_i \notin W_{t,n}^k \wedge w_i \in W_{t,n}^{k'}\})$ are set to zero. In summary, the reconstructed matrix of an agent k to another agent k' is defined as

$$\tilde{R}_{t,n}^{k|k'}(w_i, w_j \mid \forall w_i, w_j \in W_{t,n}^k \cup W_{t,n}^{k'}) = \begin{cases} R_{t,n}^k(w_i, w_j) & \text{if } w_i, w_j \in W_{t,n}^k \\ 0 & \text{if } (w_i \notin W_{t,n}^k \wedge w_i \in W_{t,n}^{k'}) \vee \\ & (w_j \notin W_{t,n}^k \wedge w_j \in W_{t,n}^{k'}) \end{cases}$$

(11)

The distance between two agents k and k' is defined with the reconstructed matrices as

$$\rho_{t,n}^{k,k'} = \sqrt{\sum_i \sum_j (\tilde{R}_{t,n}^{k'|k}(w_i, w_j) - \tilde{R}_{t,n}^{k|k'}(w_i, w_j))^2} .$$

(12)

Since the number of known words always increases in the simulation, the dimension of the matrix $\tilde{R}_{t,n}^{k'|k}$ becomes bigger and bigger and the distance $\rho_{t,n}^{k,k'}$ seldom decreases. We take the average of the distance by the number of words,

$$\bar{\rho}_{t,n}^{k,k'} = \frac{\rho_{t,n}^{k,k'}}{\mid W_{t,n}^k \cup W_{t,n}^{k'} \mid} ,$$

(13)

where $\mid W_{t,n}^k \cup W_{t,n}^{k'} \mid$ is the number of words in $W_{t,n}^k \cup W_{t,n}^{k'}$. We call $\bar{\rho}_{t,n}^{k,k'}$ the distance rate between agents k and k' at the nth sentence in a text t. The average for all pairs of agents is

$$\langle \bar{\rho}_{t,n} \rangle = \frac{\sum_{\text{all pairs}} \bar{\rho}_{t,n}^{k,k'}}{{}_K C_2} ,$$

(14)

where K is the number of agents in an ensemble and ${}_K C_2$ is the number of pairs of agents.

Development of Common Structure. We report the results of simulations in which the number of agents (K) is 5. The coefficients in (1) and (2) are $\alpha^w = \alpha^s = 0.6$. The other parameters are the same as in the simulations in the previous subsections.

All agents share an identical initial state, that is, they do not know any words or sentences. Two agents are selected randomly to converse. Note that only one pair makes a conversation in one text, and that the agents that do not participate in the conversation cannot hear sentences uttered by the participants in the conversation. Therefore, each agent has its own experience of conversations and its own way of developing its internal structure. However, the difference between agents can be reduced by joining a conversation, since the agents conversing hear the same sentences.

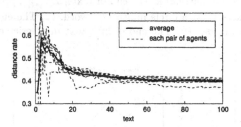

Figure 5 shows the transition of the distance rates, including the distance rate for for each pair and the average rate for all pairs, at the end of texts per each text. At first the average distance rate is large, and then it converges at around $\langle \bar{\rho} \rangle \cong 0.4$. This means that each agent has both common and not common parts in its internal structure.

Fig. 5. An example of transitions of the distance rates at the end of texts per each text. The broken lines are the distance rates for each pair $(\bar{\rho}^{k,k'}_{t,n^*(t)})$, and the solid line is the averaged distance rate for all pairs $(\langle \bar{\rho}_{t,n^*(t)} \rangle)$.

To see how the shared structure between a pair of agents is organized through conversations, we define the difference matrix as

$$E^{k,k'}_{t,n} = |\tilde{R}^{k|k'}_{t,n} - \tilde{R}^{k'|k}_{t,n}| \ . \tag{15}$$

In Fig. 6, we depict scattered diagrams of the difference matrices for a pair of agents. Figure 6(a) is at the end of text $t = 9$. This is the first text in which the pair of agents converse. Figure 6(b) is at the end of text $t = 35$ which is the fifth text of a series of conversations between the two agents. Since the agents converse with the other agents before the text $t = 9$, they develop their own structure. After the five conversations between them, the difference is more organized than at the end of first text. The common words, i.e. those that share a common relationship, and the not common words are clearly separated.

The ratio of elements for which the difference between two agents in a pair is larger than 0.5 to all elements, namely, the percentage of words for which $E^{k,k'}_{t,n^*(t)}(w_i, w_j) > 0.5$ in all elements, decays exponentially as shown in Fig. 7(a). The number of texts in which the pair converse is taken as the X axis in the figure. The degree of commonality between the agents increases through conversations.

Although the similarity among the internal structure of agents seems to increase with conversations, the agents in a pair converse with the other agents,

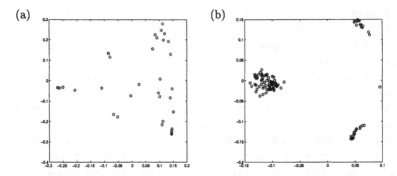

Fig. 6. Structurization of difference between two agents through conversations. These graphs are scattered diagrams of difference matrices at the end of texts, $E_{t,n^*(t)}^{k,k'}$, processed by the principal coordinate analysis. Each circle indicates a word. (a) The end of the first text in which the agents converse. (b) The end of fifth text in a series of conversations between them.

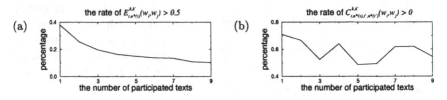

Fig. 7. (a) The ratio of elements for which the difference between two agents larger than 0.5 ($E_{t,n^*(t)}^{k,k'}(w_i, w_j) > 0.5$) for a pair of agents to all elements in a difference matrix vs. the number of texts in which the pair converses. (b) Transition of the ratio of elements for which the difference between two agents becomes larger ($C_{t,n^*(t),t',n^*(t')}^{k,k'}(w_i, w_j) > 0$) for a pair of agents to all elements in a change matrix through conversations.

and therefore disparity between the agents can again be increased. The manner by which differences between two agents change between two texts is expressed by the change matrix defined as

$$C_{t,n,t',n'}^{k,k'} = E_{t',n'}^{k,k'} - E_{t,n}^{k,k'} \quad . \tag{16}$$

If $C_{t,n,t',n'}^{k,k'}(w_i, w_j)$ is positive, the difference between two agents becomes larger, and it becomes smaller in the opposite case. Figure 7(b) shows the transition of the ratio of elements which the difference of word relationships between two agents increases with texts. The number of texts in which the pair participates in conversations is taken as the X axis. Each point shows the percentage of the elements $C_{t,n^*(t),t',n^*(t')}^{k,k'}(w_j, w_j) > 0$ at between the end of the text and the end of the next text in which the pair converses. This quantity does not decay monotonically but shows oscillatory behavior. Although the common part evolves through conversations, the non-common part does not simply become small.

Commonality and Individuality. In the present model, achieving a mutual understanding in communication means that the words used in a conversation are situated in relationship to other words in the same way by partners, i.e., that these words form an equivalent structure in word relation matrices to other agents. Actually, as we have seen, although commonality to agents develops with conversations, the whole matrix does not come to be identical. This is because an agent interacts with not only one agent but several, and its internal structure changes accordingly. This results in an ever-changing relation among agents.

Mutual understanding is, of course, important. Of great significance in communication through language, however, is the openness with which an individual construe the utterances of others, i.e. the diversity of interpretation of utterances. Such openness drives the language to be dynamic. Coping with both commonality and individuality at the local level allows for stability and dynamics of language. The characteristics of a category system that has both dynamical stability and adaptability, as discussed in the previous section, may manage the compatibility of commonality and individuality.

Here we have seen coexisting common and non-common parts of agents, but the global-level structure has yet to be clarified. Due to computational limits, both the number of agents in an ensemble and the number of texts are small. Further inquiry into the structure and dynamics of larger systems will be needed.

5 General Discussion

Dynamical Models for Origins of Languages We can often understand what a sentence means even if it does not obey "rules of syntax" or "the precise word meanings found in dictionaries." For example, even if one of the speakers in a conversation is a foreigner speaking in a faltering manner, a mutual understanding can still be reached. Such "ill-formed" usages may induce changes in a language and in the dynamics of the internal worlds of language users. Using language is a dynamical process, and is not limited to the mere recognition of idealized rules of grammar or word meanings. It is difficult to study the dynamical nature of language by abstracting these idealized aspects from an already "well-formed" language.

In this study, we have proposed one of the possible methods for modeling dynamical language phenomena. Agents in the model do not share explicit grammar, rather they share a way to infer relations among words used. As has been demonstrated, shared and non-shared categorical structures develop through conversations and these structures are modified by "new" usage of words.

The final aim of our studies is to inquire into not only development but the origins of language. Therefore, the agents in our model are given no explicit linguistic knowledge, such as of grammar or word use or meaning. And in fact, at the start of the trials they know no words at all. To this end, the conventional, i.e. descriptive, studies for languages and their development are, of course, important. But there is a limit to which we can expand our knowledge of language origins using only the descriptions of present languages. The constructive approaches described here may give possible scenarios for the origins and development of languages. These two ways of studying should be complementarily developed.

External World To investigate the dynamics of categorical structure in conversation, we have focused primarily on inter-individual interaction. Actual language phenomena, however, are not divorced from the environments surrounding individuals. We often use language in unauthorized ways to describe new situations brought on by environmental changes.

Our model should be developed to incorporate the dynamics of the external worlds of language users. It is important to clarify how shared and non-shared structures of language develop depending on the relations between external and internal worlds.

Application to Discourse Analysis Karov and Edelman (1996) have presented the algorithm to calculate similarity among words for word sense disambiguation in corpora. We have made two revisions to the algorithm. The first is that we consider correlation of appearance between words in a series of conversations. The second is that we define the new algorithm such that it can update word relation matrices per each utterance and acceptance.

These modifications improve the algorithm's ability to treat "contextual" information, as well as its ability to handle the dynamic feature of conversations. The original algorithm is to process a corpus, a static database of sentences, but conversations are dynamic streams of utterances. Although its details must be fine-tuned for natural language processing, our new algorithm may ultimately be applied to word sense disambiguation in conversations and discourse analysis.

6   Conclusion

We have studied the dynamics of categorization based on a dynamical view of language. We model the comprehension of word meaning in communication by situating them in relationship to other words. The relationship is derived from the usage of words in sentences in conversations. The agents develop categorical structure of words as clustering through conversations. There are central and peripheral members in each cluster, and the extent to which words belong to a cluster changes gradually. The cluster structure has both stability and adaptability. Common structure to an ensemble of agents is organized by communication. Individuality in agents is also maintained. This coexistence of commonality and individuality is an outgrowth of the diverse experience of communication.

Acknowledgments

I wish to express my gratitude to Takashi Ikegami, Yukito Iba, Luc Steels and Chitose Ikawa for their fruitful discussions. I thank Michael Miller and Chitose Ikawa for their editorial revisions. This work was supported by the Special Postdoctoral Researchers Program at the Institute of Physical and Chemical Research (RIKEN), Saitama, Japan.

References

N. Chomsky. 1957. *Syntactic Structure*. Mouton, The Hague.

M. Fukaya and S Tanaka. 1996. *Kotoba no ⟨Imiduke-ron⟩ (A Theory of "Making Sence" of Language)* [in Japanese]. Kinokuniya Shoten, Tokyo.

D. Geeraerts. 1985. Cognitive restrictions on the structure of semantic change. In Fisiak J, editor, *Historical Semantics*, pages 127–153. Mouton de Gruyter, Berlin.

H. P. Grice. 1975. Logic and conversation. In P. Cole and J. L. Morgan, editors, *Syntax and Semantics, Vol. 3: Speech Acts*, pages 41–58. Academic Press, New York, NY.

P.Y. Gunji, K. Ito, and Y. Kusunoki. 1997. Formal model of internal measurement: Alternate changing between recursive definition and domain equation. *Physica*, D110:289–312.

T. Hashimoto and T. Ikegami. 1996. Emergence of net-grammar in communicating agents. *BioSystems*, 38:1–14.

T. Hashimoto. 1997. Usage-based structuralization of relationships between words. In P. Husbands and I. Harvey, editors, *Fourth European Conference on Artificial Life*, pages 483–492, Cambridge, MA. MIT Press.

K. Kaneko and I. Tsuda. 1994. Constructive complexity and artificial reality: an introduction. *Physica*, D75:1–10.

K. Kaneko and I. Tsuda. 1997. *Fukuzatsu-kei no Kaosu-teki Sinario (Chaotic Scenario of Complex Systems)* [in Japanese]. Asakura Shoten, Tokyo.

Y. Karov and S. Edelman. 1996. Similarity-based word sense disambiguation. Technical Report CS-TR 96-06, Weizmann Institute.

G. Lakoff. 1987. *Women, Fire, and Dangerous Things*. The University of Chicago Press, Chicago.

D. Sperber and D. Wilson. 1986. *Relevance: Communication and Cognition*. Blackwell, Oxford.

L. Steels. 1997. The synthetic modeling of language origin. *Evolution of Communication*, 1(1):1–34.

J. R. Taylor. 1995. *Linguistic Categorization – Prototypes in Linguistic Theory*. Oxford University Press, Oxford.

I. Tsuda. 1991. *Chaos-teki-Nou-kan (Chaotic Scenario of Brain)* [in Japanese]. Saiensu-sha, Tokyo.

V. N. Vološinov. 1986. *Marxism and Philosophy of Language*. Harvard University Press, Cambridge, MA.

Stereotyping, Groups and Cultural Evolution: A Case of "Second Order Emergence"?

David Hales

Department of Computer Science, University of Essex, Colchester, Essex, UK
daphal@essex.ac.uk

Abstract. An on-going project investigating group formation, stereotyping and cultural evolution using an artificial society is outlined. Agents culturally interact by exchanging behavioural rules and cultural markers. They economically interact by playing games of the Prisoners Dilemma. The mode of game play is novel because agents apply stochastic repeated game strategies not to individuals but to subjectively stereotyped groups (based on cultural makers). Agents consequently treat stereotyped groups as single players with whom they are involved in an on-going game of iterated PD. It is envisaged that such cultural processes may display a form of "second order emergence" [11] in which agents come to recognise the cultural groupings that have emerged within the society. Some initial experimental results are presented with tentative observations.

1 Introduction

In complex social worlds, individuals are required to interact with many strangers using limited knowledge and bounded rationality. Yet in human societies the outcome is rarely pure chaos and confusion. An important cognitive tool employed by humans to deal with this situation is the generation, sharing and confirmation of social categories. Social categories can be employed by an individual or group allowing them to partition their society into more-or-less distinguishable groupings. In modern societies there are many such categories in common currency. Some persist and become common knowledge (e.g. "Intellectuals"), others appear quickly then vanish (e.g. "Mods" and "Rockers") some become official instruments of policy (i.e. governmental classifications of socio-economic class). The methods by which members of a category are identified are many and varied, as are the social behaviours for which such categories provide a rationalisation.

In this paper an Artificial Society is proposed which attempts to capture (in a highly abstracted form) the social construction, communication and dynamics of social categories and their effects on group formation and relations. Agents construct and use categories to inform a choice of behaviour towards others. Categories therefore take the form of "stereotypes" indicating the actions an agent should perform when encountering others. Agents interact culturally via the exchange of memes (see section 4.1) and economically via repeated games of the Prisoner's Dilemma (see section 2). The motivation for this study is to investigate two distinct yet possibly related phenomena: "second-order emergence" where agents come to recognise actual emergent macro-level groupings (see section 7) and sustained altruism and/or exploitation between emergent groupings (see section 6). Both these phenomena are examined within a minimal "memetic" [12] framework.

2 The Prisoner's Dilemma

The Prisoner's Dilemma (PD) game models a common social dilemma in which two players interact by selecting one of two choices: Either to "co-operate" (C) or "defect" (D). From the four possible outcomes of the game payoffs are distributed to the individuals. A reward payoff (R) and a punishment payoff (P) are given for mutual co-operation and mutual defection respectively. However, when individuals select different moves, differential payoffs of temptation (T) and sucker (S) are awarded to the defector and the co-operator respectively. Assuming that neither player can know in advance which move the other will make and wishes the maximise her own payoff, the dilemma is evident in the ranking of payoffs: $T > R > P > S$ and the constraint that $2R > T + S$.

Although both players would prefer T, only one can attain it. No player wants S. No matter what the other player does, by selecting a D move a player ensures he gets either a better or equal payoff to his partner. In this sense a D move can't be bettered since playing D ensures that the defector can not be suckered. This is the so- called "Nash" [10] equilibrium for the single round game. It is also an evolutionary stable strategy [24] for a population of randomly paired individuals playing the game where reproduction fitness is based on payoff. But the dilemma remains, if both individuals selected a co-operative move they would both be better off. But many societies (human and animal) appear to have solved (at least some) dilemmas similar to PD. How can this be explained either from purely rational action or evolutionary mechanisms?

3 Evolutionary Extensions

Evolutionary selection favours selfish individual replicators. When collections of these replicators form groups it's possible for them to co-ordinate their behaviour in ways which would make global optimisation possible. The kinds of behaviours that make this possible include, co-operation, altruism and specialisation. All of these are observed in animal and human societies. But evolutionary selection does not seem to offer an explanation for these behaviours. To address this problem three extensions of natural selection have been proposed: kin selection [14], group selection [31] and reciprocal co-operation [1]. Although each offers explanations of some of the kinds of the social behaviours of interest neither seems to offer a general framework applicable to human or artificial social systems. Kin selection only applies to highly genetically related individuals, group selection in it's simplest form is fundamentally flawed and reciprocal co-operation does not explain true altruism (i.e. co-operative behaviour in the one-shot PD). Neither does it scale-up well to large groups due to the cognitive demands from the requirement that all interactions be on-going with recognisable individuals and associated memory of past interactions.

What kinds of evolutionary process might produce the complex and co-operative social organisations found in human societies? It does not seem possible through natural selection applied to genetic replicators. The formation of highly specialised, co-operative human societies comparatively recently and their rapid evolution indicates a process much faster and more adaptive than genetic evolution. Are evolutionary perspectives of any value at this level of organisation?

4 Culture and Belief

Understanding individual or social "rationality" is not sufficient to explain complex social relations and groupings. Reason has to be applied to assumptions (beliefs) which may or may not be true. Different societies are based on distinctly different belief systems. These systems explain the society to it's members and structure their interactions. Such beliefs may emerge and evolve over long periods of time but sometimes change very rapidly. They are propagated by the combined actions of many individuals and are passed from one generation to the next. Many of these beliefs are not presented as falsifiable representations of reality but as foundational assumptions from which to reason and derive individual behaviours and explanations. To the extent that such beliefs become stable and shared they tend to define a group, we might say they form an essential element of the culture of that group. To understand the formation of complex social systems it is necessary to understand the processes which bring about these shared foundational beliefs.

4.1 Cultural Evolution

Can evolutionary selection be applied to culture? To the extent that the communication of beliefs can be seen as replication and that beliefs can be varied within individuals (through learning and creativity) and between individuals (through imperfect communication) many argue that it can [4], [5], [22], [30]. In order to apply an evolutionary perspective to culture it is necessary to identify a cultural unit, i.e. the cultural analogue of the gene. If ideas are seen as replicating and mutating entities (replicating through agent's brains via communication) then they can be viewed as "viruses of the mind". The analogy is that ideas spread through a population by "infecting" brains in a similar way to the spread of a virus. The word "meme" was introduced by Dawkins [4] as a convenient label for a unit of transmission. Dawkins states:

The 'gene' was defined, not in a rigid all-or-none way, but as a unit of convenience, a length of chromosome with just enough copying-fidelity to serve as a viable unit of natural selection. If a single phrase of Beethoven's ninth symphony is sufficiently distinctive and memorable to be abstracted from the context of the whole symphony... then to that extent it deserves to be called one meme. ([4], p.210)

Many animals have nervous systems capable of supporting the spread of memes (any imitative behaviour). This capability increases the speed and flexibility of the adaptability of the population and paves the way for the development of complex cultural (global) entities to emerge, such as hierarchies, specialisation and group behaviour.

5 Group Selection of Memetic Kin

It is argued that previously proposed extensions to basic natural selection can be applied subtlety within a meme framework to explain seemingly evolutionary unstable behaviours such as altruism (self-sacrifice for the group) and it's flip-side: exploitation.

Kin selection only applies when individuals share much of the same genetic material. Consider a group with a shared culture comprising a significant number of shared memes. Mathematical models [3] and computer simulations [2], [13] indicate that groups do emerge with relatively stable shared sets of memes. This is a result of the harmonisation of memes through a process of frequency dependant bias [3] and in the context of Axelrod's model "cultural barriers" [2]. When a group share memes, this makes them "memetic kin" [16]. Although they may be different in other respects, memetically they have a common link. Altruistic behaviours among "memetic kin" are selfish from the point of view of the shared memes, if they cause optimisation of individual behaviours which increase the size or stability of the group (sharing those memes). Selection can now operate at the group level if there are other groups with different sets of shared memes.

The argument is that many cultural practices and beliefs, are highly contingent and their evolutionary trajectory is heavily influenced by local chance conditions. If they become harmonised within a group this can result in reduced harmonisation between groups because of cultural barriers (regional languages for example). Even in small scale groups, numerous social psychological studies [27], [21] find that individuals within groups are highly oriented towards their own group both in terms of actively harmonising their beliefs and behaving in a more altruistic way towards in-group members [20] and adapting stereotyped and negative attitudes towards out-group members (so called in-group bias).

Axelrod [2] shows that simple harmonisation of cultural attributes between individuals in a 2-dimensional grid produces separate groups with different "cultures" split along "cultural barriers" of non-communication. An extension of this model into a resource sharing scenario shows that in-group altruism and out-group hostility readily emerge [13].

Nowak and May [25] reduce the number of interaction partners to small overlapping spatially determined groups playing only pure strategies in single round PD. Agents are given the ability to determine (after each round) which agent within their spatial neighbourhood of interaction got the highest pay-off and copy their strategy. Through the application of a strict spatial structure, co-operation could evolve without the need for complex strategies or memories of past interactions. However, spatial models only produce co-operation when learning is limited to some small and fixed group [17].

Macy & Skvoretz [23] show that situating individuals within a large society divided between a small fixed in-group and a much larger out-group of strangers can result in co-operation (in single round games of PD with an exit option) emerging through a form of learning based on a modified GA which captures a form of social learning. Selection operates at the group level because in-groups that do well (by establishing co-operative conventions) become models from which strangers learn and subsequently spread co-operative behaviours.

6 Group Formation

However, in these studies, the group formation processes themselves are not fully explored. The agents have no explicit representations of the groups that comprise their societies. In Axelrod's [2] model group emergence is identified by the observer of the model but is effectively a side-effect of simple agent behaviours: although groups emerge the agents have no explicit cognitive input into this process. In Macy's & Skvoretz' [23] model agents are pre-assigned in-group and out-group membership. Also, these models only address divisions between an in-group and an out-group relative to each agent. There is no mechanism allowing for agents to generate their own internal representations of possibly multiple groupings towards which differential behaviours can be applied. In the context of group formation the Sugarscape [8] models a society in which groups (or "tribes") do emerge and agents do have explicit representations of them. However, the representations in the form of behavioural rules are hard-coded and unchanging. In this sense the representations are exogenous to the model and effectively specify a priori what groups the society can divide into.

Doran & Palmer [6] and Doran [7] present models which furnish agents with explicit representations of group membership. Here agents construct subjective groups based on direct perception or interaction with other uniquely identifiable agents. "Meme-like" harmonisation processes are also implemented. This has the effect of producing "collective beliefs" concerning group membership among collections of agents. However, the groups are defined by explicit representations of individual group members within each agent's memory. Consequently these models do not explore stereotyping processes.

In order to explore these issues, this work outlines an on-going project which attempts to capture some of the dynamics which link group formation and explicit internal agent representations of groups. Minimally agents need to be able to construct categories which partition the population and use these categories to influence interactions with others. The artificial society constructed captures these features via sets of (initially) arbitrary tags (or cultural markers) attached to agents and internal agent behavioural rules (stereotypes) which map tag patterns to strategies for playing the repeated form of the PD. Both tags and rules are treated as memes and as such can be harmonised between individuals during cultural interaction.

7 Second Order Emergence?

Such mechanisms as tags and rules, it is claimed, may capture a minimal form of "second order emergence" (Gilbert 1995). Put simply, the previous models discussed are strictly "bottom-up". Macro structures and behaviours emerge from the micro-level interactions of agents but the agents have no explicit representation of those structures. Consequently any feedback from macro to micro is indirect and happens "behind the backs" of the agents or (in the context of the Sugarscape) was a priori decided by the agent designers. Here an attempt is made to allow agents to evolve macro structures and representations of those structures using a minimal uniform mechanism of cultural imitation (or social learning).

It is not just the actual macro structures that emerge (i.e. groups and actions) that are of interest but the internal representations of those structures (stereotypes) stored within each agent and the relationship between the two.

8 Stereotypes

For the purposes of this study stereotypes are defined narrowly as knowledge which associates attributes with agents based purely on observable characteristics (labels or tags). I exclude assumed, deduced, believed or relative characteristics. The role of tags as methods of increasing co-operation in iterated co-operation games has been discussed by Holland [18] and more recently in [28].

I start from the assumption that stereotypes are constructed maintained and evolved through individual agent interactions over time. Also that different agents may posses different (even conflicting) stereotypes and that the processes that generate them are due to the need for cognitive efficiency and selection of social strategies based on incomplete information. The social psychological literature refers to this as the "information processing error" explanation [27] as opposed to the "kernel of truth" position which proposes that stereotypes are based (at least in part) on true group differences embedded in the structure of society (e.g. that women are innately better homemakers). However, it can be argued that the "structural differences" from which stereotypes may be generated may themselves be the result of processes involving stereotyping (among other cognitive and social processes) and hence are reflexively related.

Labels or tags are defined as observable attributes attached to agents [1], [18], [28]. In a binary string representation of a tag, each bit can be interpreted as representing the presence or absence of some observable characteristic. The definition of labels used by Holland [18] specifies that they are fixed and unchanging intra-generationally but evolve inter-generationally. The interpretation here, therefore is one of physically observable properties linked to genetic material. However, tags have been used to represent cultural attributes which can be copied between agents in order to abstractly capture a form of cultural group formation [2], [8]. The interpretation here, therefore is one of cultural characteristics gained through cultural interactions (e.g. style of dress, social demeanour etc.) which dynamically form identifiable groups.

9 The Artificial Society

Throughout the design of the society important constants have been parameterised. Specified as exogenous parameters they open-up the system to an exploration of a space of behaviours linked to the assumptions (parameter values). This allows for searching and sensitivity analysis in order to link the assumptions to system behaviour.

Agents comprise a set of observable labels (bit strings), a set of behavioural rules (stereotypes) and some state (memory) associated with each rule. The number of bits and rules stored are exogenous parameters. Each bit of the label and each stereotype is treated as a meme. This means they can be communicated and mutated. For each meme held the agent maintains a "confidence value" [0..1] which indicates how attached the agent is to the associated meme. Confidence values are affected by cultural interactions and periodic satisfaction tests (see below).

9.1 Stereotypes and Observable Labels

In order to implement "stereotyping" agents have the ability generalise over observable labels using their behavioural rules. This is achieved by a simple form of pattern matching. Agents store some fixed number of rules which map patterns of observable labels to strategy representations:

```
<label_pattern>   ->   <strategy>
```

The label pattern is a string of the same length as the label bit strings but may comprise digits of zero (0), one (1) and don't care (#). A don't care digit matches both zero and one digits. This mechanism allows for generalisation. A label pattern containing all don't care (#) digits, would match all possible labels.

9.2 The Representation of Strategies

Strategies are represented as pairs (p,q) of real values in the range [0..1] as used in [28], [26]. These values represent the probabilities that an agent will co-operate on a move proceeded by co-operation from the last player to whom the rule was applied in a previous game (p), or co-operate on a move proceeded by defection (q). This is a stochastic representation with a memory of one. It captures many variations of reciprocity and provocability: (1,0) represents tit-for-tat-like reciprocity, (0,0) represents pure defection and (1,1) represents pure co-operation. Each stereotype rule has an associated memory storing either C or D which indicates the move made by the other agent when the rule was last used. Initially these memories are set randomly. Consequently, though agents actually play single round games, these are played by the agents as on-going games of IPD (as if all agents in the category specified by the label pattern were a single agent).

9.3 Cultural and Game Interaction

There are two kinds of independent interaction that occur between agents: game interaction (where a round of PD is played) and cultural interaction (where memes are exchanged). Both spatial and label biasing may be employed to either of these interaction types.

Label biasing consists of rejecting a potential interaction based on label distance. The number of differing bits between the two labels indicates distance. Exogenous bias parameters specify the extent of biasing. They indicate the maximum label distance allowable before an interaction rejection is triggered. Two independent parameters control label biasing for game and cultural interaction.

In order to capture the phenomena of some agents interacting with each other regularly and some less regularly and some not at all, a one dimension spatial relationship has been selected for the population structure. Each end of the line is joined to form a ring topology. Along the line are a finite number of locations (an exogenous parameter), but each location can hold any number of agents. Agents are distributed along the line initially at random. The probability that an agent interacts with another agent is a function of distance representing a gaussian-like distribution around the agents. Both the "flatness" and "width" of the curve are determined by exogenously specified parameters. Both game and cultural interaction are mediated by independent curve parameters.

9.4 Mutation

Agents start with a set of randomly generated memes. Agents can only change their memes by mutation or by accepting a meme from another agent via communication. In order to reduce complexity agents don't generate memes from scratch based on personal interactions. After a satisfaction test (see below) agents examine each of their memes to determine if a mutation should take place. The susceptibility of a rule to mutate is inversely proportional to it's associated "confidence" factor.

Since the LHS of a rule (pattern label) is a bit string (perhaps including don't care symbols), mutation takes the form of changing (with some exogenously defined probability - Mt) each digit from it's current value to one of the other two values with equal probability. When a specific bit value (0 or 1) is replaced by a don't care (#) digit then the rule is generalised. Conversely when a # is replaced by a 0 or 1 the rule is specialised.

On the RHS of the rule (the (p,q) tuple representation), mutation takes the form of changing, with probability Mt, the values of each variable by some +ve or -ve value (in the range -Ms..+Ms inclusive, where Ms is an exogenously defined parameter) Values of >1 or <0 are reset to 1 and 0 respectively. After a rule is changed by either mutation or communication the confidence associated with the rule is set to a random value.

9.5 Confidence Values

Confidence values are changed during communication (see below) and periodically through the application of an all-or-nothing satisfaction test. If an agent is satisfied all confidence values are increased by some factor, else all values are reduced by some factor. Such a scheme implements a crude form of reinforcement learning: if an agent is satisfied it increases the confidence of all memes (by a factor of Ci) otherwise confidence is reduced (by a factor of Cr). Both Ci and Cr are exogenously defined parameters.

Two limitations emerge from this crude method: 1) no attempt is made to promote or demote individual memes based on their contribution to the outcome of the satisfaction test. 2) delayed rewards may not be credited to the memes which generated them since they may have changed in the intervening time. In the context of the game theoretical scenario presented here these limitations are not considered overly restrictive (In more complex scenarios methods of tackling these limitations are discussed in [18] in the context of classifier systems). Since the outcome of each game interaction results in an instant payoff it would not be difficult to accumulate payoffs against the rules that generated them. In this way, confidence values could be differentially updated. However, it is part of the assumption of the society that individuals are highly bounded in their reasoning. Agents don't know which individual memes are responsible for satisfactory outcomes [29].

9.6 Satisfaction Test

An agent is said to be "satisfied" if it's average round payoff is above some threshold T since the last satisfaction test. A satisfaction test is performed with some probability P after each round played. Both T and P are exogenous parameters.

9.7 Cultural Interaction

Each individual rule and label bit is viewed as a meme. The labels bits can be considered to be "surface memes" the rules "hidden memes". Both are communicated in a similar manner.

Two agents are selected to communicate rules and label bits using the interaction method outlined above. Given two agents have been selected, at random, one becomes the sender, the other the receiver. Each meme held by the sender is proposed to the receiver with a probability of Pm (this is an exogenous parameter, 0 indicates no meme propagation, 1 indicates all memes are proposed). The fundamental mechanisms of meme spread are those of:

- replication: the sender replicates a meme to the receiver overwriting an existing meme.
- reinforcement: the receiver already possesses the meme proposed by the sender and this results in an increase in confidence associated with that meme by the receiver
- repelling: the receiver is likely to reject an attempted replication when the associated confidence value of the meme to be overwritten is high.

In order to implement such mechanisms each agent must posses the ability (given a proposed meme by a sending agent) to classify it's memes into one of three types with respect to the proposed meme: a) Identical memes - which can be reinforced; b) Contradictory memes - which need to be removed if the new meme is accepted; c) Other memes - which are neither identical nor contradictory. The label bits are naturally either identical or contradictory (the bits match or they don't). Two behavioural rules (stereotypes) are deemed to be identical if both the pattern and the strategy match exactly and contradictory if the patterns match exactly but the strategies don't. The process of rule communication can be characterised as:-

```
the sender proposes a meme to the receiver
IF the receiver finds an "identical" meme THEN
   the confidence associated with meme is increased
ELSE
   IF the receiver finds a "contradictory" meme THEN
      attempt replication (see 1. below)
   ELSE
      choose a meme at random
      attempt replication (see 1. below)
   ENDIF
ENDIF
```

(1) attempt replication:

```
the receiver draws a random number between 0 and 1.
IF draw > confidence associated with it's meme THEN
```

```
        overwrite receivers meme with senders meme
        (replication)
    ELSE
        sender keeps it's meme intact (repel)
    ENDIF
```

9.8 Game Interaction

When two agents are selected for game interaction (see above) the following occurs:

- each agent reads the other agents label bit string
- using this label each agent searches it's set of rules
- each rule with a LHS label pattern that matches the label is marked as "active"
- each "active" rule is assigned a score based on the number of actual bits (1 or 0) that match (specific rules are therefore scored higher than general rules)
- the rule with the highest score is "fired" and the appropriate action performed as dictated by the strategy represented on the RHS of the rule and the associated memory

If more than one rule has the same highest score then the rule with the highest confidence is used. If more than one rule has the same highest confidence then a random selection is made between them. There will always be at least one "active" rule since each agent is is forced to maintain a default rule (all don't care states on the LHS).

9.9 Consistency & Redundancy

In the scheme described, "contradictory" and "identical" rules are not allowed to coexist within a single agent rule set (see above for functions that define these two terms). Basically, the LHS of each rule must be unique. If a mutation event causes two LHS' to become identical it is reversed. A communication event is so defined (see above) that it can not result in either contradiction or redundancy. Note: This does not mean that more than one rule can not match a single agent. This is resolved via specificity, then confidence, then ultimately a random choice.

9.10 The Time Unit

In a given time unit the following events occur:

- With probability Fg and refusal bias Bg, two agents have a game interaction
- With probability Fc and refusal bias Bc, two agents culturally interact
- With probability Fm one agent moves

A "cycle" of the system is defined as 10N where N is the number of agents in the society (an exogenously defined parameter).

9.11 The Parameter Space Search

Because of the complexity of the system and the number of exogenously defined parameters, an experimental automated searching system has been constructed. Currently the system is simplistic employing multiple hill-climbers over the parameter space. These are executed in parallel across multiple processors working to optimise single pre-specified statistical values derived from the output of the simulation runs.

10 Terminology & Measures

In order to explore the relationship between the agents' internal representations of groups and the actual state of the society the following terminology in introduced.

A group is defined by a rule that partitions the population into group members and non-group members based on observable labels only. An objective group is any set of agents with identical label bits. Since the label bits mediate all interactions between agents, two agents with identical labels will elicit identical responses from any given agent in the population at a given instant in time. A subjective group intention is a string of label bits or some generalisation over the label bits (that is, any combination of "0","1" or "don't care" bits). Each agent holds exactly M rules at all times. Each rule comprises a subjective group intention (or definition) and an associated game strategy. A subjective group extension is defined as those agents that are covered by the intention at a given time for a given population. The most general subjective group intention (comprising all don't care bits) always has an extension comprising the entire population. The size of a subjective group extension is defined as the number of agents in the extension which may be zero. The order of intentional recognition of a subjective group intention is defined as the number of agents in the population at a given time possessing a rule containing the intention. Subjective group intentions can be subsets and supersets of one another. Given an incomplete range of labels in the population at a given time, different subjective group intentions may have identical extensions. An existing subjective group has an extension with a size of more than zero. A recognised subjective group has an order of recognition of more than one. A recognised existing subjective group conforms to both these constraints. For a given existing subjective group, the order of intentional self-recognition of the group is defined as the proportion of members of the group extension that store a rule containing the group intention.

The distinctive homogeneity (HM) of an existing subjective group is defined as the average "relative proportion" of the top M shared rules in the group. The "relative proportion" of a rule is the proportion of agents inside the group holding the rule less the proportion of agents outside the group holding the rule. A value of 1 indicates a rule shared by all members of the group but none outside the group. A value of 0 indicates that the proportions of the rule are equal in and outside the group. With this measure smaller groups will tend to have higher distinctive homogeneity than larger groups. It's a metric of the distinctive cohesiveness of the group with respect to behavioural rules (see equation 1 below).

In order to identify a set of groups with distinctive homogeneity the space of all existing subjective groups (of size >= 10) is searched for the gtop (10) groups with the highest HM values. The HM values for these gtop groups are averaged to give an overall measure of multiple group formation MG (see equation 2 below).

Recognition of the MG groups both inside and outside of those groups is given by averaging the number of rules which match those groups inside and outside of the groups. MGSR (see equation 3 below) indicates the average number of rules matching each group in MG stored by agents within those respective groups. MGIR (see equation 4 below) indicates the average number of rules matching each MG group stored by agents outside those respective groups.

$$HM(g) = \frac{\sum_{r=1}^{topM} (Pi(g,r) - Po(g,r))}{M} \tag{1}$$

where: $Pi(g,r)$ = proportion of out (g) group agents holding rule (r)
$Po(g,r)$ = proportion of in (g) group agents holding rule (r)

$$MG = \frac{\sum_{g-1}^{gtop} HM(g)}{gtop} \tag{2}$$

where: gtop = the highest 10 groups based on HM measure

$$MGIR = \frac{\sum_{g=1}^{gtop} IR(g)}{gtop} \tag{3}$$

where: $IR(g)$ = number of rules outside group g that match g

$$MGSR = \frac{\sum_{g=1}^{gtop} SR(g)}{gtop} \tag{4}$$

where: $SR(g)$ = number of rules inside group g that match g

11 Theory of Group and Category Formation

A speculative theory of group and related category formation can now be characterised within the terminology of the Artificial Society presented. From initially randomly placed agents and randomly generated rules and markers cultural interaction produces distinct groupings with shared memes. Cultural markers become predictors (or tell-tale signs) of groups. Rules which identify such groupings give the agent holding them an advantage (consequently stabilising its memes). Meme bundles of markers and rules which recognise those same markers are likely to propagate if they produce positive in-group behaviours. Multiple groups emerge with high self-recognition and recognition of other emerged groupings.

From this theory the following initial hypothesis was derived: In regions of the parameter space where groups with high HM form these groupings will be highly recognised by others (high MGIR) and have a high order of self-recognition (high MGSR).

In order to test the hypothesis the parameter space was first randomly sampled over 100 points giving an average measure of MG, MGIR and MGSR. These values where compared to 100 points which were each found via 100 steps of hill-climbing (maximising MG) from random starting points. Here therefor the hypothesis that high MG is correlated with high MGIR and high MGSR is being tested.

12 Results

Table 1 (below) shows the results of the runs described above. As can be seen the opposite of that predicted by the hypothesis has occurred. When MG was maximised (2) MGIR and MGSR are reduced. After inspection of the runs it was found that some 20% of the runs in (2) resulted in domination of the entire population by a single objective group (all share same marker bits). The MG measure does not exclude this. However, even when these 20% were excluded (3) there was still a negative effect on MGIR and MGSR over (1).

Table 1. Comparison of average MG, MGIR and MGSR values between random sample (1) and maximised MG (2). Each value the result of the average of 100 individual runs at different points in the parameter space.

Description	MG	MGIR	MGSR
(1) random sample	0.22	0.68	0.08
(2) maximise MG	0.53	0.22	0.03
(3) excluding singles	0.48	0.46	0.07

13 Conclusion

These initial results indicate that the simple hypothesis that high group distinctive homogeneity (MG) is correlated with high recognition within and without the group (MGSR and MGIR) is false. High MG is not a necessary and sufficient condition alone to produce such recognition. Of course there may be areas of the parameter space where the hypothesis holds – in which case those areas need to be located and identified. This is part of the on-going project here described.

The method present here for the exploration of artificial societies involves the exogenous parameterisation of each unjustified assumption and the explicit specification of what constitutes behaviour of interest within the society. The parameter space can then be searched automatically to locate those behaviours and link them to the assumptions which give rise to them.

The problems presented by such an approach are firstly, precise specification of "behaviours of interest" (in this paper these are given by MG, MGIR and MGSR) and secondly, how to search a large parameter space practically and ultimately how to identify regions of that space which produce behaviours of interest.

References

1. Axelrod, R.: The Evolution of Cooperation. Basic Books, New York (1980)
2. Axelrod, R.: The Convergence and Stability of Cultures: Local Convergence and Global Polarization. Working Paper 95-03-028. Santa Fe, N.M.: Santa Fe Institute (1995)
3. Boyd, R. & Richerson, P.: Culture and the Evolutionary Process. University of Chicago Press, Chicago (1985)
4. Dawkins, R.: The Selfish Gene. Oxford University Press, New York (1976)
5. Dennett, D.: Darwin's Dangerous Idea. Simon & Schuster, New York (1995)
6. Doran, J. & Palmer, M.: The EOS Project: Integrating Two Models of Palaeolithic Social Change. In: Gilbert, N. and Conte, R. (eds.): Artificial Societies: the Computer Simulation of Social Life. UCL Press, London (1995).
7. Doran, J.: Simulating Collective Misbelief. In: Journal of Artificial Societies and Social Simulation vol. 1 no. 1, http://www.soc.surry.ac.uk/JASSS/1/1/3.html (1998)
8. Epstein, J., & Axtell, R.: Growing Artificial Societies: Social Science from the Bottom Up. MIT Press. London (1996).
9. Gabora, L.: The Origin and Evolution of Culture and Creativity. In: Journal Of Memetics - Evolutionary Models of Information Transmission, 1. http://www.cpm.mmu.ac.uk/jom-emit/vol1/gabora_1.html (1997)
10. Gibbons, R.: A Primer In Game Theory, Harvester, New York (1992)
11. Gilbert, N.: Emergence in social simulation. In: Gilbert, N. and Conte, R. (eds.): Artificial Societies: the Computer Simulation of Social Life, UCL Press, London (1995)
12. Hales, D.: Modelling Meta-Memes. In: Conte,R. & Hegselmann,R. (eds.): Simulating Social Phenomena – LNEMS 456, Springer, Berlin (1997)
13. Hales, D.: Selfish Memes and Selfless Agents: Altruism in the Swap Shop. In: The Proceedings of the ICMAS 1998 (ICMAS'98), IEEE Computer Society, California (1998)

14. Hamilton, W.: Altrusim and Related Phenomena, Mainly in Social Insects. In: Annual Review of Ecology and Systemics 3 (1972) 193-232
15. Hardin, G.: The tradigy of the commons. In: Science. 162 (1968) 1243-1248
16. Heylighen,F. & Campbell,D.: Selection of Organization at the Social Level: Obstacles and Facilitators of Metasystem Transitions. In: The Journal of General Evolution: Special Issue on "The Quantum of Evolution: Toward a Theory of Metasystem Transitions" at ftp://ftp.vub.ac.be/pub/projects/Principia_Cybernetica/WF-issue/Social_MST.txt (1995)
17. Hoffmann, R. & Waring, N.: The Localisation of Interaction and Learning in the Repeated Prisoner's Dilemma. Santa Fe Institute Working Paper 96-08-064. Santa Fe, NM (1996)
18. Holland, J.: The Effect of Lables (Tags) on Social Interactions. Santa Fe Institute Working Paper 93-10-064. Santa Fe, NM (1993)
19. Huberman, B. A, & Lukose, R. M.: Social Dilemmas and Internet Congestion. Science, 277 (1997) 535-537
20. Kramer, R. & Brewer, M.: Effects of Group Identity on Resource Use in a Simulated Commons Dilemma. Journal of Personality and Social Psychology, Vol. 46, No.5, (1984) 1044-1057.
21. Leyens, J. et al.: Stereotypes and Social Cognition. Sage, London (1994)
22. Lynch, A.: Thought Contagion: How Belief Spreads Through Society. Basic Books, New York (1996)
23. Macy, M. & Skvoretz, J.: Trust and Cooperation Between Strangers. Presented at Santa Fe Institute, August 6, Santa Fe, N.M (1996)
24. Maynard Smith, J.: Evolution and the Theory of Games. Cambridge University Press, Cambridge (1982)
25. Nowak, M. & May, R.: Evolutionary Games and Spatial Chaos. Nature, 359, (1992) 532-554
26. Nowak, M. & Sigmund, K.: Tit for Tat in Heterogeneous populations. Nature, 355, (1992) 250-253
27. Oakes, P. et al.: Stereotyping and Social Reality. Blackwell, Oxford (1994)
28. Riolo, R.: The Effects of Tag-Mediated Selection of Partners in Evolving Populations Playing the Iterated Prisoner's Dilemma. Santa Fe Institute Working Paper 97-02-016. Santa Fe, NM (1997)
29. Simon, H. A.: A Mechanism for Social Selection and Successful Altruism. Science, 250 (1990) 1665-1668
30. Sperber, D.: The Modularity of Thought and the Epidemiology of Representations. In: Hirschfeld, L. & Gelman, S. (eds): Mapping the Mind, Domain Specificity in Cognition and Culture. Cambridge University Press. Cambridge (1994)
31. Wilson, E.: Sociobiology: The New Synthesis. Harvard University Press, Cambridge Mass (1975)

Finding the Best Partner: The PART-NET System

R. Conte [1] and R. Pedone [2]

[1] Division of AI, Cognitive and Interaction Modeling - PSS (Project on Social Simulation) -
IP/Cnr, V.LE Marx 15 - 00137 Rome, Italy
[2] Department of Psychology - University of Rome "La Sapienza" 78, Via dei Marsi, 00185
Rome, Italy

rosaria@pscs2.irmkant.rm.cnr.it; pedone@caio.irmkant.rm.cnr.it

1 The potential of computer simulation for the social sciences

The issue as to whether computer simulation can be considered a valid tool for improving the predictive capacity of social scientific theories is still controversial (e.g., Troitzsch 1997 and Scott et al. 1997, seem to deny it). Instead, the role of computer simulation for testing models and experimenting on social phenomena is denied by no-one in the field (see Halpin 1997).

However, so far agent-based simulation experiments have been based upon manipulation of *external* variables (i.e., environmental, spatial, and other agent-independent variables) rather than of agent-dependent ones. When agent-dependent variables have been tested, they consisted of numerical values assigned to agents (for example, in the Cellular Automata framework, individual capital assignment, degree of neediness, scope of individual information, etc.). With the exception of the AI-based contributions to agent-based simulation (e.g., the work by Jim Doran and his collaborators) and the SOAR architecture, the agent's *internal* variables, that is, their mental states, processes, and their architecture are essentially ignored in social simulation studies. Indeed, it is often stated that agents' internal states and processes are irrelevant for understanding observable social phenomena.

Consequently, the experimental power of computer simulation is not fully exploited, since whilst external variables can be manipulated under *ordinary* experimental conditions, internal variables can be manipulated only when carrying out a *computational* experiment. In this perspective, computer simulation represents a unique but missed opportunity for the social sciences.

But what is the use of agent manipulation? Together with Simon (1991), we think that an experimental manipulation of the internal variables of the agents would enhance the predictive capacity of social scientific theories:

"To identify mechanisms, strategic and structural, we cannot be satisfied with aggregated data of total performance (speed of performance, aggregate accuracy) but have to observe as many details of the *ongoing processes* as we can. (...) How do we know a real businessperson wants to maximize profit? Perhaps he or she wants to maximize the respect received from the community, or the friendliness of workers or of customers. This would lead to very different behavior."(Simon 1991:38)

Indeed, simulation may facilitate making predictions especially if (and to the extent that) it allows for specifying agents' internal states. More precisely, prediction presupposes that not only quantitative, but also *qualitative differences* among agents' properties are specified.

This traces back to an important neglected distinction in the conceptualization of rationality. Indeed, according to Moser (1990), there are two views of rationality:

(a) the *substantialist*, according to which, "certain ends are essential to rationality" (Moser 1990:1). This conception

"originated with Aristotle, held sway among Western philosophers in Medieval times, but lost influence with the rise of modern decision theory."(ibid.)

(b) the *instrumentalist*, nowadays, decision theorists

"take rationality to be a minister without portfolio. On their view, rationality does not require *any particular substantive ends* or *goals of its own*; it consists in the optimal pursuit of one's preferred ends, *whatever those ends happen to be*." (ibid.; our italics)

These two views bear different consequences. The instrumentalist rationality implies indeterminate ends and multiple equilibria:

"the principal (problem) has arisen because there seem to be rather a lot of settings where there are multiple rational expectations equilibria". With game-theory, "the problem is exactly the same as the one which has surfaced with respect to multiple rational expectations equilibria (...). An individual's choice is underdetermined when there are several Nash or perfect equilibria because any of the Nash/perfect equilibria will satisfy the conditions of instrumental rationality and knowledge provided it is selected by others." (Hargreaves-Heap 1993: 75-77; our italic).

Furthermore, from an *engineering* perspective, the instrumentalist view of rationality does not provide indications for designing concrete agents (their goals, their preferences, etc.).

"There are .. important issues for which the field of game theory does not seem to provide a satisfactory answer. One of them has to do with the case of multiple equilibrium points existing in a game. The question is, which one should be chosen...? For example, ... should one prefer equilibrium points that have a better payoffs, or the ones that are safer?" (Gmytrasiewicz 1995:42).

On the contrary, a substantialist view of rationality leads to not only admit that agents have different ends, but characterize agents in terms of their substantive, heterogeneous goals and strategies and use relevant properties of these goals and strategies to make predictions about the agents' future behaviors.

2 Diversity _ Hierarchy

So far, the classical model of rationality has been implemented with sub-optimal versions of rationality in Elster's (1985) sense. Therefore, more plausible versions of rationality seem to be hierarchically subordinate to the traditional one. What about a simply diverse, rather than sub-optimal, view of agent mental capacities?

Diversity can be accounted for by introducing

1. *substantial* differentiation: qualitative heterogeneity among individual agents' goals (Conte & Sichman, 1995); (but, *goal*-based rather than *preference*-based view of endogenous motivations!)
2. a *variety of social actions*, from influencing, to exchange, to cooperation (Conte & Castelfranchi, 1996);
3. a *context-bounded notion of rationality*, such that different contexts call for different rational strategies (Conte & Paolucci, 1997);
4. *architectural* differentiation: agents not only have *different goals*, but also *different decision-making rules*: f.i., a goal-based rule exists, in which utility is subordinated to goal-satisfaction rather than vice-versa.

In this paper, architectural differences, i.e., different strategies of decision-making, are integrated within a computational tool (PART-NET) developed within the framework of Multi-Agent Systems to show how partnerships may be formed among heterogeneous agents.

The notion of agent referred to here can be characterized as:

1. an *ideal-type* construct -- not to be confused with the subjective, idiosyncratic individual of differential psychology; and
2. an *AI-based* notion, where the attention is drawn on the whole process that leads a system to acting, and on its internal makeup, i.e., the internal regulatory mechanisms and representations allowing a system to act adaptively in its environment.

The objective of the present study is twofold: on the one hand, we intend to combine agent modeling and social simulation; on the other, we are interested in exploring the role of qualitative agent differences in social phenomena.

3 Substantial Diversity and Interaction Variety

Elsewhere (Sichman et al. 1994), a computational instrument (DEPNET) calculating the network of dependence relations among agents in a common environment, has been described. This is based on a very simple agent architecture, consisting of agents' goals, actions, and resources. DEPNET (cf. Conte and Sichman 1995; Conte and Castelfranchi 1996; etc.) has been applied to allow a complex structure of agents' interdependencies to emerge. In our terms, an agent x is socially dependent on another agent y when x does not at least have one of the actions achieving one of its goals, while y has one.

Social dependence may be unilateral, when one agent depends on a given (set of) agent(s) but no-one depends in turn upon him, or bilateral, when the dependence works in the two directions at the same time. In the latter case, there are two further possibilities: since, in our terms, dependence is a goal-dependent notion, we may have two agents depending on each other to achieve the same goal, or two distinct goals. In the former case, we speak about mutual dependence and expect the agents to initiate a *cooperative* interaction. In the latter, we speak of reciprocal dependence and expect the agents to initiate an *exchange* interaction. Indeed, on the grounds of our dependence model, a variety of rational social (inter)actions can be predicted (influencing, exchange, and cooperation; cf. Conte and Sichman 1995).

4 PART(nership)NET

PART-NET forms real partnerships among heterogeneous agents in a common world. It exclusively deals with reciprocal dependence, and therefore with exchange interactions, rather than cooperative ones.

The PART-NET architecture includes two basic components: the first one gives as an output the agent structure; the second deals with the formation of effective matches among the agents. Let us examine each component in turn.

4.1 Agent Structure

At the onset of each simulation, PART-NET edits the structures of the agents in the population. Each structure includes:

1. a set of *goals*, defined by status, expressed as a boolean variable (0, for active goals, and 1 for satisfied), type (how to achieve it) and priority (subjective importance, expressed as a cardinal value);
2. a set of *actions,* again defined by status (0, for action not spent, 1 for action spent), type (its predicted effect) and cost (subjective) - to be noted, in our system at its present stage of development, actions achieve goals directly, in a one-to-one correspondence;
3. *knowledge* about dependence relationships, in particular about bilateral dependencies;
4. a given decision-making *strategy*, either substantialist (more colloquially called "hedonist"), which orders existing alternatives according to goal-priority, that is, to the importance of the goal each allows to achieve, or instrumentalist (more colloquuially called "utilitarian"), which orders alternatives in order to maximize the difference between benefits (goals achieved) and costs; miser, which orders alternatives in order to minimize action costs.

The output of this component is an ordered list of desirable exchange partners for each agent. Out of all agents, only those reciprocally dependent on the agent in question will be selected and ordered according to their strategies. Essentially, the hedonists' best partner is expected to achieve the agents' most-valued goal at any cost; the utilitarians' best partner is expected to achieve the agents' most-valued goal at their lowest cost; while the misers' best partner is one which asks for the agents' lowest cost at any benefit. In other words, while hedonists will never give up their most important goals unless these cannot be achieved, utilitarians negotiate between what they get and what they give. Utilitarian agents are prepared to give up their most-valued goal and turn to a lower-valued one if the difference between benefits and costs in the latter case is lower than in the former. Indeed, goals are interchangeable for utilitarians and misers, but not for hedonists. In other words, utilitarians and misers are one-goal systems, guided by either utility or frugality. Specific goals are therefore superseded by, and are achieved only, in order to maximize either principle. With hedonists, instead, no criterion of choice is applied other than one provided by the goals themselves. A hedonist will try to achieve precisely that specific goal of its, if active and achievable, at any cost, and won't barter it with anything else.

In the assumption of rationality, hedonists are less rational than utilitarians (cf. Harsanyi 1990). This is probably true if one takes a strongly economic perspective on rationality (but Chattoe and Gilbert in press, show that this is not necessarily the case even in the context of budgetary decision-making). But certainly this assumption must be relaxed if one takes either a social, or a biological, or a political, or a merely interpersonal perspective. In any of these fields, it is much less clear whether an utilitarian strategy is more rational, meaning more convenient and effective, than others. In particular, how to combine the rationality assumption with the matter of fact, initially understood by Aristotle and recently modelled by cognitive scientists (cf. Miller et al. 1960; Simon 1991), that natural intelligent systems, and human beings in particular, are goal-based, rather than utility-based? Human beings, indeed, do not act in order to maximize utility but to achieve goals. At most, utility maximization is a modality of their action, regulating problem solving, planning and decision-making often in interaction with other principles. But action, intention formation, planning, problem solving etc. are activated to achieve goals, possibly *while* maximizing utility. Now, goals call for a substantive form of rationality, while utility requires an instrumentalist one. Natural intelligence is never indifferent to the substance of the goals to be achieved. On the contrary, rational agents must be indifferent to the contents of their preferences and sensitive to the ordering of such prefernces in order to be able to maximize utility. Utility maximization is a function aimed at maximizing the distance between benefits and costs. Benefits and costs are condensed into this function. One may happen to satisfy one's utility function in several ways, independent of the benefit achieved. Some authors (for example, Steedman and Krause 1986; Elster 1986) have realized the existence of qualitatively different criteria and viewpoints in decision-making. But the solution found consists of "merging alternatives" (cf. Krause 1991) according to a lexicographic, or more generally, hierarchical, ordering. However, Steedman and Krause clearly state that a rational agent defined in terms of an overall preference relation equals to a *Faustian* utopia. They propose a more realistic differential modelling, in which agents' types or personalities are identified on the grounds of the level of integration among ordering criteria. Although interesting, this model shows a typical problem of rationality theory. To render the rational agent model more plausible and realistic, authors aim at modelling the *individual* agent, and turn to *differential* psychology.

In this paper, we take a radically different approach: rather than developing models of individual agents, we aim at modelling different modules or components of an ideal-type architecture. We believe, indeed, that such modules do not meet different personalities, lifestyles, etc. but that each may be required in different social contexts and answer different requirements.

4.2 Match Formation

PART-NET achieves the formation of effective partnerships through successive prunings of the list of potential partnerships.

1. *reciprocal matches filtering*: all the matches in which the same two agents form a partneship are recorded in a new list (the list of effective matches: EML) and erased from the old list of potential matches (PML).
2. *Update*: in the old list, all matches containing members of the reciprocal matches are erased (since only one action for agent is allowed at each cycle!).
3. *Incompatible matches solution*: in PML, the dyads where one agent is matched with more than one partner are identified. The common agent (which plays the role of a contended for resource) will choose the match that rewards it most; this will be recorded in EML, while the other match will simply be cancelled. This function will be applied until completion of the PML list.

At each cycle of the simulation, the matches are executed simultaneously and the agent structures are updated; in particular, the statuses of their actions and goals are (possibly) modified, and their benefits and costs are computed. A simulation ends when no further matches are possible.

4.3 Hypotheses

First, and somewhat obviously, we expected hedonists to obtain highest *gross* benefits; utilitarians to get highest *net* benefits; and misers to sustain the lowest costs. Secondly, and more interestingly, on the grounds of a pivotal study (see Conte 1997) conducted on a simpler system (MICROdep, see Veneziano et al. 1996), we expected hedonists to behave less flexibly than utilitarians. Previous findings had shown that hedonists obtain results comparable to utilitarians only in large-size populations. This result was interpreted as an indicator that hedonists need a larger social choice than utilitarians do because only under such conditions hedonists can find their best partners. Precisely because they are not indifferent to the contents of their goals, to the specific benefits they get from partnership, the larger the set of agents among which they can search for their partners, the higher the chances that they will find exactly the one(s) they need for. On the contrary, and precisely for the same reason, the utilitarian strategy is more flexible: utilitarians will adapt to any social condition since they are indifferent to the quality of the benefits to be received. Their strategy can be interpreted as intrinsically more adaptive because it is more flexible (provided they have an overall preference relation). However, in the previous study, the two strategies were found to perform almost equally in larger populations even in terms of net benefits. A repetition of that study was necessary in order to investigate such convergence more extensively in an envioronment more plausible than was allowed by MICROdep.

5 Preliminary findings

We will present three orders of results.

5.1 Checking the previous study

Confirming the results obtained in the previous study, hedonists get higher benefit (Y axis) as a function of increasing number of goals (X axis)(see Fig. 1) and population size (Fig. 2).

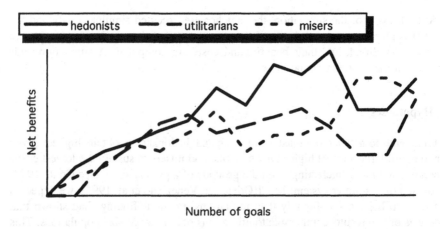

Figure 1: Net benefits with increasing number of goals

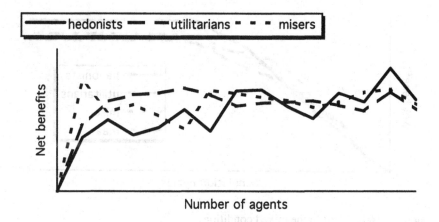

Figure 2: Net benefits with increasing populations

Hedonists confirm themselves as less flexible than utilitarians: to obtain good results, they need a larger social choice, in terms of larger sets of agents and/or goals.

5.2 The efficiency of strategies vary as a function of interaction

In the standalone condition, the different strategies get not very different results (see Fig. 3).

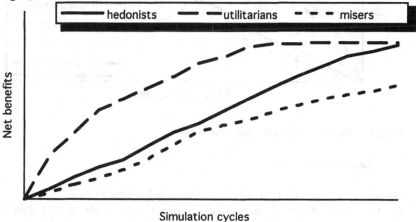

Figure 3: Net benefits in the standalone condition

But in the mixed condition (see Fig. 4), hedonists get the highest benefits, while utilitarians do better in the standalone than in the mixed condition.

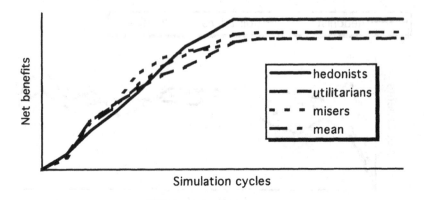

Figure 4: Net benefit in the mixed condition

Interestingly, by the way, the whole population gets better results than in the stanadalone condition (see Fig. 5).

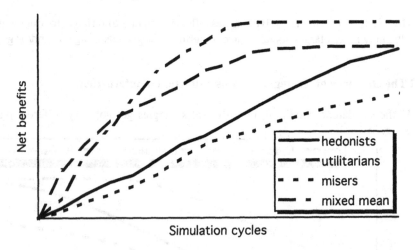

Figure 5: Net benefits: Standalone vs Mixed

Two questions arise here:

(a) Why do hedonists perform better in the mixed condition?
(b) Why the net benefit is on the average higher in the mixed than in the standalone condition?

As we will see, answering the first question will also provide a reasonable solution to the second problem.

5.3 The Social Role of Hedonists

Here, we will attempt to feedback from the results obtained to our model, and will put forward a further hypothesis concerning the nature of the hedonistic strategy, a hypothesis which will be tested against further simulation evidence.

The first result obtained indicate that hedonists are more rigid than utilitarians because they are not indifferent to the goals to be achieved. However, while hedonists care for goals, they do not care for costs. To state it in social psychological terms, hedonists care about what they receive but do not care about what they give. In this sense, hedonists can be considered as a neutral social strategy, not necessarily anti-social. On the other hand, utilitarians care about both what they get and what they give, and a fortiori misers care about what they give to others. The two last strategies are indeed more anti-social than the first one. Therefore, it can be expected that utilitarians and misers form fewer partnerships than hedonists. Indeed, they should less frequently be requested as partners than hedonists. Hedonists, in other words, should enter more frequently the others' Lists of Potential Partners.

This is exactly what happens. In fact, in the mixed condition,

(a) utilitarians match less while
(b) hedonists match more than in the standalone condition (see Fig. 6 and 7).

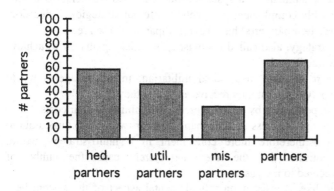

Figure 6: Number of partners in the mixed condition

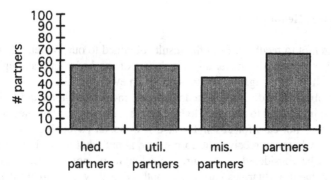

Figure 7: Standalone vs mixed partners

This seems also to explain why a mix of strategies gives higher benefits on the average than a one-strategy world. A multi-strategy world seems to be more convenient than a univocal one: not surprisingly, when nice people are around, the number of associations increases!

To sum up, strategy's convenience depends upon circumstances: a hedonistic strategy is more convenient in larger and heterogenous (mixed) groups, while mixed groups match more frequently and get higher benefits than homogeneous ones.

6 Concluding Remarks

Using the PART-NET simulator - a system which executes partnerships among heterogeneous and possibly complementary agents - different strategies of decision-making for seeking one's best partner(s) have been compared. These are:

(a) a *substantialist* strategy, also called hedonistic, in which agents try to achieve the next-best (mostly valued) goals;

(b) an *instrumentalist* strategy, also called utilitarian, in which agents try to maximize the distance between what they receive and what they give;

(c) a *control* strategy, performed by misers which try to minimize their costs.

While the first strategy proved less flexible than the other two, it also turned out to be less anti-social, and therefore more convenient in a multi-strategy world. Hedonists are more requested than the others and thereby cause the number of matches effectively executed to increase.

Secondly, we would like to insist upon a fundamental aspect of the system here described. PART-NET will allow the hypotheses discussed here to be tested in a detailed and procedural way, by exploring the effects of each cycle of simulation on the agents' structures. Thanks to this characteristic, it will be possible to check qualitatively (and not only quantitatively and statistically) whether our hypothesis about the social utility of hedonists is true. This will require an investigation of the agents' PMLs in a stepwise way, which is made possible by PART-NET. Indeed, thanks to the system's agent structures, a qualitative record is kept of the simulation events.

Certainly the simulation results so far obtained need to be checked with a careful examination of the parameter space. However, the reader is asked to conceptualize simulation not only as a hypothesis-*confirming* but moreover, as a hypthesis-*constructing* tool. The present simulation study has constructed a social phenomenon (the interplay of goal-based and utility-based agent architectures) which strongly demands theoretical attention.

References

Chattoe, E. & Gilbert, N. in press. A simulation of budgetary decision-making based on interview data. Paper presented at SimSoc '95, University of Florida, Boca Raton, 15-17 September 1995. To appear in the Journal of Artificial Societies and Social Simulation.

Conte, R. & Castelfranchi, C. (1996). Simulating interdependence networks. A two-way approach to the micro-macro link. In K.G. Troitzsch, U. Mueller, N. Gilbert, J. Doran (Eds) *Social Sience Microsimulation*. Heidelberg: Springer.

Conte, R. & Paolucci, M. (1997). Tributes or norms? The context-dependent rationality of social control. In R. Conte, R. Hegselmann, P. Terna (Eds) *Simulating social phenomena*, Heidelberg: Springer.

Conte, R. & Sichman, J. (1995). DEPNET: How to benefit from social dependence, *Journal of Mathematical Sociology*, 20(2-3), 161-177.

Conte, R. (1997). Diversity in strategies of partnership formation. Paper presented at the Dagstuhl Seminar on *Social Science Microsimulation. Tools for Modeling, Parameter Optimization, and Sensitivity Analysis*,Schloss Dagstuhl, 1-5 May, 1997.

Elster, J. (1985). *Sour grapes. Studies in the sub-version of rationality*. Cambridge: Cambridge UNiversity Press.

Gmytrasiewicz, P.J. (1995). On Reasoning About Other Agents. In DIMAS'95 - *Proceedings of the First International Workshop on Decentralized Intelligent and Multiagent Systems* - 22 Nov., Krakov, Poland (p.I/38-49).

Halpin, B. (1997). Simulation in Sociology: A review of the literature. Paper read at the Workshop on "Potential of the computer simulation for the social sciences", Centre for Research in the Social Sciences (CRESS), University of Surrey, 14-15 January, 1998.

Hargreaves-Heap, S. (1993). Post-modernity and new conceptions of rationality in economics. In Gerrard, B. (Ed) *The economics of rationality*. London: Routledge.

Harsanyi, J.C. (1990). Advances in understanding rational behavior. In P.K. Moser (ed) *Rationality in action. Contemporary approaches*. Cambridge, Cambridge University Press, 1990.

Krause, U. (1991). On the resolution of conflict by compensation. In E.J. Nell, W. Semmle (eds) Nicholas Kaldor and mainstream economics. London: Macmillan.

Miller, G. , Galanter, E., Pribram, K.H. (1960). Plans and the structure of behavior, New York: Holt, Rinehart & Winston.

Moser, P.K. (1990). Rationality in action: general introduction. In P.K. Moser (ed) *Rationality in action. Contemporary approaches*. Cambridge, Cambridge University Press.

Moss, S. , Edmonds, B., Wallis, S. (1997). Validation and Verification of Computational Models with Multiple Cognitive Agents, CPM Report No.: 97-25.

Sichman, J.S., Conte, R., Castelfranchi, C., & Demazeau, Y. (1994). A social reasoning mechanism based on dependence networks. In A G. Cohn (Ed.), *Proceedings of the 11th. European Conference on Artificial Intelligence* . Baffins Lane, England: John Wiley & Sons, pp. 188-192.

Simon, H.A. (1991). Cognitive architectures and rational analysis: Comment. In K. VanLehn (ed) *Architectures for intelligence*. Hillsdale, N.J.: Lawrence Erlbaum.

Steedman, I. & Krause, U. (1986). Goethe's Faust, Arrow's Possibility Theorem and the individual decision-taker. In J. Elster (ed) The multiple self. Cambridge: Cambridge University Press. Elster 1986

Troitzsch, K.G. (1997). Social science simulation - Origin, prospects, purposes. In R. Conte, R. Hegselmann, P. Terna (Eds) *Simulating social phenomena*, Heidelberg: Springer.

Veneziano, V, Conte, R, Castelfranchi, C. (1996). *MICROdep The formation of partnerships*. Paper presented at the Workshop on Multi-Agent Systems and Social Simulation (MASSIM '96), University of Ulm, Germany, March.

Dependence Relations Between Roles in a Multi-agent System:
Towards the Detection of Inconsistencies in Organization*

Mahdi Hannoun[1], Jaime Simão Sichman[2], Olivier Boissier[1], and Claudette Sayettat[1]

[1] Département Systèmes Industriels Coopératifs, SIMADE,
École des Mines, 158 cours Fauriel, 42023 Saint-Etienne Cedex 02, France
{hannoun,boissier,sayettat}@emse.fr
[2] University of São Paulo, Computer Engineering Department,
av. Prof. Luciano Gualberto, 158, tv. 3, 05508-900, São Paulo, SP, Brazil
jaime@pcs.usp.br

Abstract. With the growing interest in Multi-Agent Systems (MAS's), the need of useful tools to design and make such systems evolve has become an important domain of research. In this context, on the one hand, we are interested in modeling the organization of a MAS and on the other hand, in adapting this organization to environmental changes during the execution of the system. In our sense, the organization has to deal with the structure of the system according to the definition and the allocation of responsibilities regarding execution of tasks among agents. In this paper, we present our organizational model whose core notions are roles and links. By combining this organizational model with the dependence theory, we explore a way that allows the detection of inconsistencies in the organization of a MAS.

1 Introduction

At the beginning of Distributed Artificial Intelligence (DAI), the research projects were mainly focused on the design of architecture of agents with sophisticated reasoning capabilities [9, 18]. Recently, the focus has moved onto the social aspects of knowledge and action [13, 4, 1]. Research is now directed toward the definition of social mechanisms that install cooperative modes in the system, in particular the agents' organization (structural aspect of a cooperative collection of agents [22]).

Organizations presented in MAS range between implicit and explicit structures. On the implicit side, the organization is mixed up with the interaction protocols [21] or like in emergent computation [8], the organization is just an observed result by the user of the system. Expression of causal graphs [6, 7], of

---

* This work has been partially financed by CNPq, Brazil, grant number 301041/95-4 and FAPESP, Brazil, grant number 98/03489-9 and an Eurodoc grant from the Région Rhône-Alpes, France.

production latices [12, 16], of commitments [4, 3] or dependence relations [5, 19] are examples of explicit representations on which the agents can reason. Orthogonally to these criteria, taking into account how the design of the organization is made, we can further classify MAS organization in a bottom-up (we call it *emergent*) or a top-down manner (we call it *normative*). In a bottom-up approach, the organization is the result of computation done at the agent level interacting with the environment and with the others agents [8, 17]. In the normative approach, the organization is pre-defined by the designer or by the agents in order to constrain the functioning of the agents [16, 3].

As initiated in the ASIC model [2], we envision the modeling of a complex and decentralized system along the four main axes of the "Vowels" approach [10] : agent, interaction, organization and environment. In this context, using a normative approach, we are mainly interested in an explicit representation of the organization [14, 15] in order to enable agents to take it into account and to reason about it. But, when building a MAS that works in complex and changing environments, it is crucial for its organization to be able of adapting itself to the changes, since organizations may not always define sufficient and complete roles and links.

Bearing that in mind, we need to detect the inadequacy of a predefined organization regarding the current relationships existing among the agents in the system and make it evolve. The dependence theory [5, 19] can help to make explicit relations (dependencies) among agents. We hereafter aim at showing that it also offers a rational framework that can help to detect inconsistencies in an organization. As result we will be able to make these organizations evolve.

First we present the global context that underlies our approach and our model of organization in a MAS. Then, in sections 4 and 5, we present the use of the "dependence theory" for verifying the consistency of this model. We will illustrate these notions with an example of a Groupware application which we are working on. This application concerns the functioning of master educational training.

2 Context of our Approach

In order to design a MAS, characteristics of the problem must be analyzed and made explicit. These characteristics are the foundations which the architecture will nuilt upon : they are used in the definition of interactions, in the configuration of the agents and also in the definition of the organization. In our case, these characteristics are the *goals* to be achieved, the *plans* to be followed and the *actions* and the *resources* involved in these plans. We call a *task* a set composed of a goal, of one or more plans that can achieve this goal. The definition of plans adds the needed actions and resources to this set. We will use the letters g, p, a, r to represent goals, plans, actions and resources respectively.

When we analyze a sub-part of the functioning of the groupware application, we can identify different tasks : "RedactCourse", "GiveExamination", "SuperviseActivities", etc. We can further analyze these tasks and decompose them in terms of goals and plans (cf. Table 1). For example, the task **"RedactCourse"** is defined by the goal g_1 **"RedactDoc"** that is achieved by the plan p_1. This plan is concerned with the sequential execution of the actions a_1 "WriteDocument", a_2 "Type" using resource r_1 "LaTeX" or resource r_2 "WinWord", and action a_3 "Print".

Table 1. Task Decomposition for the GroupWare application

Tasks
RedactCourse $= g_1$ following p_1
GiveExamination $= g_2$ following p_2
SuperviseActivities $= g_3$

Goals	Plans
$g_1 =$ "RedactDoc"	$p_1 = a_1;a_2(r_1 \text{ or}^{(*)} r_2);a_3$
$g_2 =$ "GiveExam"	$p_2 = a_1;a_2(r_1 \text{ or}^{(*)} r_2);a_3;a_4;a_5$
$g_3 =$ "SuperviseAct"	

Actions	Resources
$a_1 =$ "WriteDocument"	$r_1 =$ "LaTeX"
$a_2 =$ "Type"	$r_2 =$ "WinWord"
$a_3 =$ "Print"	
$a_4 =$ "TakeExam"	
$a_5 =$ "MarkPaper"	

$^{(*)}$ we can choose between the two resources to execute a_2.

We will now define some predicates that will be useful in the following sections. We use the predicates is_{ac} and is_{re} with a plan as first parameter to express that an action or a resource belongs to that plan. The predicate $is_{pl}(g, p)$ expresses that a goal g is achieved by the plan p and the predicate $sub_{pl}(p_i, p_j)$ that the plan p_i is a sub-plan of p_j[1] (for example $sub_{pl}(p_1, p_2)$ in the table 1). The predicate is_{go} expresses that a task (first parameter) is attached to a goal (second parameter). In the example, the task **"RedactCourse"** is described by:

$$is_{go}(RedactCourse, g_1) \qquad is_{pl}(g_1, p_1)$$
$$is_{ac}(p_1, a_1), \; is_{ac}(p_1, a_2), \; is_{ac}(p_1, a_3)$$
$$is_{re}(p_1, r_1), \; is_{re}(p_1, r_2)$$

As well, each agent can be described externally with the same characteristics. The predicates $is_{go}(ag, g)$, $is_{pl}(ag, p)$, $is_{ac}(ag, a)$ and $is_{re}(ag, r)$ express respectively that, the goal g, the plan p, the action a or the resource r belongs to the external description of the agent ag.

In the next sections we explain how we structure the organization of the system from these tasks and how we analyze the dependencies in the organization by taking into account the external description of the agents and the structure of the system.

---

[1] p_i is a sub-plan of p_j if the sequence of actions and resources involved in p_i is included with the same order in p_j

3 Our Organizational Model for a MAS

In this section, we give a brief overview of our modeling of a MAS organization [14, 15] in order to define the framework in which the detection of inconsistencies takes place. This model is based on two notions : organizational *roles* and organizational *links* between these roles similar to [23, 11]. A role makes explicit *what* we have to do, whereas a link determines *how* and with *who* to solve the problem, by constraining the exchanges between the organization's members.
From the section 2, we define the organizational roles in the same terms of tasks. The organizational links are divided into three types : *authority*, *communication* and *acquaintance* links. Using these links, an agent playing a given source role may respectively control, communicate or represent the role of other agents playing the target roles. In order to be brief, we will not give the formal definition of the semantics of roles and links.

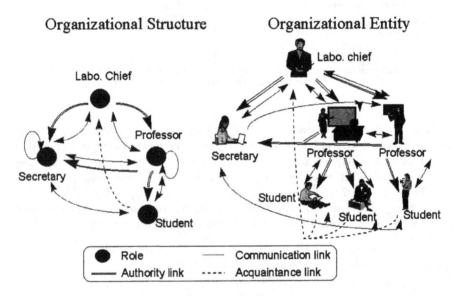

Fig. 1. Organizational structure and organizational entity of the GroupWare application. The OS defines four roles that are "Labo. Chief", "Secretary", "Professor" and "Student". Several links bind these different roles. In the OE based on this OS, we can see that several agents play the roles "Professor" and "Student".

Links and roles represent (cf. Fig. 1) respectively edges and nodes of a graph that we call an *organizational structure* (OS). However, a real MAS is defined in terms of an *organizational entity* (OE), where agents are associated to OS roles.

An OE can be viewed as an instantiation of an OS.

$$
\begin{aligned}
os_i &= \ < Ro_i, L_i > \\
oe_j &= \ < Ag_j, os_j, dist_j > \ \text{with } dist_j \text{ a multi-valued function} \quad (1) \\
& \quad dist_j : Ag_j \rightarrow Ro_j.
\end{aligned}
$$

Ro_i and L_i represent respectively the set of roles and the set of links of the organizational structure os_i. Ag_j is the agent's set of oe_j and $dist_j$ a function from the agent's set Ag_j to the role's set Ro_j of os_j that defines the roles played by each agent of the organizational entity oe_j.

3.1 Organizational Roles

A role ro_i of an Organizational Structure os is a coherent collection of *missions* M_i.

$$
ro_i = < M_i > . \quad (2)
$$

A mission $m_i \in M_i$ specifies the part of a task to be fulfilled for which the role is responsible. It specifies also how the player of the role has to behave during the execution of the mission. It is defined by a quadruple of four sets : *goal* G_i, *plans* P_i, *actions* A_i and *resources* R_i :

$$
m_i = < G_i, P_i, A_i, R_i > . \quad (3)
$$

The agent that plays the mission m_i of this role is constrained in the sense that he will *have to* achieve the goal of G_i, to follow the plans of P_i, to execute himself only the actions of A_i and to use only the resources of R_i even though he has the capabilities to define other goals, plans, actions or to control other resources. Each set can also be the set { any }, which means that the agent is constraint-free regarding the elements of this set (see the examples below). We

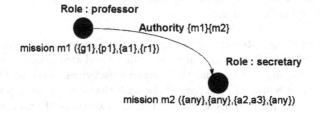

Fig. 2. Example of organizational role and link of the GroupWare Application.

refine the predicates of section 2 in order to express the membership to one of this set[2] :

$$is_{ac}(m_i, a_k) \stackrel{\triangle}{=} a_k \in A_i \qquad is_{re}(m_i, r_k) \stackrel{\triangle}{=} r_k \in R_i$$
$$is_{pl}(m_i, p_k) \stackrel{\triangle}{=} p_k \in P_i \qquad is_{go}(m_i, g_k) \stackrel{\triangle}{=} g_k \in G_i \qquad (4)$$
$$is_{mi}(ro_i, m_k) \stackrel{\triangle}{=} m_k \in M_i \qquad is_{ro}(os_i, ro_k) \stackrel{\triangle}{=} ro_k \in Ro_i$$

Table 2. Roles and Missions for the GroupWare Application

"Professor" $ro_1 = <\{m_1, m_4, m_5\}>$	"Secretary" $ro_2 = <\{m_2\}>$
"Student" $ro_3 = <\{m_3\}>$	"LaboChief" $ro_4 = <\{m_6\}>$

$$m_1 = <\{g_1\},\{p_1\},\{a_1\},\{r_1\}>$$
$$m_2 = <\{\text{ any }\},\{\text{ any }\},\{a_2, a_3\},\{\text{ any }\}>$$
$$m_3 = <\{\text{ any }\},\{\text{ any }\},\{a_4\},\{\text{ any }\}>$$
$$m_4 = <\{\text{ any }\},\{\text{ any }\},\{a_5\},\{\text{ any }\}>$$
$$m_5 = <\{g_2\},\{p_2\},\{a_1\},\{\text{ any }\}>$$
$$m_6 = <\{g_3\},\{\text{ any }\},\{\text{ any }\},\{\text{ any }\}>$$

The combination of these four sets, allows us to define and constrain a mission with more flexibility (cf. Fig. 2 and Table 2) :

- let an agent be assigned the role ro_1.
  In the context of m_1, he has to achieve the goal g_1 by following the plan p_1, executing locally **only** the action a_1 and using only the resource r_1. In this context, the agent can't execute the actions a_2 and a_3 involved in the execution of the plan p_1. Even if the agent is able to execute these actions, he will have to delegate their execution to another agent.
  In the context of m_4 the agent is assigned to execute action a_5 despite the goals and plans involved in m_4.
- another agent who is assigned ro_2 has only to fulfill m_2. He has to execute only the actions a_2 and a_3.

Please note that the "RedactCourse" task of the Groupware example is specified in the OS by missions m_1 and m_2, the "GiveExamination" task by the missions m_2, m_3, m_4 and m_5 and the "SuperviseActivities" task by the mission m_6. Each mission represents the part of the task that the role is responsible for. Also note that the mission m_2 is involved in the two tasks "RedactCourse" and "GiveExamination".

---

[2] In sections 4 and 5, we use an extended version of the predicate $is_{pl}(m, p)$ noted $is^*_{pl}(m, p)$. This new predicate takes into account the case where $P_i = \{\text{any}\}$ by returning true iff the plan p is formed by a combination of the actions and resources specified in the mission m and related to the defined goal.

3.2 Organizational Links

An organizational link is a directed relation between two roles (source role ro_s and target role ro_t) that is labeled by a type and a possibly "any" subset of missions of the source role and subset of missions of the target role. These two sets of missions define the context in which the link can be used. The type is used to define the link as an *acquaintance*, a *communication* or an *authority* link.

$$
\begin{aligned}
&link_i = < type, ro_{s_i}, \{m_j\}_{ro_{s_i}}, ro_{t_i}, \{m_k\}_{ro_{t_i}} > \\
&type \in \{acquaintance, \; communication, \; authority\}.
\end{aligned}
\tag{5}
$$

The authority link defines the degree of control/influence that agents playing the source role may carry on agents playing the target role. The aim of the communication link is to better represent and to constrain the exchanges of information in the system. The acquaintance link allows the agent playing the source role, to maintain a representation of the role of the target agents. This acquaintance link defines the part of the organization that an agent is allowed to represent.

For example (cf. Fig. 2), we can define an authority link regarding mission m_1 of ro_1 "**Professor**" and mission m_2 of ro_2 "**Secretary**". This means that one agent playing ro_1 can exert control while executing the mission m_1 on the agent playing ro_2 while executing the mission m_2.

Roles, on one side, and authority, communication and acquaintance links on the other side, define respectively a control, a communication and an acquaintance graph. We can then draw control *paths*, communication *paths* and acquaintance *paths* among roles.

4 Dependence in Organizational Structure

According to social power and the dependence theory [5], cooperation and social exchanges are based on agents' complementarity. The main notion of this theory is *dependence relation* : an agent i depends on an agent j if the latter could help him in achieving one of his goals or prevent him from achieving one of his goals. Dependence relations lead to different dependence situations that can be the basis of social interactions. For example [19], if two autonomous agents i and j have a common goal g and if they infer a mutual dependency for this goal, i.e each one needs the other to satisfy his goal, then they may decide to cooperate.

Based on the external description of agents (cf. section 2) the dependence theory can explain in a rational framework the social exchanges that can occur between agents. The dependencies can also help to analyze the relationships between roles in the organization. We suggest to extend the notion of agents' complementarity, used in the dependence theory, to the OS. We could then infer dependencies among the roles. These dependencies are useful to detect inconsistencies in the definition of the roles and links within the OS. After the definition of the role dependence, two notions of consistency are introduced :

- *autonomy of a role* guaranteeing that for each of its missions that must delegate some actions, there exists missions in the OS that can execute these actions;
- *consistency of roles* guaranteeing that the adequate communication paths are present between the dependent roles in the OS.

We shall consider hereafter action dependence only, but we can generalize our reasoning by taking resource, plan and goal dependence into account.

Before defining the dependence between two roles, let us introduce one relation and two predicates (to ensure readability we have simplified these definitions by assuming that all the operands belong to the same OS) :

- $m_i \overset{*}{\subseteq} m_j$: expresses that the mission m_i can be considered as a sub-mission of m_j, i.e we can find an allowed plan p_i for m_i, and an allowed plan p_j for m_j such as p_i is a sub-plan of p_j :

$$m_i \overset{*}{\subseteq} m_j \overset{\triangle}{=} \exists p_i, p_j \ / \ is^*_{pl}(m_i, p_i) \wedge is^*_{pl}(m_j, p_j) \wedge sub_{pl}(p_i, p_j). \qquad (6)$$

- $uses_{ac}(ro, m, a)$ expresses that the mission m of the role ro uses the action a :

$$uses_{ac}(ro, m, a) \overset{\triangle}{=} \exists p \ / \ is^*_{pl}(m, p) \wedge is_{mi}(ro, m) \wedge is_{ac}(p, a). \qquad (7)$$

- $needs_{ac}(ro, m, a)$ expresses that the mission m of the role ro needs the action a but doesn't allow to execute this action, i.e this action must be delegated.

$$needs_{ac}(ro, m, a) \overset{\triangle}{=} uses_{ac}(ro, m, a) \wedge \neg is_{ac}(m, a). \qquad (8)$$

We can define now the action dependence between roles. A role ro_i depends on a role ro_j if a mission m_j of ro_j can be a sub-mission of a mission m_i of ro_i, and m_j can execute the action a needed by mission m_i. Formally we have :

$$dep_{ac}(ro_i, ro_j, a, m_i, m_j) \overset{\triangle}{=} \begin{cases} m_j \overset{*}{\subseteq} m_i \wedge needs_{ac}(ro_i, m_i, a) \wedge \\ uses_{ac}(ro_j, m_j, a) \wedge \neg needs_{ac}(ro_j, m_j, a). \end{cases} \qquad (9)$$

Consider the two roles "**Professor**" and "**Secretary**" with only the two missions m_1 and m_2 of the application. The table 3 is an example of what we can deduce using the precedent definitions.

By analyzing the action dependencies among the roles of the organizational structure, we can detect inconsistencies in the definition of the roles and the links.

4.1 Autonomy of the Role in a OS

Based on the dependence among roles, we can use these dependencies to reason about the other roles. In particular, for a given role, we can compute its own dependencies relatively to each role of the organizational structure.

Table 3. Characteristics of the roles ro_1 and ro_2

ro_1	$is_{mi}(ro_1, m_1)$, $is^*_{pl}(m_1, p_1)$
	$uses_{ac}(ro_1, m_1, a_1)$, $uses_{ac}(ro_1, m_1, a_2)$, $uses_{ac}(ro_1, m_1, a_3)$
	$needs_{ac}(ro_1, m_1, a_2)$, $needs_{ac}(ro_1, m_1, a_3)$
ro_2	$is_{mi}(ro_2, m_2)$, $is^*_{pl}(m_2, p_4)$ with $p_4 = a_2(r_1$ or $r_2); a_3$
	$uses_{ac}(ro_2, m_2, a_1)$, $uses_{ac}(ro_2, m_2, a_2)$
$m_2 \overset{*}{\subseteq} m_1$ and $dep_{ac}(ro_1, ro_2, a_2, m_1, m_2)$ and $dep_{ac}(ro_1, ro_2, a_3, m_1, m_2)$.	

Let us define first the concept of autonomy : a role ro is autonomous noted $aut_{ac}(ro)$ if no action of their missions must be delegated :

$$aut_{ac}(ro) \overset{\triangle}{=} \forall a \ \forall m \ uses_{ac}(ro, m, a) \ \Rightarrow \ \neg needs_{ac}(ro, m, a). \tag{10}$$

From then, we can infer a particular situation of dependence : let $\mathcal{R}_{ro}$ be the set of roles which ro depends on.

$$\mathcal{R}_{ro} = \{ro_i \ / \ \exists a \ \exists m \ \exists m_i \text{ such that } dep_{ac}(ro, ro_i, a, m, m_i)\}. \tag{11}$$

In the context of $\mathcal{R}_{ro}$, we consider the autonomy of the role ro, noted $aut_{ac}(ro, \mathcal{R}_{ro})$, which expresses that the missions of the role ro are feasible with the cooperation of the roles of the set $\mathcal{R}_{ro}$:

$$aut_{ac}(ro, \mathcal{R}_{ro}) \overset{\triangle}{=} \begin{cases} \forall a \ \forall m \ needs_{ac}(ro, m, a) \Rightarrow \\ \exists ro_i \in \mathcal{R}_{ro} \ \exists m_i \ / \ dep_{ac}(ro, ro_i, a, m, m_i). \end{cases} \tag{12}$$

This implies that for each role ro, we can find a complementary set of roles $\mathcal{R}_{ro}$ in the OS, that makes the set of missions of the role feasible. Otherwise there is a problem with the definition of the missions of the role.

In the Groupware example, from the different dependencies deduced in the previous section, we can compute the following autonomy situations for the roles ro_1 and ro_2 : $aut_{ac}(ro_2)$ and $aut_{ac}(ro_1, \{ro_2\})$

4.2 Consistency of the Role Definition in the OS

We now introduce the notion of role consistency. A role ro is consistent if the definition of the OS allows all the missions of the role to be feasible, that is to say, that we can find in the OS, a set of roles $\mathcal{R}_{ro}$ in which ro is autonomous. However, we can't ensure that the links are sufficient to enable the achievement of the missions of the role. To control the consistency of these links according to a role, we introduce the predicate $path(ro_i, ro_j, m_i, m_j)$. It expresses that there exists a succession of organizational communication links in the OS that binds the roles ro_i in the context of mission m_i and ro_j in the context of m_j (see Fig. 3). The consistency of the organizational role definition can be defined as follows :

$$\text{path}(ro_1, ro_k, m_1, m_k)$$

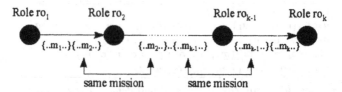

Fig. 3. Path of communication between two roles

$$cons\_def\_role_{ac}(ro_i) \triangleq \begin{cases} auto_{ac}(ro_i, \mathcal{R}_{ro_i}) \text{ and} \\ \forall a \, \forall m_i \ is_{mi}(ro_i, m_i) \wedge needs_{ac}(ro_i, m_i, a) \Rightarrow \\ \exists ro_j \, \exists m_j/ro_j \in \mathcal{R}_{ro_i} \wedge is_{mi}(ro_j, m_j) \wedge \\ dep_{ac}(ro_i, ro_j, a, m_i, m_j) \wedge path(ro_i, ro_j, m_i, m_j). \end{cases}$$
(13)

This means that for the role ro_i we can find a set $\mathcal{R}_{ro_i}$ where ro_i is autonomous regarding this set, and we can find a communication path between ro_i and each mission of the roles of $\mathcal{R}_{ro_i}$ which ro_i depends on.

Naturally, we can deduce the following consistency :

$$cons\_def\_os_{ac}(os) \triangleq \forall ro \ is_{ro}(os, ro) \Rightarrow cons\_def\_role_{ac}(ro). \tag{14}$$

Consider the two roles ro_1 and ro_2 with the two missions m_1 and m_2 of the GroupWare application example : from $aut_{ac}(ro_2)$ we can deduce $cons\_role_{ac}(ro_2)$. Concerning the second role ro_1, we have $aut_{ac}(ro_1, \{ro_2\})$. ro_1 is consistent because there exists a path between m_1 and m_2 of the roles ro_1 and ro_2.

5 Dependence in Organizational Entity

At the organizational entity level, we suggest to extend the dependence theory to deal with the agents. We define a new dependence : dependence between two agents in terms of action relatively to a role of the first agent. This dependence allows us to study the complementarity of the organizational entity agents taking into account the assignment of the roles among them. After the definition of the agent dependence, the notion of consistency is introduced along two points :

- *autonomy of an agent* guaranteeing that each of the actions used by the role of the agent is available in the OE ;
- *consistency of role distribution* guaranteeing that the distribution of the roles is adequate regarding the actions of the agents.

As in the last section, we consider only the action dependence, but we can generalize our reasoning to take into account the resource, plan and goal dependence.

In all the following definitions, we assume that the organizational structure is consistent as defined in the last section. Furthermore, to ensure readability we have simplified the definitions by assuming that all operands belong to the same OE. Before introducing a formal definition of dependence in the OE, let us define some predicates :

— $needs_{ac}(ag, ro, m, a)$ expresses that the agent ag needs the help of another agent to execute the action a required by the mission m of the role ro :

$$needs_{ac}(ag, ro, m, a) \triangleq uses_{ac}(ro, m, a) \wedge (needs_{ac}(ro, m, a) \vee \neg is_{ac}(ag, a)). \tag{15}$$

— $has\_all_{ac}(ag, ro, m)$ expresses that the agent ag has all the actions to achieve the mission m of the role ro.

$$has\_all_{ac}(ag, ro, m) \triangleq \forall a / uses_{ac}(ro, m, a) \Rightarrow is_{ac}(ag, a) \wedge \neg needs_{ac}(ro, m, a). \tag{16}$$

We now can define the action dependence : an agent ag_i playing the role ro depends on action a required for the mission m of ro, from an other agent ag_j if this latest has this action and the agent ag_i needs this action in the context of the mission.

$$dep_{ac}(ag_i, ro, m, a, ag_j) \triangleq needs_{ac}(ag_i, ro, m, a) \wedge is_{ac}(ag_j, a). \tag{17}$$

Consider two agents ag_1 and ag_2 which play the role "Professor" and "Secretary" respectively. ag_1 possesses the actions a_1 and a_3, and ag_2 the action a_2 only. We can deduce their characteristics as shown in table 4

Table 4. Characteristics of ag_1 and ag_2 in the application example

agent ag_1	agent ag_2
$is_{ac}(ag_1, a_1)$ and $is_{ac}(ag_1, a_3)$	$is_{ac}(ag_2, a_2)$
$needs_{ac}(ag_1, ro_1, m_1, a_2)$ and $needs_{ac}(ag_1, ro_1, m_1, a_3)$	$needs_{ac}(ag_2, ro_2, m_2, a_3)$
$dep_{ac}(ag_1, ro_1, m_1, a_3, ag_1)$ and $dep_{ac}(ag_1, ro_1, m_1, a_2, ag_2)$	$dep_{ac}(ag_2, ro_2, m_2, a_3, ag_1)$

5.1 Autonomy of the agents in a OE

Based on dependence among agents regarding their roles, we can reason about the other agents of the OE. In particular, for a given agent ag_i and a role ro, we can compute its own dependencies.

As viewed before for a role, we define the notion of autonomy of an agent in the OE. The agent ag is action autonomous regarding the role ro, noted

$aut_{ac}(ag, ro)$, if ag has all the actions used by the missions of ro, and no action must be delegated :

$$aut_{ac}(ag, ro) \triangleq \forall m \ is_{mi}(ro, m) \Rightarrow has\_all_{ac}(ag, ro, m). \tag{18}$$

From then we can infer a particular situation of dependence : let $Ag_{ag,ro}$ be the set of agents on which ag depends regarding ro :

$$Ag_{ag,ro} = \{ag_i \ / \ \exists a \ \exists m \ \text{such as} \ dep_{ac}(ag, ro, m, a, ag_i)\}. \tag{19}$$

In the context of $Ag_{ag,ro}$, we consider the autonomy of the agent ag regarding the role ro, noted $aut_{ac}(ag, ro, Ag_{ag,ro})$, which expresses that all the actions needed by ag to achieve the missions of ro are available in $Ag_{ag,ro}$:

$$aut_{ac}(ag, ro, Ag_{ag,ro}) \triangleq \begin{cases} \forall a \ needs_{ac}(ag, ro, m, a) \Rightarrow \\ \exists ag_i \in Ag_{ag,ro} \ / \ dep_{ac}(ag, ro, m, a, ag_i). \end{cases} \tag{20}$$

Let us consider the two agents ag_1 and ag_2 of the application example. We have : $aut_{ac}(ag_1, ro_1, \{ag_1, ag_2\})$ and $aut_{ac}(ag_2, ro_2, \{ag_1\})$, $Ag_{ag_1,ro_1} = \{ag_1, ag_2\}$ and $Ag_{ag_2,ro_2} = \{ag_1\}$.

5.2 Consistency of the Role Distribution in the OE

Unfortunately, the autonomy of the agent in an OE does not ensure that the missions of the agent's role can be done by this agent. To achieve the missions of the role, we need an adequate distribution of the roles among the set of agents $Ag_{ag,ro}$.

Let $D_{ag,ro}$ represent the current distribution of roles for the agents' set and the roles' set which ag depends on regarding ro :

$$D_{ag,ro} = \{(ag_i, ro_i) \in Ag_{ag,ro} \times \mathcal{R}_{ro} \ / \ ag_i \ \text{plays the role} \ ro_i\}. \tag{21}$$

A consistent distribution of roles in $D_{ag,ro}$, that makes the missions of ro feasible for ag, noted $cons\_dist\_roles_{ac}(ag, ro)$, can be defined as follows :

$$cons\_dist\_roles_{ac}(ag, ro) \triangleq$$
$$\begin{cases} aut_{ac}(ag, ro, Ag_{ag,ro}) \quad \text{and} \\ \forall a \ \forall m \ needs_{ac}(ag, ro, m, a) \Rightarrow \\ \exists(ag_i, ro_i) \in D_{ag,ro} \ \exists m_i \ / \ dep_{ac}(ag, ro, m, a, ag_i) \wedge \\ dep_{ac}(ro, ro_i, a, m, m_i) \wedge path(ro, ro_i, m, m_i). \end{cases} \tag{22}$$

Considering the consistency of the role definition of the OS, this implies that for each action needed by the agent ag regarding the mission m of ro, we are able to find in the OE an agent ag_i having this action and being able to execute it in the context of a sub-mission m_i of m, and we also know thatthat there exists a communication path between m_i and m.

In case of inconsistency, one way to avoid the problem is to reorganize the OE by choosing a new distribution of the roles among the agents, i.e finding a subset D' of $\mathcal{R}_{ro} \times Ag_{ag,ro}$ that makes the predicate $cons\_dist\_roles_{ac}(ag, ro)$ true.

The two agents ag_1 and ag_2 of the application example have all the actions needed by their roles. However we detect an inconsistency in the distribution of the roles for the two agents due to the impossibility of finding an agent that can ensure the execution of the action a_3 within a submission of m_1 or m_2. If we add the role ro_2 to ag_1, the distribution of the roles would be consistent.

6 Conclusion

The dependence theory explains, within a rational framework, the social exchanges that can occur among autonomous agents. In this paper, we have shown how to use the dependence theory to detect inconsistencies in a MAS organization. This work has to be continued and developed, especially the study of dependence regarding resource, plan and goal, and their combination. But we may foresee at least two potential applications of our work:

- *validation* : the use of dependence relations between roles, in a formal context, allows the validation of an existing OS by detecting the inconsistencies of organizational links and roles, which could be helpful to the designer of a system using the "Vowels" approach, in the sense that the design of an organization is a difficult task that leads very easily to inconsistencies.
- *adaptation* : both OS evolution (creating and deleting links, ...) and OE reorganization (redistribution of roles among agents) may be achieved from the validation results and through organizational heuristics. This can be done by the designer of the application or by the agents themselves.

References

1. Baeijs, C., Demazeau, Y.: Les Organisations dans les Systèmes Multi-Agents, 4èmes Journée Nationale du PRC-IA sur les Systèmes Multi-Agents, PRC-IA, Toulouse, France, (February 1996).
2. Boissier, O., Demazeau, Y.: A multi-agent architecture for open and decentralized vision systems, Techniques et Sciences Informatique. 16(8), (October 1997).
3. Bond, A.H.: PROJECTS : A normative model of collaboration in organizations, 10th International Workshop on DAI, Bandera, Texas, (October 1990).
4. Bouron, T.: Structures de Communication et d'Organisation pour la Coopération dans un Univers Multi-Agents, PhD thesis, Université de Paris VI, France, (1992).
5. Castelfranchi, C., Miceli, M., Cesta, A.: Dependence relations among autonomous agents, Decentralized A.I 3, Werner E., Demazeau Y., editors, (1992) 215–227.
6. Chaib-Draa, B., Desharnais, J., Lizotte, S.: A Relation Graph Formulation for Relationships among Agents, In 13th Int. DAI Workshop, Lake Quinalt WA USA, (March 1994).
7. Chaib-Draa, B.: Causal Reasoning in Multi-Agent Systems: A Formal Approach based on Relation Algebra, Canadian Conf. on AI, BC Vancouver, (June 1998).

8. Corbara, B., Drogoul, A., Fresneau, D., Lalande, S.: Simulating the Sociogenesis Process in Ant Colonies with MANTA, in Towards a Practice of Autonomous Systems II, MIT Press, Cambridge, (1993).

9. Corkill, D.D., Lesser, V.R. : The Distributed Vehicle Monitoring Testbed : a tool for investigating Distributed Problem Solving Network, In AI Magazine, **3(4)** (Fall 1983) 15–33.

10. Demazeau, Y.: From interactions to collective behaviour in agent-based systems. European conference on cognitive science,Saint-Malo, (Avril 1995).

11. Foisel, R., Chevrier, V., Haton J.-P.: Modèle pour la réorganisation de système multi-agents, in JFAIDSMA'97, Joël Quinqueton, Marie-Claude Thomas and Brigitte Trousse editor, Hermes, (April 1997), 261–277.

12. Gasser, L., Rouquette, N., Hill, R.W., Lieb, J.: Representing and Using Organizational Knowledge in DAI Systems, in Distributed Artificial Intelligence, vol II, L. Gasser and M. Huhns (Ed.), Pitman, (1989), pp 55-79.

13. Gasser, L.: Social Conception of Knowledge and Action : DAI Foundations and Open Systems Semantics. Artificial Intelligence. **47(1-3)**, (1991), 107–138.

14. Hannoun, M.: Modeling the organization in a multi-agent system. RR 98.02, Laboratoire SIC - ENSMSE, (January 1998).

15. Hannoun, M., Boissier, O., Sayettat, C., Sichman, J.S.: Towards a Model of Multi-Agent Systems' Organization. Workshop on Computational and Mathematical Organization Theory. Montréal - Canada, (April 25-26, 1998).

16. Pattison, H.E., Corkill, D.D., Lesser, V.R.: Instantiating Description of Organizational Structures, in Distributed AI I, Huhns M.N. editor, Morgan Kaufman Pitman, (1987), 59–96,

17. Proton, H., Bousquet, F., Reitz, P.: Un outil pour observer l'organisation d'une société d'agents : le cas d'une société d'agents chasseurs agriculteurs, in actes JFIAD-SMA, (1997), 159–172.

18. Rosenschein, J.S., Genesereth, M.R.: Deals Among Rational Agents, 84-44 HPP Report, Stanford University (1984),

19. Sichman, J.S., Conte, R., Demazeau, Y., Castelfranchi, C.: A social reasoning mechanism based on dependences networks, Proceeding of the 11th European Conference on Artificial Intelligence, Cohen T. editor, Amsterdam, The Netherlands, (August 1994), 182–192.

20. Sichman, J.S.: Du Raisonnement Social chez les Agents : Une Approche Fondée sur la Théorie de la Dépendance. PhD thesis, Institut National Polytechnique de Grenoble - France, (1995).

21. Smith, R.G.: The Contract Net Protocol : High-Level Communication and Control in a Distributed Problem Solver, IEEE Trans. on Computer, **29(12)**, (December 1980), pp 1104-1113.

22. So, Y., Durfee, E.H.: An Organizational Self-Design Model for Organizational Change, In Working Notes of the AAAI-93 Workshop on AI and Theories of Groups and Organizations, (July 1993).

23. Tidhar, G., Rao, A.S., Sonenberg, E.A.: Guided Team Selection, in ICMAS'96, Mario Tokoro editor, Kyoto, Japan, (December 1996), 369–376.

When Agents Emerge from Agents: Introducing Multi-scale Viewpoints in Multi-agent Simulations

David Servat[1,2], Edith Perrier[1], Jean-Pierre Treuil[1], and Alexis Drogoul[2]

[1] Laboratoire d'Informatique Appliquée, Orstom
32, rue H. Varagnat, 93 143 Bondy, France
[servat, perrier, treuil]@bondy.orstom.fr
[2] Laboratoire d'Informatique de l'Université de Paris 6
4, place Jussieu, 75 252 Paris Cedex 05, France
[David.Servat, Alexis.Drogoul]@lip6.fr

Abstract. Current multi-agent simulations, which have many individual entities evolve and interact, often lead to the emergence of local groups of entities, but provide no means of manipulating them. To our mind, giving full a sense to multi-agent simulations would consist though in making use of such dynamically created potential groups, by granting them an existence of their own, and specific behaviours. Brought into operation, they would provide effective and new tools for modelling purposes : for instance, encapsulating physical laws which depend on scaling, thus giving means of apprehending micro-macro links in multi-agent simulations, or introducing the experimentater's viewpoints on the specific behaviours of such groups. We thus have to imagine how to give any set of agents means of becoming aware of their mutual interaction, and giving birth to new types of agents out of their collective activity. In other words we look for a computer equivalent to our own emergence recognition ability. We present here a conceptual reflexion on such matters in the light of our own experience in the development of the RIVAGE project at Orstom, which aims at simulating runoff and infiltration processes. Conversely, we believe that the development of our methods in such a novel and original field of research as the multi-agent simulation of pure physical processes will provide new ideas and tools useful for many multi-agent architectures and modelling purposes.

Keywords : multi-agent simulations, multiple level of abstractions and scales, emergent phenomena, micro-macro link.

This research is supported by a grant from the french Department of Higher Education and Research, and by Orstom.

1 Introduction

The context of our research is the application of multi-agent systems to the simulation of complex phenomena. Such an approach has aroused an increasing interest among the scientific community for the last few years. However, the design process proves much more difficult when studying complex situations involving both different time and space scales. Current multi-agent simulations have so far provided but means of observing and *a posteriori* interpreting emergent phenomena that occur in such situations, and have not taken enough interest in the handling of multiple viewpoints within a simulation : for instance, when we want to adopt both a reductionist and a holistic point of view on the same phenomenon.

To build effective tools of simulation, we have to find an explicit *tangible* computer equivalent to such an emergence recognition process. We are convinced that such an issue may be tackled by giving full a sense to the agent concept : allowing the dynamic creation of agents by agents themselves. Within the computer simulation, higher level entities are locally and dynamically created by a set of agents which share for some time a structurally stable interaction and give shape to this interaction in the form of an agent of higher granularity.

These issues have echos in the community of multi-agent systems as a whole, namely in the field of distributed planning and reasoning (see Rao *et al* 1992 and their notion of social agents, a discussion on boundaries and identity of aggregated agents in Gasser 1992, or Wavish 1992). In this paper however, we have deliberately decided to quote mainly works from the simulation community.

We shall start our discussion with a short historical account of the development of the RIVAGE project at Orstom, which aims at simulating runoff and infiltration processes in a distributed way (see section 2). We show how we have come up to the idea of agents emerging from agents as a way to solve some important computational problems in the building of such a simulator. Then we go back to some fundamental questions as emergence, group creation in Social Sciences, scale transfer in Physics, which inevitably come into question when trying to cope with multiple scales and viewpoints in simulations (sections 3 and 4). From this dicussion we draw some guidelines for the design of such simulators (end of section 4). Eventually we present some preliminary results in the implementation of a discrete version of a RIVAGE simulator (section 5).

2 The RIVAGE Project

The RIVAGE project aims at modelling runoff, erosion and infiltration on heterogeneous soil surfaces. Such an issue has for a long time motivated lots of experimental studies (e.g. EMIRE program at Orstom Senegal, Planchon and Estèves 1995), because of the impact of runoff and erosion on tropical soils, but also in temperate countries (e.g. Cros-Cayot 1996). It has also motivated lots of modelling researches (e.g. Perrier 1992, Abbot *et al* 1986, Crave 1995).

At the beginning of the RIVAGE project is the meeting of two communities : computer scientists specialists of multi-agent simulations and hydrologists concerned by on field studies as well as models. For the last few years, we have experienced the benefits of multi-agent simulations in the field of complex system modelling, in a wide range of domains (e.g. Cambier *et al* 1992, Treuil and Mullon 1996). As a result we think of applying such a formalism to represent and simulate natural objects and physical processes, as described by researchers working on natural complex environments. More precisely, many factors have an impact on the hydrological surface behaviour of a soil - topography and nature -, of the vegetation and of different flowing networks, either natural (hydrological networks, ravines or streams, ponds or lakes, etc.) or human made (permeable ditch and impermeable road networks, anti-erosion layouts, etc.). Classical approach try to superpose all these different types of information - which are assumed constant - and make them fit in one unique lattice of given scale, so as to use a unique hydrological model based on different theoretical and integrating parameters. The diversity of the underlying scales and mechanisms is more or less erased, which nevertheless does not preclude from obtaining good prediction capacities - at least in so far as only global variables are concerned (e.g. input rain intensity vs. output flow relationship). However it is much more difficult to take into account the influence of different local factors, heterogeneous and dynamic, or to introduce specific behaviours which do not let themselves easily translate in terms of numerical parameters of equations distributed on the whole domain of study.

We are leading a methodological research without *a priori* precise time and space scale. We are willing to reproduce not only water flows at the outlet of a domain, but also to simulate the spatial distribution of water paths, level and extension variations of a pond or a ravine, as well as the creation of new water storage points, and eventually to handle the apparition of local interactions (such events as drawing water from a pond or building of walls to prevent erosion and runoff).

The idea of our modelling approach is to consider water as a set of multi-scale agents which evolve independently in the environment from which they locally extract the information they need. The first level of this configuration consists of a population of individual entities, waterball agents, which move according to their local environment. In (Perrier and Cambier 1996) this environmental information is given by several parallel discretisations of *a priori* independent levels of information (soil or vegetation maps, topographical map, map showing human layouts, etc.). Waterballs are the actual mediators between those different spatial information types, in so far as they introduce, when needed, a local superposition of information sources relative to the studied processes.

The computation of waterball motions at the surface depends on the topographical map. It is done in a deterministic way - the motion is assumed to be that of a mobile on an inclined plan with acceleration and friction forces (Solignac 1996). The basic idea is to make such a motion computation as independent as it may from the type of geometric representation used by the topographical map : the waterball motion is determined by the local normal vector which is internally computed by the topographical agent on request of a waterball. Thus we try to consider the action space of waterballs - which we perceive as continuous - as being independent from the structure of the information which determine this action - topographical and other information. The first implementations are promising as far as the openness of the model is concerned - addition of new actors, such as a new soil map for infiltration or an obstacle dynamically set up on a slope which waterballs perceive when drawing near and which locally alters waterpaths (Solignac 1996).

In the course of its motion on the surface a waterball may come down to a local minimum, which leads to the creation of a pond. From a general point of view, the accumulation of water in certain points (ponds and streams already existing and ravines created in the course of the simulation) leads to different hydrological behaviours (volume, height and spatial extension variation of a pond, flow rate and spatial extension variation of a ravine). Therefore we try to define new types of hydrological agents (ponds, ravines, etc.) which interact with waterballs and to specify the conditions of their creations and evolutions. A pond is dynamically created when the speed of a waterball becomes null on a local minimum of the topography. But the determination of its variable spatial extension and outlet from topographical data leads to important geometrical problems (Solignac 1996). Such computations have been possible for specific topographical representations but with a consequent loss of independence between the pond agent and the spatial support of its states and actions. The idea we have come up to then consists in considering the pond as a collective set of waterballs. Each waterball agent is provided with a capacity of memory (historical record of the path followed), which enables the consistution of a representation of the drainage area on the sole basis of the information stored by waterballs. Thus pond and waterballs share the same representation of space linked to action and coexist at different levels of organisation.

3 Capturing Scale Transfer Processes in Simulations : Why?

3.1 Reality Is Perceived at Different Scales

When looking at a sand pile, the first thing we perceive because of the poor keenness of our vision is a whole. Of course we know that this whole is made up of lots of sand grains which we could see if we drew closer. Fortunately enough we do not constantly think of the sand pile as a collection of grains and we naturely perceive it as a whole, disregarding its "particularness".

When looking at a traffic jam, we do not only see a collection of cars, but a self-organized object which actually grows in the opposite direction that the cars slowly follow. The same phenomenon occurs when taking part in a demonstration. We may talk with friends that are walking beside us as if the whole procession did not exist. But we may as well feel ourselves carried along by the crowd as if all the people taking part in the demonstration were a unique whole, moving individuals along the streets, constraining our own behaviours.

Moreover we commonly reify the group we feel we belong to. Gilbert gives an example of such a situation (Gilbert 1995b), for instance when people are influenced in their consumption decisions by their adoption of a lifestyle : "there are some people who quite consciously adopt lifestyles and others who discover that they have adopted a lifestyle. These people are quite likely to categorize themselves as the sort of people who follow this lifestyle, to band together as a group (e.g. punks, students, old age pensioners) and to contribute explicitly to the evolution of the lifestyle".

This ability to change our way of perceiving the world, according to where we sit so to speak, accounts to a wide extent for our capacity for modelling reality. We are able to conceptualize part-whole relations according to our perception of correlations or constraints and at the same time disregard non fundamental peculiarities so as to build new abstractions : that is precisely the basic exercise in the intellectual gymnastics of the scientist, to simultaneously adopt different points of view on observed phenomena.

Indeed, as underlined by Stöckler (1991a), such a capacity becomes truly essential when apprehending complex systems : "Contrary to the ideal of complete description with as many details as possible, complex systems require a simplified characterization which nevertheless saves the essential features of the system. For practical reasons, details which are not important in a particular context should be neglected." And moreover, it is useful to introduce new concepts on the higher levels if the macro-level exhibits constant structures. Such higher level abstractions prove more useful for explanations than irrelevant atomistic details, even if they do not point at irreducible new entities or forces (Stöckler 1991a). Such abstractions help us to apprehend reality and build models which are by essence simplifications of the actual reality.

3.2 Simulations Should Integrate Different Scales

Having said that, we are inclined to expect simulators, which are models put in process, to inherit from such an ability. As a matter of fact, most simulators show poor capacities as far as handling multiple viewpoints and scales is concerned. They often deal with one unique level of analysis, whatever the modelling formalism : for instance, the level of the ants in MANTA, a multi-agent simulation of ant societies (Drogoul et al 1995), the level of gaz particles in lattice gaz methods - cellular automata dedicated to hydrodynamics - (e.g. Fredkin 1990, Toffoli and Margolus 1990), the level of fishes in SEALAB, an individual-based modelling of fish demographic behaviour (LePage and Cury 1996).

Some simulations do handle objects that belong to different granularity levels. In (Bousquet et al 1994) for instance, fishermen, ethnic groups and fishing ponds are represented. But in those cases, all the different entities - and thus levels - that are present in the simulation are static objects built at design time : groups neither dynamically appear from the lower level nor vanish in the course of the simulation.

To be fair, these simulators do not rest upon one unique level of analysis, rigourously speaking. They exhibit emergent phenomena : interactions among objects at the ground level give rise to different types of objects at a higher level. For instance in MANTA, social structures such as a division of labour emerge as a consequence of the behaviour and interactions of individuals. However such emergent phenomenon must be analysed after the simulation process in the light of the data produced. At the end of (Drogoul et al 1995), the authors admit that such post-analysis requires a huge amount of work before being able to conduct new experiments on its basis.

Instead, we believe that simulators *should* be able to handle processes at different time and space scales and integrate such emergent phenomena. Two main reasons account for this.

On the one hand, it is a question of cost-efficiency. Simulator designers express major concern about the ability of simulators to scale up when the number of simulated objects increase. For instance, Scheffer *et al* (1995) admit that a major problem with individual-based models is that the typically large number of individuals needed requires impractically large computation times. They suggest to add an extra feature to each model individual : the amount of individuals that it actually represents. In the course of the simulation, some global process regroups similar individuals into super-individuals, so as to reduce the computational burden. It is all the more important to try and cope with such a problem, as it is precisely when large number of individuals interact and lots of computation is required, that the most interesting phenomena occur : Darley (1994) considers for instance that "emergence is purely the result of a phase change in the amount of computation necessary for optimal prediction of certain phenomena".

On the other hand, there are more conceptual reasons that account for such a need. Recall the example of the consumption decision making. Not only can we as observers distinguish patterns of collective action but the agents themselves can also do so and therefore their actions can be influenced by their recognition of these patterns. In other words, a simulation of such a process would have to model (Gilbert 1995b) :

1. The emergence of patterns of consumption in the society as a result of social imitation of individual agents' consumption decisions,
2. The perception by agents that these patterns exist,
3. The categorization, or social construction, by agents of these patterns into some small number of lifestyles,
4. Eventually the influence of agents' adoption of these lifestyles on their consumption decision making, leading to the evolution of adapted or new consumption patterns.

In the case of the RIVAGE project, suppose we want to model the action of drawing water from a pond. We cannot possibly do so by describing each interaction between the agent that draws water and each waterball. We do need to introduce the pond agent, as a realistic counterpart.

We say that both reasons essentially call for the same type of recognition process, which we nately and constantly do in reality : to recognize the relevant level of analysis for describing interactions. Simulators should be able to provide means of doing the same. Indeed we have to find a tangible computer equivalent to our ability to perceive scale transfers : when individuals might be rightly consider as a group, that is as an individual of higher level, and conversely when the group as a whole no longer exists or is not sufficient to account for the underlying reality.

4 Capturing Scale Transfer Processes in Simulations : How?

4.1 From Individuals to Individual

So as to be able to build such simulators that would handle multiple viewpoints and scales and dynamical change of scale, a good starting point is to analyse our own ability to perceive an individual entity out of a collection of individuals. Put it differently, how do we recognize that "something macro" is going on?

Emergence Obviously this is related to the issue of emergence. We shall take a look at some definitions of this concept.

Stöckler (1991b) stresses that the notion of emergence has a pragmatic aspect : his main idea is that emergent properties occur if the tools of explanation, which are sufficient for the parts of a whole, are not adequate for a real understanding of the composed system. "I have proposed calling those properties of complex systems emergent which cannot be explained by those parts of the fundamental theory which are sufficient to understand the behaviour of the isolated components".

We may find another close definition of emergence in (Darley 1994), who considers an emergent phenomenon as "a large scale, group behaviour of a system, which does not seem to have any clear explanation in terms of the system's constituent parts". For him, emergence results from our inability to predict the outcome of accumulating interactions among objects. In those cases, the optimal means of prediction is simulation. Cariani (1992) would call it emergence-relative-to-a-model, which involves a change in the relationship between the observer and the physical system under observation - when the behavior of the system deviates from the observer's model of it.

Gilbert (1995a) speaks for considering that there are multiple levels of emergence, forming a complex hierarchy. "It may be the case that individual identity is best regarded as an emergent phenomenon, where the micro-level agents are sub-cognitive, such as neurons". Here as well the level of emergence depends on the relevant level of analysis according to an observer of the phenomenon.

The concept of emergence seems rather ambiguous indeed (see M.R. Jean 1997 for a more thorough discussion). We would like to retain two main aspects. First, the emergence phenomenon lies to a certain extent in a shift in our vision of things. Secondly, emergent phenomena reveal a shift in the behaviour of the whole.

Collective Individuals in Human Sciences In Human Sciences, the question of the observer's viewpoint and of the right level of analysis has continuously aroused conflicts among scientists. We will not try to summarize the debate which has divided the defenders of methodological reductionism and those of structuralism (see for instance Gilbert 1995a, Treuil 1995 or Caillé 1992 for an account of this debate). Rather we will echo some hints expressed by some authors in favour of an in-between way.

In (Smith 1998), the author says that : "Ever since social sciences first began to analyze groups of people as if they comprised a single entity or structural componenet a constant objection has been raised : social structural entities do not really exist save as heurisitcs". As a matter of fact, even if human consciousness so to speak is needed to observe such structures, they can be empirically shown to exist. For instance in Axelrod's experiments on the emergence of political actors (1995), the new organization resulting from alliance formations between states is shown to possess all the required conditions to be assumed as a state in its own right : effective control over subordinates - little rebellion and no independent foreign policy -, collective action - paternalism and joint foreign policy -, and recognition by others as an actor. This last feature is crucial. For some social simulation specialists (Gilbert 1995a), "simulations may have oversimplified important characteristics of specifically human societies, because the actors (agents) in these societies are capable of reasoning, and do so routinely, about the emergent properties of their own society."

From this, we shall keep in mind that the knowledge of the existence of a group is part of the group itself. In other words, what seems to found a group is the acknowledgment from individuals that they belong to it.

Individual-Based Methods Historically individual-based methods have been used by biologists and ecologists, whereas agent-based simulations come mainly from computer scientists. In essence they are similar. When spatially distributed, these methods easily account for spatial heterogeneity of phenomena. Moreover they are easy to apprehend by the profane : individuals are taken as the natural units, which is both more realistic and intuitively straightforward. Besides, they are sometimes more cost-effective than other methods, especially when complex systems and demographical processes are concerned.

However it is not always easy to decide whether or not the phenomena require that we trace the actual evolution of each individual in the course of events, instead of simply describing them in statistical terms - in other words, when the continuity of identity becomes as essential as that of existence.

For instance in Lotka-Voltera like dynamics, there are two individual states : either prey or predator. The macroscopical state is given by the numbers of preys and predators. The microscopic state is given by the state - prey or predator - of every individual. Thus, to each macroscopic state corresponds many microscopic states. If any permutation of individuals results in changes in the macroscopic state *destiny*, it is necessary to take individual behaviours into account (DeAngelis and Rose 1992). Otherwise the interactions among individuals are likely to be numerically integrable and should not be considered at the individual level.

So a topical question we are faced with in the course of an individual-based simulation is *when* we can soundly assume individuals as interchangeable with respect to the global destiny of the population. Indeed this question determines the validity of the adopted scale of analysis.

Scale Transfer in Physics The problems at issue have a special echo in Physics: the scale transfer.

Perrier (1990) gives a thorough account on that matter, in the field of hydrodynamics. Classically in Hydrology each model accounts for a unique specific level of study. For instance, hydrodynamic modellers are interested by porous media at a micro-level, whereas agronomists study the evolution of water stocks on a parcel and hydrologists develop their own models at the level of a watershed. In a sense this does seem to be rather normal and satisfactory an approach. As a matter of fact phenomena which have very different characteristic lengths generally have little influence on one another (Wilson 1989). We may separately study them. Water waves for example pulse through the medium but at every stage of their travel they are made up of different collections of water molecules. Fortunately enough we may accurately describe waves as perturbations in a continuous medium, disregarding the molecular structure of water.

However there are occasions when the need to take into account scale transfers becomes urging.

Sometimes, we are compelled to go deeper in complexity and consider things at a micro-level. For instance, the law of Darcy which accounts in a simple way for the flows in a macroscopically homogeneous porous medium with specific boundary conditions, fails to be extended to heterogeneous media. Unfortunately, at this level, local heterogeneities, geometrical and structural organizations of the soil might no longer be neglected. Working at the micro-level arises the question of how to extract global macro properties - that interested us in the first place -, from local micro processes. In other words how do we *computationnaly* proceed to a scale transfer?

For that purpose lots of methods have been used : mainly integrating differential equations in a continuous medium or using numerical simulations which rest upon a discretization of the porous space and even sometimes of the flows themselves (e.g. lattice gaz methods). The scale transfer essentially consists in some averaging. For instance in lattice gaz methods, in order to lighten the computational burden of huge sized networks, renormalisation group techniques have been introduced (Lesne 1995) : a macro-lattice stands for a particular area of the initial network, and is given macroscopic speed computed as the average of micro-speeds (coarse-grain averaging). Thus a smaller network is computed instead of the huge initial one. In this sense it is rather close a method such as that put forward by individual-based simulation designers, as seen above.

Yet we know even more critical situations, phase transitions for instance, for which we have to take into account a wide range of scales at the same time. For instance the phenomena associated with sandpiles manifest themselves only when all the sand grains are said to communicate globally with one another, that is when correlations occur at all length ranges.

So eventually the most important question that comes up with scale transfers in Physics is to detect phase transitions, so as to dynamically adapt our scale of analysis.

4.2 Hints for the Building of Simulators

We shall try and sum up the elements that result from our brief overview of the previous section.

Multi-agent simulations rest upon interacting entities. With respect to the intensity of their mutual interactions, such entities may show "various ways of being together". When interactions are rather loose, we are likely to perceive the entities as disorganized. On the contrary, when the interactions are more intense, the entities show various organizational structures. A structure emerges from another on phase transitions.

Such changes in the organization of the entities result in shifts in the vision of an external observer.

What actually happens during these phase transitions? Let us follow each individual entity which moves in some description space. When interactions are loose, individuals move about in the description space, in rather a free way so to speak, and thus may potentially visit the whole description space. Then under some circumstances, individuals adopt similar or coordinated trajectories, thus creating or entering a specific mode of existence, an ordered kind of mode (Prigogine and Stengers 1992).

Our hypothesis is that entities can locally and in a collective way *recognize* what their current mode of organization is, or at least that they are organized in some way. Such recognition can proceed locally (and not at a global level as in Marcenac *et al* 1997) because entities can detect a decrease in their own degree of freedom - their trajectories are somewhat constrained by others - and notice a correlative decrease in the others' degrees of freedom. Such process happens in a collective fashion as it is through communicating with one another that entities may be mutually aware of their correlations. As a result, a new entity is created by the decision of all correlated entities and incarnate their group.

So the agents must be provided with means of recognizing the emergence of structures in their environment. Some sort of a dynamical emergence recognition process must be built. The agents must be aware of the fact that their correlations between one another have lasted long enough, and consequently, that it is both more cost-effective and more accurate from a conceptual point of view, to consider them as a whole. This emergent whole would be represented as an agent in the simulation.

The next question is whether we should predefine such groups or not. In the case of RIVAGE, should waterballs agglutinate in completely general water groups or specifically in ponds and ravines? Both approaches have advantages and drawbacks.

A possible approach could be to look for some signature in the description space, or phase space, of the different predefined types of organization : for instance waterballs regrouping in a pond are immobile, their trajectories are a set of close points, on the contrary waterballs regrouping in a ravine have very close linear kind of trajectories.

However we may as well favour an all-emergence kind of approach, without any predefinition of groups. Indeed this may be necessary when we do not have clues about the groups that may appear and would help us create new ways of seeing the world.

But once the group created, the interaction rules between group and entities - control issue -, group and other groups, and group and observers of the simulation - how groups are seen by observers -, have to be specified. We may not do without a predefinition of the latter. Indeed, if we could, that would mean that such notions as volume, temperature, etc., could emerge as concepts in a simulation. This is by far too unrealistic, which seems to call for a predefinition of groups.

So it seems we have to deal with two different steps intimately connected with one another. Schematically, on the vertical axis an emergent process creates higher level entities out of lower ones, and some guided process rules the interactions between entities on the horizontal axis. The next section gives preliminary hints for implementational matters in the light of our own experience in the development of such a computer organization.

5 Emergence and Coexistence of Groups for Distributing Action Control : RIVAGE application. Preliminary Results

The implementation of a discrete version of the simulator in the RIVAGE project has allowed us to start an investigation on the means of introducing and making to coexist agents which emerge from the collective activity of other agents, within one simulation (Servat 1997).

In the simulator (see figures 1, 2 and 3), the space is represented by a tridimensional network, where each cell is an agent and may receive a unique waterball. Rain is simulated by periodically introducing waterballs. At every cycle, balls move from one cell to the first free cell, among the lowest ones in a cubic neighbourhood of 26 cells. If there are several possible cells, one is randomly chosen. A cell, situated at the edge of the surface, gets rid of its ball and the ball is removed from the simulation. The cells may take three inner states : state 0 if free, state 1 if occupied, state 2 if occupied by a ball which is trapped and may no longer move, due to the overcrowding of its neighbourhood.

Cells update an historical account of their states, on the basis of which they proceed to regroupings and give birth to ravine and pond agents. Their history account for several cycles and actually determine their belonging to one of the following categories :

1. A cell belongs to the category of *potential ravines*, when its history shows only states 1.
2. A cell belongs to the category of *potential ponds*, when its history shows only states 2.
3. Otherwise a cell belongs to the category of *potential hillsides*, that is when it is sometimes not occupied by a waterball.

Such a categorization tries to take into account the fact that some cells are more frequented than others.

Among the first two categories neighbouring cells may form clusters. When these clusters comprise a sufficient number of cells and obey to some preconditions, groups are created. A pond agent is created when a sufficient number of neighbouring cells are in the same cluster of potential ponds. A ravine agent is created when a sufficient number of neighbouring cells belonging to the potential ravines are in the same cluster, and when at least one of them is on the border of the surface or close to another already existing group : such a cell represents the outlet of the ravine.

These new agents take control over the regrouping cells, which are restrained to play a role of interface with the medium : they keep on receiving balls coming from other cells outside the group, but no longer handle waterball exchanges from cell to cell within the group.

The group agents handle waterball *flows* themselves, *via* their outlets, from groups to groups without having balls moved from cells to cells. Each group is given a maximum capacity of waterballs or stock (so far it is simply the number of cells in the group). Cells within the group accept waterballs to the extent of the group capacity, beyond this limit they act as impermeable membrane.

Periodically, groups try to get rid of their stock of waterballs, *via* their outlets. If the agent does not have an outlet towards the exterior of the surface, it asks other group agents which are linked to itself to take some or all of its stock.

The group agents are given self-observation capacities which enable them to decide their own partial dissolution, when, in the case of a pond, a free neighbouring cell is found, or in the case of a ravine, the stock of waterballs received in one cycle decreases. The dissolution process so far amounts in the case of a ravine to free a number of randomly chosen cells proportional to the decrease of the flow received from outside, and in the case of a pond to free all cells. When the number of cells in a group falls below some critical threshold the group no longer exists.

Eventually we have to consider the interactions between different groups and between groups and individuals. This point is still under reflexion. The recursive regrouping of entities which share the same granularity - for instance the creation of a ravine network - can obey the same principles regardless of the level. Yet further work is needed as far as the interactions between entities of different granularities and between different group types are concerned. A possible way of research may consist in trying to formalise these interactions in the form of rules. May a pond merge directly with a ravine or does it have to dissolve itself ball after ball in the ravine? Is a waterball coming accross a pond always absorbed by the pond? All these questions have not been answered so far, and perhaps a reason for this is that we have made our investigations in a discrete representation of space, for which it is easy to test whether or not a cell is free, but which also hides the problems of interaction between entities and group borders.

We are currently working on an adaptation of the processes implemented in the discrete version of the simulator to a continuous one. In this continuous version, waterballs no longer move from cell to cell in a discrete lattice, but move in a tridimensional continuous space, which is much more in keep with our own vision of the physical reality. Such an adaptation needs that we be able to handle interactions among agents - to spot them as well as to put agents in interaction. The absence of a fixed frame of reference - no discrete lattice - leads us to think about setting up, besides a distributed control of action, a distributed control of space which puts action entities in relation. We have started to implement such a control of space in the form of a dynamic structure of mediator agents.

6 Conclusion

Our discussion about such concepts as scale transfer, emergence, individual-group relation in social sciences gives us a much more precise vision of the type of system we need for the applicative goals of the RIVAGE project. This vision rests upon such notions as groups, inclusion of groups, which are at the heart of the multi-agent formalism and enable us to model the reality in much more faithful a way to the hydrologist's.

Moreover it seems to us that the question of handling multiple viewpoints and scales in simulations is shared by a wide community of researchers from different domains (ecology, social sciences, ethology, physics, etc.). We hope that some of the reflexions we have presented here will contribute to start a fruitful debate on those topics.

From an implementational viewpoint, lots of further work is needed. We have mainly dealt with the dynamic creation of groups but have not quite formalized what it actually means for an agent to belong to a group - inhibition of some individual behaviour, inheritance of other behaviour, internal variables restrained to a certain range, etc. Undoubtedly this research will bring new aspects of the agent programming paradigm into light. If we give agents means of creating new agents out of their collective activity, we will have to implement new architectures which provide means of dynamically creating their own organizations.

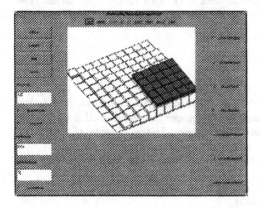

Fig. 1. Initial state. The user has set up a pond agent, shown in dark gray. The white cells represent the relief

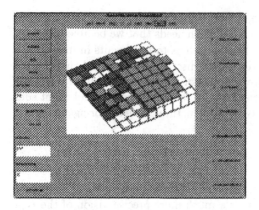

Fig. 2. The pond agent from Fig.1, obviously too extended, dissolves itself, freeing its cells, in light gray, and giving birth to the regrouping of cells in medium gray on the slope

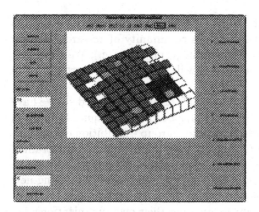

Fig. 3. Final state. The pond reappears in dark gray, with proper dimensions. The regrouping of cells in medium gray goes on, in one big ravine agent. A few free cells are also found, in light gray

References

Abbot M.B., Bathurst J-C., O'Connel P.E., Rasmussen J. : An Introduction to the European Hydrological System - Système Hydrologique Européen - S.H.E.- 2 : Structure of a Physically-Based, Distributed Hydrological System. Journal of Hydrology, 87 :61-67, 1986.

Axelrod R. : A Model of Emergence of New Political Actors. Artificial Societies, Conte and Gilbert Eds., 1995.

Bousquet F., Cambier C., Mullon C., Quensiere J. : Simulating Fishermen Society. Simulating Societies, Gilbert Ed., 1994.

Caillé A. : Sujets individuels et sujet collectif. in *Philosophie et anthropologie*, Editions du Centre Pompidou, 1992. (in French).

Cambier C., Bousquet F., Dansoko D. : Un univers multi-agent pour la modélisation du système de pêche du delta central du Niger. CARI Yaoundé, 1992.

Cariani P. : Emergence and Artificial Life. Artificial Life II, Langton et al Eds., 1992.

Crave A. : Quantification de l'organisation des réseaux hydrographiques. PhD Thesis, Thèse de l'Université de Géosciences de Rennes, 1995. (in French).

Cros-Cayot S. : Distribution spatiale des transferts de surface à l'échelle du versant. Contexte armoricain. PhD Thesis, ENSAR Rennes, 1996. (in French).

Darley V. : Emergent Phenomena and Complexity. Artificial Life IV, Brooks and Maes Eds., 1994.

DeAngelis D.L., Rose K.A. : Which Individual-Based Approach Is Most Appropriate for a Given Problem? Individual-Bades Models and Approaches in Ecology, Populations Communities and Ecosystems, DeAngelis and Gross Eds., 1992.

Drogoul, A., Corbara B., Lalande S. : MANTA : New Experimental Results on the Emergence of (Artificial) Ant Societies. Artificial Societies, Conte and Gilbert Eds., 1995.

Fredkin E. : Digital Mechanics, an Informational Process Based on Reversible Universal Cellular Automata. Cellular Automata, Theory and Experiment, H. Gutowitz (Eds) MIT/North-Holland, p254-270, Amsterdam, 1990.

Gasser L. : Boundaries, Identity and Aggregation : Plurality Issues in Multi-Agent Systems. Decentralized A.I.-3, Eric Werner and Yves Demazeau (Eds.), Elsevier, 1992.

Gilbert N. : Emergence in Social Simulation. Artificial Societies, Conte and Gilbert Eds., 1995.

Gilbert N. : Simulation : an Emergent Perspective. Transcript of a Lecture first given at the conference on New Technologies in the Social Sciences, 27-29th October 1995, Bournemouth, UK, and then at LIP6, Paris, 22nd January 1996, http ://www.soc.surrey.ac.uk/research/simsoc/tutorial.html.

LePage C., Cury P. : How Spatial Heterogeneity Influences Population Dynamics : Simulation in Sealab. Adaptive Behaviour, 4(3/4) :249-274, 1996.

Lesne A.: Méthodes de renormalisation. Eyrolles Sciences, 1995. (in French)

Marcenac P., Calderoni S., Courdier R., Leman S. : Construction expérimentale d'un modèle multi-agents. Proceedings of the 5th JFIADSMA, Hermès, 1997. (in French).

M. R. Jean: Emergence et SMA. Proceedings of the 5th JFIADSMA, Hermès, 1997. (in French).

Perrier E. : Modélisation du fonctionnement hydrique des sols. Passage de l'échelle microscopique à l'échelle macroscopique. SEMINFOR IV Le transfert d'échelle, Orstom Editions, Brest, Septembre 1990. (in French)

Perrier E. : Simsurf. Simulation numérique et graphique de l'infiltration et du ruissellement sur une surface de sol. Influence du relief et des états de surface. Document Orstom, 1992. (in French).

Perrier E., Cambier Ch. : Une approche multi-agents pour simuler les interactions entre acteurs hétérogènes de l'infiltration et du ruissellement d'eau sur une surface de sol. Tendances nouvelles en modélisation pour l'environnement, Elsevier Ed., 1996. (in French).

Planchon O., Estèves M. : EMIRE : Expérimentation et Modélisation physique de l'Infiltration, du Ruissellement et de l'Erosion. Programme Orstom, 1995.

Prigogine I., Stengers I.: Order out of Chaos. Bantham Books, 1992.

Rao A. S., Georgeff M. P., Sonenberg E. A. : Social Plans : a Preliminary Report. Decentralized A.I.-3, Eric Werner and Yves Demazeau (Eds.), Elsevier, 1992.

Servat D. : Emergence et coexistence de groupes en multi-agents. Master Thesis at the University of Paris VI in Artificial Intelligence Pattern Recognition and their Applications, Paris, Septembre 1997. (in French).

Sheffer M., Baveco J.M., DeAngelis D.L., Rose K.A., van Nes E.H. : Super-Individuals a Simples Solution for Modelling Large Populations on an Individual Basis. Ecological Modelling, 80(1995), 161-170, 1995.

Smith R.D. : Social Structures and Chaos Theory. Sociological Research Online, vol.3, no.1, http ://www.socresonline.org.uk/socresonline/3/1/11.html, 1998.

Solignac Ch. Projet RIVAGE (Ruissellement et Infiltration Vu par des Agents). Master Thesis at the University of Paris VI in Artificial Intelligence Pattern Recognition and their Applications, Paris, Septembre 1996. (in French).

Stöckler M. : Reductionism and the New Theories of Self-Organization. Advances in Scientific Philosophy, Schurz and Dorn Eds, 1991.

Stöckler M. : A Short History of Emergence and Reductionism. The Problem of Reductionism in Science, Agazzi Ed., 71-90, 1991.

Toffoli T., Margolus N.H. : Invertible Cellular Automata : a Review. Cellular Automata, Theory and Experiment, H. Gutowitz (Eds) MIT/North-Holland, p229-253, Amsterdam, 1990.

Treuil J-P., Mullon Ch. : Expérimentations sur mondes artificiels : pour une réflexion méthodologique. Tendances nouvelles en modélisation pour l'environnement, Elsevier Ed., 1996. (in French).

Treuil J-P.: Emergence of Kinship Structures : a Multi-Agent Approach. Artificial Societies, Conte and Gilbert Eds., 1995.

Wavish P. : Exploiting Emergent Behaviour in Multi-Agent Systems. Decentralized A.I.-3, Eric Werner and Yves Demazeau (Eds.), Elsevier, 1992.

Wilson K. : Les phénomènes de physique et les échelles de longueur. in *L'ordre du chaos*, Bibliothèque Pour la science, Editions Belin, 1989.

ACTS in Action: Sim-ACTS – A Simulation Model Based on ACTS Theory

Harko Verhagen

Department of Computer and System Sciences,
Stockholm University and the Royal Institute of Technology,
Electrum 230, S-164 40 Kista, Sweden,
email: verhagen@dsv.su.se,
WWW home page: http://www.dsv.su.se/~verhagen/welcome.html

Abstract. Sim-ACTS is an agent-based computer simulation model of some aspects of ACTS theory [5]. It is the first of a series of models in which increasingly more aspects of ACTS theory will be encompassed. Sim-ACTS studies the effects of communication and organizational structure on organizational problem solving. It is a follow-up study of the TASSCS research project [15],[16]. The simulation experiments from the TASSCS project are replicated using the Sim-ACTS model.The article compares the results of TASSCS' simulations with those of the Sim-ACTS experiments. Sim-ACTS is implemented in SOAR [8], the implementation of a general cognitive theory [11].

1 Introduction

The rise of the agent paradigm within artificial intelligence has given a new impulse to the application of computer simulation in the social sciences. The agent paradigm makes the study of the micro-macro link (i.e., the problem of the relation between the behavior of individuals comprising a social system and the behavior of that system as a whole) more feasible. The use of multiagent simulation models is a natural tool to study the interdependence between individual problem-solving and system behavior.

Organization theory has always used models to represent real world situations and to predict what will happen when parameters change. Instead of simulating existing organizations (sometimes called emulation), fictional organizations can be simulated in order to study propositions of an organization theory or to develop a new organization theory. These simulation models are abstracted away from particular organizations, individuals or tasks, but try to use generic concepts related to these three elements. Using agents to simulate individuals seems a natural choice. However, one has to deal with the question of what an agent is or more precisely what type of agent is suited for the particular research goal.

The properties of agents can be used to characterize different types of agents as well as the agents' and system's possibilities and limitations [4], [17], [18]. The research goal can thus be used to decide on the type of agent and system to be implemented [1], [2].

This article is organized as follows. First, ACTS theory, the theoretical basis of the simulation model, is introduced. After this, computational organizational theory models will be compared to multiagent systems. Then Soar, the programming language and cognitive theory, is discussed. After this, the simulation model itself is described. Following this is a description of the task that is used to study the interplay between individual properties and behavior and the properties and behavior of the organization as a whole. The results of the simulations are then compared to the results of the models predecessor TASSCS in order to validate the model. Finally, some conclusions will be drawn and recommendations for future work will be given.

2 ACTS theory

ACTS theory [5] is an extension of the model of bounded rationality [12], [13]. The model of bounded rationality not only specifies that the rationality of human beings is restricted, but also that the environment and the relations between the environment and the individual restrict the individuals possibilities. ACTS theory also views agents as limited and constrained by the environment, but extends the model of bounded rationality by specifying the environment and the limitations of the agents' rationality. In ACTS theory, organizations are viewed as collections of intelligent Agents who are Cognitively restricted, Task oriented and Socially situated. The general concept of bounded rationality is replaced by a full model of a cognitive agent, exhibiting general intelligence. The environment is split into two components, the task and the social situation. Organizational performance and behavior are explained by an interlinked set of computational models. The links are a model of the organizational design. At the micro level, ACTS theory tries to explain how an organizational design affects the behavior and performance of the individual agents communicating and reasoning within a social situation while trying to accomplish a task. At the macro level ACTS theory tries to explain the behavior and performance of groups and organizations with differing organizational designs while the groups or organizations consist of intelligent agents who are socially situated and task oriented. The research questions ACTS theory addresses includes those in which individual decision-making and group decision-making play a key role. What an agent knows and to whom it communicates are important components of ACTS theory. ACTS theory coheres with the ideas in [4] on the nature of the social agent in that the agents' actions depend on the agents' cognitive architecture and knowledge. The cognitive architecture does not change over time and is constant over the agents. The information processing, decision making and learning mechanisms are all a function of the cognitive architecture. The agents' knowledge may change over time, by learning (or perhaps forgetting). The knowledge depends on the agent's position in the social structure, the task and the problems the organization encompasses. ACTS theory articulates collective organizational constraints and opportunities and how these constraints and opportunities restrict and enable the individual. It thus lets collective phenomena emerge in a dynamic organizational setting. ACTS theory is embodied in a set of fundamental axioms and an expandable set of testable propositions functioning as theorems derived from the axioms. This enables us to implement ACTS theory as a multiagent system that can be used to conduct simulation studies in order to verify its predictions. Earlier work in organization theory can be seen as laying the foundations for ACTS theory. Simon [12] has earlier discussed some issues on the dimensions mentioned in [4], but used a different categorization. Simon argues that some of the (at that time) accepted administrative principles can be on the wrong foot with each other. Instead of giving new proverbs, he argues for more attention on the members of the organization and to the limits on the quantity and quality of the individual's output. The limits include limits on the ability to perform and limits on the ability to make correct decisions. The limits can be specified as limits that are unconscious (skills, habits, reflexes), limitations on the knowledge needed to perform the task and limits on decision making through the norms and values of the individual. The limits to make correct decisions however, are not analyzed as detailed as in [4].

3 Computational organizational theory models and multiagent systems

Computational organization theory (COT) research uses computational models of organizations in order to either test or develop new organization theories or to simulate the behavior of a real life organization under different circumstances so as to choose the best alternative. The first type of research uses intellectual models based on generalizations, the second type of research is based on emulation models with very detailed specifications. The computational model may thus be to a different extent specified on the level of the agents, the tasks the organization works on, the organizational structure, and the environment of the organization. On the level of agents, COT can make use of the development in multiagent systems research. However, few multiagent systems surpass trivial levels of agency and organizational structure. For a COT model to be close to the behavior of real humans (which is what COT research is interested in, not in the engineering type of MAS research that focuses on optimal solutions for distributed problems), it needs agents who are at least goal autonomous, but preferably value autonomous (as described in [17], [18]) to make for real life type of social interactions. MAS research using reactive agents may give rise to emergence of organizational structure, however, this phenomenon is in the eye of the observer and thus external to the MAS as such.

4 SOAR

Soar is the computer equivalent of the human problem solving paradigm. Using Soar, one can imitate the behavior of humans solving a particular problem. The underlying structure and the use of operators are all taken from the theory as posed in [10], [11]. Soar, which is derived from the cycle of taking a State, applying an Operator And generating a Result, searches in problem spaces using operators to change the state. Operators are generated and selected in order to pursue the goals of the system. In order to find correct and efficient paths from the initial state of the system to the desired state, knowledge is needed. This knowledge can be of two forms: directly available as operators or indirectly available through problem resolution. The operators are stored in long-term memory as sets of production rules. Problems occur when either more than one or no decision can be made (e.g., two operators can be applied, among which the system then has to choose). The problem resolution becomes the new goal of the system; a technique called *subgoaling*. When the problem is solved, the knowledge used to solve the subproblem can be stored as a learned production in long-term memory (this is called *chunking*). Soar's decision cycle consists of two parts. It first tries to elaborate the current situation with relevant information retrieved from the long-term memory. When all applicable operators have been found, the decision procedure starts. Preferences for operators are processed, and in the end either an impasse is reached or the selected operator is added to the state, enabling a new set of productions to fire. The impasse creates a subgoal (as described above). The result of this subgoaling can be stored as a learned operator, with the objects in working memory that caused the impasse as the antecedent and the results of the search in the subgoal problem space in the consequent of the new operator.

5   Sim-ACTS

The Sim-ACTS model is intended to grow into a computational model of organizational behavior that can be used to analyze the limitations of ACTS theory. The simulations that will be presented further on will show the usability and limitations of the current model. As for now it will suffice to show that the results of Sim-ACTS are in accordance with its direct predecessor TASSCS [15],[16].

5.1   History of Sim-ACTS

Double-AISS [9] was the first completed effort to build an AI-based model of organizational decision making. It was intended as a follow-up study of Cohen et al.'s the garbage can model [6] of organizational decision making. The garbage can model was also implemented on a numerical computer simulation model. In the Double-AISS model, the influence of various parameters on both individual and organizational level on the problem solving behavior of the individual agents and the organization as a whole was studied. In 1990 Plural Soar [3] was developed at Carnegie Mellon University. This model tries to examine the influence of communication and learning capabilities on the problem solving behavior of independent agents working on a simple task. The TASSCS [15], [16] simulation model was developed to integrate some features of Double-AISS in the Plural SOAR model. Starting from the source code of Plural Soar, a model of communication in organizations was added, reflecting the idea of role taking in Double-AISS and replacing the broadcasting type of communication in Plural Soar. Added was also the psychological mindset of an agent (egoistic or altruistic) from Double-AISS. Some simulations were carried out and the results were compared to the initial Plural Soar model's outcomes and theoretical predictions. Sim-ACTS is based on the source code for TASSCS.

5.2 The agents in Sim-ACTS

The agents in Sim-ACTS are implemented in Soar [8]. This implies that they are cognition-based since Soar is based on [11]. Since ACTS theory describes the individual members of the organization as cognitive, the use of Soar is a logical choice. Sim-ACTS' agents have knowledge on how to solve the task at hand, what parts of the task they can solve (i.e., what skills they have with respect to the task), know with whom they may communicate and how they are placed relative to other agents in the organization structure. The organization structure is implicit in the communication mode that can be used to address other agents. Agents at the same organizational level can be addressed using requests, whereas agents at a lower level in the organization can be commanded. The current implementation does not have a separate communication mode for communicating with agents at higher levels in the organization, however the request mode can also be used for this. The evaluation of received messages is in this first version of Sim-ACTS steered by the used communication mode, e.g., an agent receiving a command to carry out some work for another agent will obey to this command. Requests may be argued about. Agents also have a general, non subtask or agent-related, psychological mindset, they are either egoistic or altruistic. Their psychological mindset influences their behavior via the preference ordering among the strategic alternatives that were part of the Double AISS model, i.e., attracting work from another agent, moving work to another agent or reducing the agent's workload by carrying out the subtask. The ordering of the strategies is determined by the motivation of an agent. An altruistic agent is concerned with the workload of the organization as a whole, while an egoistic agent is only concerned with its own workload. So, an altruistic agent has the following ordering of strategies:

reduce > attract > move,

and an egoistic agent:

move > reduce > attract.

The agents can be characterized as type III agents in the typology as developed in [17], [18] that is they have norms (implemented as the psychological mindset), goals (the different strategies), an action repertoire (the skills), can be communicated with and react to changes in the environment. The agents however are not value autonomous and currently do not have the ability to build models of other agents.

5.3 The warehouse task

The warehouse task consists of the filling of a list of orders from a warehouse where the ordered items are stored. The location of the items is unknown to the agents. In search of an ordered item, an agent moves from stack to stack, examining the stacks for the presence of the ordered item (this is the find subtask). When an item is found, it is taken from the stack if it is the top item of that stack. If not, the items on top of the ordered item are moved to another stack in order to free the ordered item after which it can be taken by the agent (this is the get subtask). The ordered item is then placed on a conveyer belt and the agent is finished with the processing of this order (this is the put subtask). In the initial model, all agents are able to perform all subtasks (i.e., finding an item, getting it from the stack and putting it on the conveyerbelt) of which the warehouse task consists.

6 The results of the simulations

The implementation of Sim-ACTS is based on the source code of TASSCS and simulation experiments were carried out to test the results of Sim-ACTS against the outcomes of TASSCS. The simulation experiments consist of the filling of a list of orders from the warehouse. The length and order of the items on the list of orders and the distribution of items over the stacks in the warehouse were not varied. The experiments that were carried out in the TASSCS project were repeated using the Sim-ACTS model in order to compare the results of both models. THe TASSCS model was only run using two agents due to the unavailability of hardware facilities needed to run more agents. TASSCS was run in two setups. In the first the two agents were independent of each other, that is no communication between the agents was possible. In the second setup, one agent was defined as being able to command the other agent to perform a specific subtask on a specific item and supplying the agent with all information necessary to perform the subtask. Since the commanding agent was also defined as being egoistic and the agent being commanded altruistic, the first agent preferred to let the other agent do all the work (except for the taking of the orders which is not defined as a subtask of the warehouse task in the current implementation). The results of these simulations can be found in table 1.

Table 1. Results of the simulations with TASSCS

	independent agents			agents forming an organization		
	agent 1	agent 2	Σ	agent 1	agent 2	Σ
agent moves	88	70	158	0	158	158
Item moves	26	19	45	0	50	50
Waited cycles	10	62	72	1621	577	2198

These simulations were repeated with the Sim-ACTS model using the same set-ups. The results of these simulations are summarized in table 2.

Table 2. Results of the replication simulations with Sim-ACTS

	independent agents			agents forming an organization		
	agent 1	agent 2	Σ	agent 1	agent 2	Σ
agent moves	78	78	156	0	312	312
Item moves	27	16	43	0	43	43
Waited cycles	15	35	50	1430	525	1955

Apart from these replication simulations, Sim-ACTS was also run with three agents. Again, two different set-ups were used. The first set-up consisted of three independent agents, whereas the second set-up consisted of an egoistic agent being able to command the other two, altruistic agents while these altruistic agents had no communication between them. The mean value results of these simulations can be found in table 3.

Table 3. Mean values of the results of the simulations with Sim-ACTS and three agents

	independent agents				agents forming an organization			
	agent 1	agent 2	agent 3	Σ	agent 1	agent 2	agent 3	Σ
agent moves	54	46	56	156	0	143	169	312
Item moves	13	16	14	43	0	18.25	24.75	43
Waited cycles	29	49	58	136	1413.5	1378	1265.5	4057

7 Interpretation and comparison of the simulation results

7.1 Intra model comparison

In the TASSCS simulations the addition of communication and organizational structure increased the number of item movements slightly while the number of agent movements was constant. The number of waiting cycles however increased explosively. This increase in waited cycles when communication and organization structure are added has been addressed in [15], [16]. In the model without communication and organization structure the waiting cycles are caused by physical interdependencies (one agent is processing a stack and the other agent wants to do the same but has to wait for the first agent to finish). In the set-up with communication and organizational structure, the waiting time is not caused by physical interaction but by the interdependence of the subtasks. After moving a subtask to another agent, the original subtask owner waits for its subordinate to report the accomplishment of the subtask before deciding what to do with the next subtask. This means that roughly speaking only one agent is working at the same time, while the other agent is waiting. The slight increase in the number of item movements is due to the fact that instead of two agents moving themselves and orders around in the warehouse in the second setup there is only one agent moving itself and items, thereby changing the physical interdependencies.

In the Sim-ACTS simulations with two and three agents, the total amount of agent movements doubles when communication and organizational structure are added. The number of item movements is constant while the number of waiting cycles shows roughly the same explosive increase as the TASSCS simulations showed. The doubling of the total amount of agent movements is caused by a difference in the implementation of Soar5 and Soar7 with regard to operators added to a superstate of the current problem state. In Soar5, adding an operator which is preferred over other operators to a superstate results in a retraction of the substate, whereas in Soar7 the problem solving in the substate is first brought to an end before returning to the problem solving in the superstate.

7.2 Inter model comparison

There are some minor differences between the code for TASSCS and Sim-ACTS. One of them is a minor change to the way the moving of items on top of an ordered item is carried out. Therefore there is no increase in item movements. The number of item movements has decreased in the Sim-ACTS model compared to the TASSCS results. This is also due to the minor change in the item moving code. The doubling of the agent moves is in Sim-ACTS as compared to the static number of agent moves in the TASSCS experiments is already addressed in the previous section. The number of decision cycles spend waiting has also decreased in Sim-ACTS as compared to TASSCS. Both agents wait less. This may be caused by a different working of the Soar decision cycles, i.e. superstate and substate retractions.

The results of the Sim-ACTS simulation with three agents differs from the Sim-ACTS results with two agents in two ways. The system has four possible results, depending on the distribution of the find and get subtasks. If a get subtask for a found item is moved to the agent not responsible for finding it, this agent waits less cycles. This only goes for items that were found at the end of the row of stacks, where the commanding agent needs less time to make up its mind on to which agent to move the get subtask than it takes the finding agent to return to the order stack. This also makes the commanding agent wait less since the item is found quicker. The four possible results occur with the same frequency since the choice of agents is random.

8 Conclusions and discussion

The main difference between TASSCS and Sim-ACTS is the use of the Soar7.x environment instead of the Soar5.x environment. Since Soar5 was implemented in Lisp, it was both slow and required a lot of memory (e.g., one complete simulation run of the TASSCS model with two agents forming an organization needed anywhere between 12 and 20 hours on two DEC 3100 machines to finish). Since every agent needed its own Soar process, limitations of access to hardware and networking problems made the use of more than five agents almost impossible. It is therefore that the TASSCS simulations were limited to two agents only. The Soar7 environment is implemented in C++ with a Tcl interface for interprocess communication, which makes Soar not only platform independent, but also much faster and less memory hungry (e.g., one complete run of the Sim-ACTS model for three agents forming an organization needs about 5 minutes to run on one machine comparable to the two used for the TASSCS experiments). Within one Tcl process, several Soar agents can be run with even modest hardware constellations. Future simulations can thus examine more interesting organization structures than the ones discussed in this work. This will get the simulation model closer to ACTS theory, since Plural Soar, TASSCS and thus Sim-ACTS all lack possibilities to vary the organizational structure sufficiently to investigate its influence on the behavior of individual members of the organization and the organization as a whole. The agents will consequently more closely approximate the Model Social Agent as described in [4].

The current implementation of the receiving of communication is still both highly inefficient and unrealistic. This is one of the major changes proposed for Sim-ACTS-II. Some of the issues already mentioned in the discussion section of [16] are not addressed in the Sim-ACTS model since it is a direct translation of the TASSCS model into the new Soar programming environment. These issues include:

- implementation of the attract strategy
- implementation of bounded rationality
- use of revisable belief models of other agents to serve as a guideline for communication
- test the effect of different evaluation strategies of communication (e.g., based on skills, workload and preferences instead of only based on commitment)
- test the influence of skill distribution
- subtask reduction should be able to run in parallel mode to make the advantages of communication and cooperation more clear and more natural in view of human problem solving. This will also eliminate the doubling of the agent moves
- removal of the constraint to hand over an item to the agent that originally owned the subtask

This forms the agenda for the development of Sim-ACTS-II. With Sim-ACTS-II, the influence and acquisition of models of other agents will be studied. Generalizing these agent models to role descriptions bring topics such as role switching and inheritance of roles from agents that leave the organization to their replacements within reach. The general mindset (i.e., altruistic or egoistic) as used in Sim-ACTS-I will then also be replaced by preferences for subtasks and agents.

The results of these simulations can then be tested in domain like robotic soccer [7], where agents in real time interact in an ever changing environment and are organized in a soccer team competing with another soccer team. Even though a soccer team lacks some of the features of real life organizations (e.g., a special legal status), it shares most other characteristics of organizations (such as being comprised of multiple agents, goal directed, able to affect and be affected by its environment, and having knowledge, culture, memory, history and capabilities distinct from any single agent). When these agents sufficiently master the basic skills, strategies and roles become the main focus for progress of the level of play. An interesting question is whether an abstract organization theory such as ACTS theory will be able to expand into a down to earth domain as robotic soccer.

References

1. Carley, K.M., "Artificial intelligence within sociology", in: Sociological methods and research 25: 1, pp 3-30, 1996.
2. Carley, K.M., "A comparison of artificial and human organizations", in: Journal of economic behavior and organization, forthcoming.
3. Carley, K.M., Kjaer-Hansen, J., Newell, A. and Prietula, M., "Plural-SOAR: capabilities and coordination of multiple agents", in: Masuch, M. and, Warglien M. (eds.), Artificial intelligence in organization and management theory, Elsevier Science, 1991.
4. Carley, K.M. and, Newell, A., "The nature of the social agent", Journal of mathematical sociology, 19, 1994, pp. 221-262.
5. Carley, K.M. and Prietula, M., "ACTS theory: extending the model of bounded rationality", in: Carley, K. and Prietula, M. (eds.), Computational organization theory, Lawrence Erlbaum Associates, 1994a.
6. Cohen, M.D., March, J.G., and Olsen, J.P., "A garbage can model of organizational choice", Administrative Science Quarterly, 17, 1972, pp. 1-25.
7. Kitano, H., Asada, M., Kuniyoshi, Y., Noda, I., and Osawa, E., "RoboCup: the robot world cup initiative", in: Proceedings of IJCAI-95, Workshop on entertainment and AI/ALife, Montreal, 1995.
8. Laird, J.E., Newell, A. and Rosenbloom, P.S., "SOAR: An architecture for general intelligence", Artificial Intelligence, 33: 1-64, 1987.
9. Masuch, M. and Lapotin, P., "Beyond garbage cans: an AI model of organizational choice", Administrative Science Quarterly, 34, 1989, pp. 38-67.
10. Newell, A. and Simon, H.A., Human problem solving, Prentice-Hall, 1972.
11. Newell, A., Unified theories of cognition, Harvard University Press, 1990.
12. Simon, H.A., "The proverbs of administration", Public Administration Review, 6, 1946, pp. 53-67.
13. Simon, H.A., "A behavioral model of organizational choice", Quarterly Journal of Economics, 69, 1955, pp. 99-118.
14. Smit, R.A. and Verhagen, H.J.E., "On being social: degrees of sociality and models of rationality in relation to multi-agent systems", in: Proceedings of the AAAI-95 fall symposium series Rational agency: concepts, theories, models and applications, 1995.

15. Verhagen, H.J.E., "TASSCS: A computer simulation model for simulating organizational behavior", CCSOM Report 92-78, University of Amsterdam, 1991 (Master thesis).

16. Verhagen, H.J.E. and Masuch, M., "TASCCS: a synthesis of Double-AISS and Plural-SOAR", in: Carley, K.M. and Prietula, M. (eds.), Computational organization theory, Lawrence Erlbaum Associates, 1994.

17. Verhagen, H.J.E. and Smit, R.A., "Modelling social agents in a multiagent world", in: van de Velde, W. and Perram, J.W. (eds.), Position papers MAAMAW 1996, Technical report 96-1, Vrije Universiteit Brussel- Artificial Intelligence Laboratory, 1996.

18. Verhagen, H.J.E. and Smit, R.A., "Multiagent systems as simulation tools for social theory testing", poster presentation at ICCS & SS 1997, Siena.

Towards Modeling Other Agents:
A Simulation-Based Study[*]

Leonardo Garrido,[1] Ramón Brena[1] and Katia Sycara[2]

[1] Centro de Inteligencia Artificial.
Tecnológico de Monterrey.
Monterrey, N.L. 64849. México
{lgarrido,rbrena}@campus.mty.itesm.mx
[2] The Robotics Institute.
Carnegie Mellon University.
Pittsburgh, PA 15213 USA
katia@cs.cmu.edu

Abstract. In this paper, we present some of our ongoing experimental research towards investigating advantages of modeling other agents in multiagent environments. We attempt to quantify the value or utility of building models about other agents using no more than the observation of others' behavior. We are interested in empirically showing that a *modeler agent* can take advantage of building and updating its beliefs about other agents. This advantage can make it perform better than an agent without modeling capabilities. We have been conducting a simulataion-based study using a competitive game called *Meeting Scheduling Game* as a testbed. First, we briefly describe our multiagent simultaion testbed. Then, we describe in detail our experimental study. We explore a range of strategies from least- to most-informed, and present some of our preliminary results on the relative performance of these strategies. Decreasing the *a priori* knowledge about the others and increasing the modeling capabilities we are able to define a series of "modeler" agents. Finally, we present a method for using probabilistic models about the others in such a way that the expected utility is maximized.

1 Introduction

One of the most crucial forms of agent beliefs are beliefs about other agents in the agent's neighborhood. The other agents are in many cases the most important part of the agent's environment in multiagent settings, specially in situations where interaction is important. In this paper, we pay special attention to competitive situations, where a collection of heterogeneous agents are competing one against each other.

In this particular research, we are interested in investigating the competitive advantage an agent can obtain by *knowing* (i.e. modeling) some important aspects of its rivals. We want to show that a *modeler agent* can take advantage of

[*] This research has been sponsored in part by ITESM and CONACYT in México and by NSF —grant number IRI-9508191— in USA.

building and updating beliefs about other agents. This advantage can make it perform better than an agent without modeling capabilities.

Moreover, we are interested in: modeling other agents using no more than the observation of others' behavior; exploring a range of agent strategies, from blind randomized strategies to "oracle" strategies that know other agents' preferences and strategies; measuring, in an experimental way, the advantage attained by a modeler agent; guaranteeing optimality of agent beliefs, as well as the construction process itself, through the use of sound probabilistic and decision-theoretic techniques, instead of arbitrary heuristics.

In our previous experimental work [9], we explored how group quality and performance, in the distributed meeting scheduling process is affected by the privacy of calendar and preference information of each agent. Later, in [8] we presented some of our motivations and perspectives towards agent cognitive modeling for group adaptation in decentralized meeting scheduling environments with information privacy.

Currently, we have established a simulation-based study using a testbed where competition takes place in a game that has some characteristics of meeting scheduling problems. That is, a group of people (i.e. agents) trying to arrange a meeting in such a way that certain meeting slot is available for as many as possible group members. Furthermore, this meeting slot should be as convenient as possible for everyone —in the sense that it maximizes fulfillment of individual preferences. We call this game the *Meeting Scheduling Game* (MSG), described later in more detail.

In the framework of the MSG, we explore —in an experimental way— how modeling other agents can affect individual and group performance after a series of meetings. Our basic research-driving hypothesis is that both individual and group performance are better when each agent tries to explain the other agents' behavior in terms of internal cognitive structures or models —creating and adapting these agent models in an incremental way.

2 Related work

Modeling other agents is an issue that has been approached from many diverse perspectives. In this section, we present related work mainly considering three major issues regarding agents' modeling: what it is to be modeled, how it is modeled, and how models are built.

Agent models range from very specialized, task-oriented models (like other agents' capabilities [18] or organizational roles [5]) to structural models using BDI structures [15] or other internal structure of the agent being modeled. The latter are also called "cognitive" or "deep" models, while the former are called "surface" models. Of course, some combine deep and surface models, modeling from other agents' capabilities to intended actions and plans [5]. One advantage of deep models is that they allow to predict others' behavior, which can give an advantage in non-cooperative or non-communicating situations.

In competitive settings it is important to model others' strategies in order to perform better against them [2]. Strategies can be represented in terms of game theory [16]. A decision-theoretic approach has been also taken in the Recursive Modeling Method [10]. Finite automata has been used to represent rational-bounded strategies [12]. Some proposals model the others' plans [20].

Concerning the model construction method, the simplest case arrives in cooperative settings, where honest agents "tell" the others what their characteristics are [4]. Obviously, this does not work in competitive situations. The most complex situation is when others' models are built entirely from the observation of their behavior –like in the case of competitive games.

In the game-theoretic approach to agent modeling [16], agents usually model strategic interactions in terms of agents' alternative actions and payoffs, encapsulated in the classic payoff matrix. This approach assumes that all the information enclosed in the payoff matrix is common knowledge. However, these models do not explicitly represent complex symbolic representations of the internal traits of the other agents nor how agents reason in order to achieve a solution. This approach takes an external perspective and analyzes the problem of all agents together in order to provide overall efficiency and stability by means of negotiation protocols (see [17] for further details).

Gmytrasiewicz [10] has presented a research work that combines game theory with decision theoretic mechanisms. Assuming that agents are rational and the common knowledge of their payoff functions, he presents a decision theoretic mechanism that aims to let agents be able to reason about nested models about the others' possible moves. This work takes the perspective of the individual agent instead of the classic external game-theoretic perspective.

Vidal and Durfee have continued this work on nested modeling [21]. They have developed an algorithm in order to see which of the nested models of the other agents are important to consider when choosing an action in an effective manner.

A different approach is used by Tambe and Rosenbloom who have presented an agent architecture that conforms the requirements to provide support for flexible and efficient reasoning about other agents' models [20]. This work is closely related to plan recognition [11] because the goal is to discover the other agents plans based on their observed actions and execution of models about the others.

Nadella and Sen [13] have reported some mechanisms for learning partners and competitors' skills in soccer domains (e.g. the agents' passing efficiency). In this work, agents learn simple playing skill abilities (represented, for instance, as ratios of effectiveness) instead of complex symbolic structures about the others' thinking. However, since they use a learning approach, agents indeed build models about the other agents by experience.

Zeng and Sycara have [22] developed Bazaar which is a sequential decision making model of negotiation. In Bazaar, agents can have models about other agents that can be decomposed into three categories of beliefs: beliefs about factual factors about the others (e.g. payoff functions), beliefs about their decision making processes (e.g. reservation prices), and beliefs about meta-level issues (e.g. negotiation style, risk-taking attitudes). They present an experimental example with a pair of agents in a buyer-supplier domain where the buyer agent's models are beliefs about the supplier agent's reservation price. Here, the buyer models the supplier under a probabilistic framework using a bayesian representation.

3 The Meeting Scheduling Game

In this section, we briefly describe the basic features of the *Meeting Scheduling Game (MSG)* which is an extended version of the work presented in [1].

Some of our main concerns creating this testbed were: to allow self-interested as well as cooperative behavior, show and/or hide agent's private information and goals, and define different agent models or roles.

The players try to arrange a meeting at some convenient time slot. By "convenient slot" we mean one which has an acceptable *utility* for a specific player, according to his *preference profile* or *utility function*. Each player proposes a slot taken from his own calendar composed of a working week (as usual, a working week is composed of five days, each one with 8 hours ranging from 9 a.m. to 5 p.m.). Each player's calendar is randomly set at a predefined specific *calendar density* which is the proportion of busy hours in the calendar.

As in any other competitive game, the goal of a player in the MSG is to accumulate more points than his competitors in a match. A *match* consists of a fixed number (e.g. ten) of *games* with two *rounds* per game.

In the first round of each game, each player bids for (i.e. proposes) the slot which maximizes his utility, according basically to his own role (i.e. its individual preference profile). However, the player bids are not completely determined by the own player's role because some of the slots can be busy in his calendar. Thus, the player chooses the most preferable of his available slots. The information about each player's bid is *public knowledge* announced by a referee, who then calls for the second round of bids.

The second round is much like the first one. However, each player may now follow different strategies, taking into account the first-round information of the current game, historic records of past games, and/or models about the other agents. After all the players make their second-round proposal, several *teams* arise. Each team is composed of all those players who proposed the same calendar slot. Then, each *team utility* is calculated, summing up all the team members' individual utilities:

$$TU(t) = \sum_{\forall m \in t} IU(m)$$

Here, t is a team, m is a member of the team, and TU and IU are team and individual utilities respectively. Finally, the game is won by the team which accumulates the greatest team utility.

Then, each player in the winning team accumulates utility according to the predefined scoring procedure. We have defined three basic scoring procedures: the *Individual scoring procedure* which makes agents accumulate just its individual utility when they are in the winning team (i.e. agents accumulate utility according to their own contribution to the winning team utility); the *Group scoring procedure* which makes each agent, in the winning team, accumulates the team utility (i.e. agents accumulate the same number of points: the winning team utility; the *Mixed scoring procedure* which makes agents, in the winning team, accumulate its own individual utility plus the team utility of the winning team (the purpose of this mixed procedure is to promote a balance between selfish and collaborative attitudes).

The players outside the winning team accumulate zero points for that game. Points earned by each player are accumulated from one game to another in an individual point counter through all the match. Finally, the winner for a complete match is the player with the maximum individual accumulated points.

After a game, each player's calendar is randomly reset at the predefined calendar density and another game is started. All this process is repeated until the predefined number of games is accomplished.

It is worthy to note that, after each round, each player knows only the the other agents' bids and, after each game, s/he knows only his/her own accumulated utility. The referee has the responsibility of keeping private the others' calendars and any other agent information such as their roles and strategies.

The four preference profiles we consider in the MSG are: the *early-rising*, who prefers the early hours of the day; the *night owl*, who prefers the meetings to be scheduled as late as possible; the *extreme*, who tries to have meetings early in the morning or late in the afternoon but not in the middle of the day; and the *medium*, who wants the meetings to be around noon. All the players prefer to schedule meetings in the first days of the week. These preferences are coded as slot utility functions.

The MSG is a competitive game, since each player's goal is to accumulate utility over a series of meetings. However, each player needs to collaborate by joining a team that will eventually make him win.

Finally, we would like to note some of the main assumptions we have made: the agents' attitudes are modeled only by four different and fixed agent roles; there is a simple linear relation between an agent's preference profile and its role; the agents' preference profiles are static and independent of calendar density; each proposal is public knowledge; we do not require a meeting to be scheduled at a free slot for every attendee; agent roles and strategies do not change through all the games of a match; and agents are honest (e.g. they never cheat about their first-round bid).

4 The simulation testbed

In this section, we present some of the basic characteristics of our MSG simulation testbed. A more detailed description can be found in [7].

We have basically created only two kinds of agents:

Referee. This agent has all the enough data and methods to ensure the rules of the MSG. Only one instance of this kind of agent is created per match.

Player. This agent is needed for creating an instance for each player in the MSG. Each player instance may has its own "agenthood" (i.e. its own role and strategy).

When the Referee agent is started, it is necessary to pass as parameters some data, such as: the number of players and the number of games per match. The communication protocol is already programmed inside of the Referee and Player agents. This protocol is simple and centralized by the Referee agent following the MSG rules described in the previous section.

The MSG testbed is flexible. When starting the Referee agent, one can easily and directly change the following game parameters:

- Number of agents.
- Number of games per match.
- Scoring procedure.
- Calendar density.
- Roles and strategies for each Player agent.

Creating new roles is relatively easy. It is just necessary to modify an internal structure which stores the calendar slot utility function (in fact, it stores numbers between 1 and 40 for each calendar slot of the eight-hours one-week calendar).

Creating new strategies is also easy. One just needs to create a new method (perhaps together with other complementary methods) where we should procedurally define the agent behavior that the agent with that game strategy needs to follow when reacting to the first-round proposals.

Sometimes it could be desirable to change some rules of the game. For instance, if one wants to disclose the calendar information to all the other agents, we just need to modify the Referee agent in order to broadcast this information (inside the "First Round" message) to all the agents. A similar procedure can be done in case of being interested in disclosing the agents' roles or strategies.

The MSG testbed has been programmed in Java[3], using also the JATLite[6] software for multiagent systems development. We have saved some time and effort using JATLite which is a set of Java classes that allow programmers to quickly create new software agents. [1]

5 Design of the experiments

Besides its role, each agent should also have a particular game *strategy*. Strategies are rules which tell agents what actions to choose at some specific decision point —at the second round of each game, in the MSG. A *modeler agent* is just an

---

[1] An introduction to JATLite can be found in [14].

agent using a strategy which builds models about the others, and uses them in order to improve its behavior.

We wanted to explore a range of strategies, ranging from least-informed to most-informed. Our research path can be described as follows: First, we define simple basic strategies without modeling features, in order to establish the least-informed end of the spectrum. Later, we jump to the other end of the spectrum, creating the *oracle strategy* that correctly guesses all the information about the other agents – this is the most-informed end of the spectrum. Next, we generate a series of modeling strategies by decreasing the knowledge about others and increasing the modeling capabilities. At the end, every piece of information about the internal traits of other agents is obtained directly from their behavior.

First of all, we defined the following, perhaps the simplest, strategy:

Random Strategy: An agent using this strategy chooses his next bid among its action set using an uniform probability distribution (i.e. any action from the set of possible actions has the same probability of being chosen).

A *random agent* does not take into account any information about the other agents nor its own agent role. However, it takes into consideration its own calendar information because it should select an *available slot*, as should all the other strategies.

This strategy's performance is taken as a reference point to compare other "reasonable" strategies, whether or not they including other-agent modeling. Of course, it could be possible to define strategies behaving worse than the random does. This kind of strategies could not be considered as reasonable.

Another simple strategy, but a little bit more complex, is:

Team-Size Strategy: Using this strategy, the agent's next bid has the goal of joining the biggest team seen at the first round of each game, such that this slot is available.

As the random strategy, this one does not take into account individual agent roles (i.e. preference profiles). The next strategy tries to maximize the agent's utility based on its preference profile:

Preference Strategy: This strategy tells the agent to choose the action which maximizes its individual utility based on his own role defined by his preference profile. This comes to simply choose the same slot in the first and second round of each game.

As in the previous strategies, a *preference agent* does not take into account information about the other agents.

Now, let us characterize the relative performance of the basic strategies described so far. The **first experimental scenario** is composed of three different experiments. In the first one, we run matches with only team-size and random agents. In the second experiment, we run matches with preference and random agents. In the third one, we run team-size and preference agents but we did not run any random agent (the goal is to directly compare preference and team-size strategies). Our experimental results are presented in the next section.

As we previously mentioned, random agents lead us to some kind of performance lower limit. Now, in order to get an agent performance upper limit, we defined the following strategy:

Oracle Strategy: An *oracle agent* is capable of correctly guessing the other agents' roles and strategies —hence its "oracle" name. Using this strategy, the agent chooses the best possible action which maximizes his expected individual utility based on all the information about the roles, strategies and calendars of all the other agents.

Though the oracle is supposed to correctly guess the other agents' information, in the actual implementation the referee agent gives the *oracle agent* the other agents' information (roles, strategies, and calendars). Thus, the oracle agent can always see in advance the others' second-round bid and calculate all the possible profits he could get under all its different playing options, according to its own calendar availability.

Clearly, an oracle agent has the best chances of winning each game —and winning the match as well. However, an oracle agent not always can win! This is because of its calendar availability.

Now, in order to get a refined upper limit, we defined the following strategy:

Semi-oracle Strategy: This strategy is similar to the previous one. It guesses information about the others' roles and strategies; however, it ignores all the calendar information about the other agents.

A *semi-oracle agent* takes into consideration the calendar density information in order to calculate the most probable bids of the other agents. The main idea is to maximizes its *expected utility*, which is the product of an utility and the probability of getting it.

Let us see the general behavior of a semi-oracle agent:

1. For each other agent a, make a set S_a of all the possible slots that can be proposed for agent a.
2. For each possible slot s_a in each set S_a, calculate the probability $P(s_a)$ of being actually selected by agent a.
3. Combining all the possible slots that each agent can propose, generate the set O of all the possible outcomes or playing scenarios that could arise at the second round. Each possible outcome o in O is a vector $o \stackrel{\text{def}}{=} (s_1, \ldots s_n)$ of slots that can be proposed by each other agent at the second round.
4. For each possible outcome $o \in O$ do:
    4.1 Calculate the probability that o arises at the second round; that is: $P(o) = \prod_{\forall s_a : s_a \in o} P(s_a)$.
    4.2 Find which would be the slot s_o that gives the maximum utility u_o that can be earned by the semi-oracle agent in this outcome o.

4.3 Calculate the semi-oracle's expected utility due to slot s_o under this outcome o; that is: $U(s_o) = u_o P(o)$

4.4 Accumulate $U(s_o)$ to the previous expected utilities due to the same slot s_o obtained in the previous outcomes.

5. Choose the slot s_m with the maximum accumulated expected utility.
6. Bid for the slot s_m.

Let us see in detail steps 1 and 2: it is worthy to note that all the possible slots that can be proposed by any preference agent is just the same slot proposed at the first round (because of their *preference strategy*); obviously, its probability is 1; however, the set of possible slots that can be proposed by any team-size agent is composed of the different slots proposed by all the other agents; in order to calculate the probability of each possible slot, the semi-oracle must perform the following steps:

1. See what teams show up at the first round of the game.
2. Make sets of teams according to the team sizes (i.e. make sets of teams with the same number of members).
3. Make a vector $\mathbf{v} \stackrel{\text{def}}{=} (e_1, \ldots e_n)$ with all the sets of teams made previously. Arrange this vector in descendant order —according to the size of the teams of each set— from the set e_1 with the biggest teams to the set of teams e_n which contains the team that contains the team-size agent a ($a \in t_j \in e_n$ for some team t_j).
4. For each set of teams $e_i \in \mathbf{v}$, calculate the probability of being chosen by the team-size agent, given the known calendar density d:

$$P(e_i) = \begin{cases} 0 & \text{if } i = 0 \\ (1 - d^{|e_i|})(1 - P(e_{i-1})) & \text{if } 0 < i < n \\ 1 - \sum_{j=0}^{i-1} P(e_j) & \text{if } i = n \end{cases}$$

5. Calculate the conditional probability $P(t_a|e_n)$ of choosing team $t_a \in e_n$ which contains the team-size agent a given that e_n is already chosen:

$$P(t_a|e_n) = \sum_{k=0}^{|e_n|-1} \frac{b(k; |e_n| - 1, d)}{k+1}$$

6. Now for each team $t_j \in e_i$ of each set of teams e_i, calculate the probability of being chosen for joining this team:

$$P(t_j) = \begin{cases} \frac{P(e_i)}{|e_i|} & \text{if } \forall m[t_m \in e_i \Rightarrow a \notin t_m] \\ P(e_i)\frac{1-P(t_a|e_n)}{|e_i|-1} & \text{if } a \notin t_j \wedge \exists m[a \in t_m \in e_i] \\ P(t_a|e_n)P(e_i) & \text{if } a \in t_j \wedge \exists m[a \in t_m \in e_i] \end{cases}$$

The first case of this formula is when the team-size agent a is not in any team t_m of the set e_i; the second case is when the team-size agent a is not member of the team t_j but it is member of some other team $t_m \in e_i$; and the third case is when the team-size agent a is member of the team t_j and it is in set e_i.

7. Assign this probability $P(t_j)$ to the slot proposed by t_j —this slot is one of the slots s_a that each team-size agent a could propose in step 2 of the previous algorithm.

Although the semi-oracle agent seems to be very similar to the oracle agent, it is much more complex. While the oracle agent can predict the others' moves in an exact way, the semi-oracle agent must calculate the probabilities of all the possible bids of the other agents. This is because of the semi-oracle's ignorance of the others' calendar information.

Now, let us see in detail step 4.2 of the general algorithm of the semi-oracle agent: each possible outcome is seen, by the semi-oracle agent, as composed of a set of teams t's. Then, for each t the semi-oracle checks:

- If the slot s_t proposed by t is available in the semi-oracle's calendar, calculate the utility u_t it could earn if it joined this team; that is: $u_t = IU(sm) + \sum_{\forall m \in t} IU(m)$, where $IU(sm)$ is the semi-oracle's individual utility and $IU(m)$ is the individual utility of the team member m.
- If the slot is not available, forget team t and go directly to the next unvisited team.

When the slots proposed by all the teams have been checked, the semi-oracle looks for the team that offered the maximum utility u_t; then, the semi-oracle chooses the slot proposed by that team as the slot s_o.

As we have seen, the oracle strategy can give us an upper limit performance for any modeler agent. Furthermore, the semi-oracle strategy can give us a smaller upper limit. In our **second experimental scenario** we show these upper limits empirically obtained by simulation with the oracle and semi-oracle strategies. This scenario is composed of two experiments: in the first one, we run team-size and preference agents with an oracle agent; in the second experiment, we run a semi-oracle agent with team-size and preference agents.

6 Experimental results

We set up matches of ten two-rounds games and, in our experiments, we have set up series of matches in order to measure —after many matches— how agent performance is affected by different strategies. Our experiments are composed of 500 independent matches. Once a match is completed, we call it a "success" if the strategy under consideration wins. Otherwise it is considered a "failure" from the probability theory standpoint. Assuming that the success probability p remains constant through all the matches, it is easy to realize that we run binomial experiments. [2]

We are interested in obtaining the expected agent performance after an infinite number of matches. Thus, we want to estimate the proportion p in these

---

[2] The probability distribution of a binomial random variable X, the number of success in n independent matches, is: $b(x; n, p) = \binom{n}{x} p^x q^{n-x}$, $x = 0, 1, 2, \ldots, n$ where p is the success probability and q the failure probability ($q = 1 - p$).

binomial experiments. From basic sampling theory we see that this parameter is given by the statistic $\hat{P} = X/n$ where X is the number of successful matches and n the number of matches. Therefore, we can use the sampling proportion $\hat{p} = x/n$ as the estimator of p with a $(1 - \alpha)100\%$ confidence of getting an error not greater than $z_{\alpha/2}\sqrt{\hat{p}(1 - \hat{p})/n}$. [3]

In all the experiments presented here, we used the Mixed scoring procedure, described earlier, in order to promote a balance between selfish and collaborative attitudes. We have also set up the calendar density at 50%; we have conducted some experiments —not presented here— that show how low calendar densities lead us to scenarios of little interest and high calendar densities lead us to chaotic scenarios because agents almost never can play their strategies —agents show a kind of pseudo-random behavior.

In each experiment, we show the estimation of the success probability of each involved strategy (it is showed as a percentage). As we said in the previous paragraph, this estimation is the sampling proportion which is calculated just counting the number of successful matches of each strategy and dividing it by the number of matches. We also show the maximum error expected with a 99% confidence.

The goal of the first experimental scenario is to compare the performance of the random, team-size, and preference strategies. In experiment 1.1, we run random vs. team-size agents. In the second experiment, we run random vs. preference agents. In experiment 1.3, we compare directly team-size and preference agents. In all these three experiments, we run 6 agents. The results are shown in the following table:

Experimental Scenario 1			
Experiments	**Strategies**		
	Random	*Team-size*	*Preference*
Experiment 1.1	8.04% (5% error)	91.96% (5% error)	—
Experiment 1.2	0.60% (1% error)	—	99.40% (1% error)
Experiment 1.3	—	50.30% (6% error)	49.70% (6% error)

Experiment 1.1 shows that the team-size strategy clearly outperforms the random strategy, as expected. Furthermore, the second experiment shows that the preference strategy also outperforms the random strategy.

Later, in the last experiment of this scenario, we compare team-size and preference agents without any random agent. As we can see, from these results it is not clear which strategy is better.

Thus, we have also conducted another set of experiments —not detailed here— which relates the relative team-size and preference performances with the number of agents. Our results have confirmed that the team-size strategy has better performance if the number of agents is bigger than a specific threshold. This is explained by the fact that team-size agents tend to gather altogether in

---

[3] $z_{\alpha/2}$ is the value of the random variable z with standard normal distribution which defines an area of $\alpha/2$. For a deeper discussion about all the statistical formulae we refer the reader to any probability and statistics text such as [19].

the same team. After a specific number of running agents, the team-size team outperforms any other team.

Next table presents our results of the *second experimental scenario*:

Experiments	Experimental Scenario 2			
	Strategies			
	Oracle	Semi-oracle	Team-size	Preference
Experiment 2.1	59.11% (7% error)	—	19.57% (7% error)	21.32% (7% error)
Experiment 2.2	—	53.40% (7% error)	23.76% (7% error)	22.84% (7% error)

Experiment 2.1 shows the upper limit obtained by the oracle strategy. The oracle strategy clearly outperforms the other two strategies. In experiment 2.2, the semi-oracle agents also outperforms the other two strategies.

As expected, the oracle strategy showed a relatively high performance when compared with the other two strategies' performances. This upper limit seems to be far enough from the other two basic strategies performances. Therefore, this shows that there is a relatively big gap where we can locate the performance of any modeler agent.

In the last experiment, we can see the semi-oracle performance. As expected, it shows a lower performance than the oracle's. This is close to the oracle's performance, as expected too. However, the team-size and preference agents showed significantly lower performance than the semi-oracle strategy.

7 Ongoing research

Currently, we are continuing our research using strategies which do take into account models about other agents. Intuitively, we think the performance of this kind of strategies must be somewhere between those performance limits we have empirically obtained.

Let us first introduce our term *probabilistic models* about others. We can see a probabilistic model about another agent as a simple linear structure which records each particular probability of having a specific possible feature of a given feature set. Thus, we can visualize a model as a vector of the form:

$$\mathbf{m}_a \stackrel{\text{def}}{=} (f_1, \dots f_n)$$

where $\mathbf{m}_a$ is the probabilistic model about agent a and each f_i represents the probability that agent a shows the particular feature i. It is worthy to note that the sum of all the probabilities of each vector always must be 1, since each vector (i.e. model) is a partition of the feature probabilities. A model about another agent is always a probabilistic approximation to the actual character of the modeled agent.

In the context of our MSG, each agent has two models about each other agent. The first one is the role model $\mathbf{r}_i$:

$$\mathbf{r}_a \stackrel{\text{def}}{=} (r_1, \dots r_n)$$

where each r_i is the probability that agent a has the particular role i. The second model is the strategy model s_i:

$$s_a \stackrel{\text{def}}{=} (s_1, \ldots s_n)$$

where each s_i is the probability that agent a follows strategy i.

Our next research step is the following strategy:

Pre-Modeler Strategy: This strategy tells agents to choose the action which maximizes his expected utility calculated from the probabilistic models about the other agents. (note that this strategy does not create the models, it just uses them).

A *pre-modeler* agent is not an oracle agent! This strategy does not guess the other agents' roles, strategies, nor calendars. This strategy just uses the probabilistic models about the other agents. However, it does not create these models; the models are given and the strategy just use them.

Thus, the pre-modeler agent uses two models about the others: the role and strategy models described earlier. However, the others' calendar information is not known nor used by the pre-modeler agent. As in the case of the semi-oracle strategy, it is not realistic to do so because each agent calendar dynamically changes after each game. This strategy also uses the probabilistic approach taken by the semi-oracle strategy for calculating all the probabilities of all the other agents' possible free slots.

The general pre-modeler's behavior is given by the following algorithm:

1. Given the probabilistic role and strategy models about the others (each agent's models **r** and **s**). For each agent a, generate a set Y with all the possible role-strategy scenarios y's and their probabilities. For each agent a, each role-strategy scenario probability is calculated as follows:

$$P(y) = r_i s_j$$

where y is the role-strategy scenario of agent a created by the combination of role i and strategy j.

2. Combine all the role-strategy scenarios of each agent and generate a set G with all the possible playing scenarios for the pre-modeler agent. Each playing scenario $g \in G$ is a combination of some particular role-strategies scenarios y's. The probability of each playing scenario g is given by:

$$P(g) = \prod_{\forall y \in g} P(y)$$

3. For each playing scenario $g \in G$, follow the *semi-oracle strategy*, and get the better slot proposal s_g for scenario g and its expected utility $U(s_g)$.

4. Update the expected utility of each proposal obtained in the previous step:

$$U(g) = P(g)U(s_g)$$

5. Choose the playing scenario g_w which gives the maximum expected utility to the pre-modeler agent.

6. Bid for the slot of the scenario g_w.

Remember, a pre-modeler agent does not create the probabilistic models about the others. We assume that these models are given, and the pre-modeler agent just uses them in order to act in the most convenient manner.

The next obvious step is the following strategy:

Modeler Strategy: This strategy incrementally creates probabilistic models about the others. Then, it chooses the action which maximizes his expected utility calculated from those models.

The *modeler agent* is the most complex agent of all the agents we have created. It does not guess any thing about the others. It will create models about the other agents in an incremental way, updating those models after each game during a match. All the probabilities of each model are incrementally updated, approaching to the actual character of the agent being modeled.

Currently, we are working on the mechanisms for creating and updating these models about the other agents. One of our primary concerns is to preserve our probabilistic approach in order to assure optimality in the models without using any kind of heuristic rules.

We are considering to adopt a bayesian approach for creating the probabilistic models about the others. Using these kind of bayesian mechanisms, the modeler agent could create the probabilistic models about the others' roles and strategies based on the others' actions at the first round of each game. We are also investigating how this models can be globally updated after each game based on the historical record of all the played games during a match.

8 Conclusions

In the preceding sections we have described an experimental framework where it is possible to assess the relative performance of different playing strategies for the MSG. This allows to experimentally evaluate the performance of strategies that build and use models of the competitors; other modeling-agents proposals fail to provide such an evaluation.

The natural object-oriented modularity of Java and JATLite has help us in developing a flexible testbed. It is easy to change parameters, such as: number of agents, number of games per match, calendar density, and scoring procedures. The roles and strategies of each agent are also easily set and reset. If one wants, it is also relatively easy to create new agent roles and game strategies.

We have used a collection of reference points for a modeler agent's performance: The random agent and the oracle provide the extremes of the spectrum, ranging from least-informed to most-informed strategies. We have formally defined the strategy of a "pre-modeler", which is capable of using a pre-built probabilistic model. The pre-modeler's strategy aims to be optimal in the sense that no other non-oracle strategy could outperform it.

Finally, we have sketched the design of a "full modeler" agent –capable of incrementally building probabilistic models of its competitors, which is part of our current research.

References

1. R. Brena and L. Garrido. The schedule game. Technical Report CIA-RI-026, Center for Artificial Intelligence, ITESM-Campus Monterrey, Monterrey, N.L., México, September 1996.
2. D. Carmel and S. Markovitch. Opponent modelling in a multi-agent systems. In G. Weiss and S. Sen, editors, *Lecture note in AI, 1042: Adaptation and Learning in Multi-agent Systems*, Lecture Notes in Artificial Intelligence. Springer-Verlag, 1996.
3. Sun Microsystems Inc. Copyright ©. All rights reserved. The source for java technology. URL: http://java.sun.com/.
4. R. Davis and R. G. Smith. Negotiation as a metahpor for distributed problem solving. *Artificial Intelligence*, pages 63–109, 1983.
5. K. Decker, Sycara K., and M. Williamson. Modeling information agents: Advertisements, organizational roles, and dynamic behavior. In *Working Notes of the AAAI-96 workshop on "Agent Modeling"*. *AAAI Report WS-96-02*. AAAI Press, 1996.
6. Center for Design Research at Stanford University. Copyright ©. All rights reserved. Jatlite: Java agent template, lite. URL: http://java.stanford.edu/.
7. L. Garrido and R. Brena. The meeting scheduling game. Technical Report CIA-RI, Center for Artificial Intelligence, ITESM-Campus Monterrey, Monterrey, N.L., México, 1998. In preparation.
8. L. Garrido, R. Brena, and K. Sycara. Cognitive modelling and group adaptation in intelligent multi-agent meeting scheduling. In C. Lematre, editor, *First Iberoamerican Workshop on Distributed Artificial Intelligence and Multiagent Systems*, pages 55–72. LANIA-UV, 1996.
9. L. Garrido and K. Sycara. Multi-agent meeting scheduling: Preliminary experimental results. In M. Tokoro, editor, *Second International Conference on Multi-Agent Systems*, pages 95–102. AAAI Press, 1996.
10. P.J. Gmytrasiewicz. On reasoning about other agents. In *Intelligent Agents II*, Lecture Notes in Artificial Intelligence (LNAI 1037). Springer Verlag, 1996.
11. A. Kautz and J. Allen. Generalized plan recognition. In *Proceedings of the National Conference on Artificial Intelligence*, pages 32–37. AAAI press, 1986.
12. Y. Mor, C. Goldman, and J. Rosenschein. Learn your opponent's strategy (in polynomial time)! In G. Weiss and S. Sen, editors, *Lecture note in AI, 1042: Adaptation and Learning in Multi-agent Systems*, Lecture Notes in Artificial Intelligence. Springer-Verlag, 1996.
13. R. Nadella and S. Sen. Correlating internal parameters and external performance: Learning soccer agents. In G. Weiss, editor, *Distributed Artificial Intelligence Meets Machine Learning - Learning in Multiagent Environments*, Lecture Notes in Artificial Intelligence, pages 137–150. Springer-Verlag, 1997.
14. C. Petrie. Agent-based engineering, the web, and intelligence. *IEEE Expert*, December 1996.

15. A. S. Rao and M. P. Georgeff. Modeling rational agents within a bdi-architecture. In *The Twelfth International Joint COnference on Artificial Intelligence (IJCAI-91)*, 1991.

16. J. S. Rosenschein and Genesereth M. R. Deals among rational agents. In *The Ninth International Joint Conference on Artificial Intelligence*, 1988.

17. J.S. Rosenschein and G. Zlotkin. *Rules of Encounter*. Artificial Intelligence Series. MIT Press, 1994.

18. J. Sichman, Y. Demazeau, R. Conte, and C. Castelfranchi. A social reasoning mechanism based on dependence networks. In A.Cohn, editor, *The 11th European Conference on Artificial Intelligence (ECAI-94)*, pages 188–192. John Wiley and Sons, Ltd., 1992.

19. Charles M. Stone. *A Course in Probability and Statistics*. Duxbury Press, 1996.

20. M. Tambe and P. Rosenbloom. Architectures for agents that track other agents in multi-agent worlds. In *Intelligent Agents*, volume II of *Lecture Notes in Artificial Intelligence (LNAI 1037)*. Springer Verlag, 1996.

21. J.M. Vidal and E.H. Durfee. Using recursive agent models effectively. In *Intelligent Agents II*, Lecture Notes in Artificial Intelligence (LNAI 1037). Springer Verlag, 1996.

22. D. Zeng and Sycara K. Benefits of learning in negotiation. In *Fourteenth National Conference on AI*, pages 36–41, Providence, RI., July 1997. AAAI, AAAI Press.

Multi-agent Architecture Integrating Heterogeneous Models of Dynamical Processes: The Representation of Time

Edem Fianyo[1], Jean-Pierre Treuil[1], Edith Perrier[1], and Yves Demazeau[2]

[1] Laboratoire d'Informatique Appliquée ORSTOM, 32 av. Henri Varagnat - 93143 Bondy CEDEX France - {fianyo,treuil,perrier}@bondy.orstom.fr
[2] Laboratoire LEIBNIZ - Institut IMAG 46 av. Félix Viallet 38041 Grenoble Cedex France - Yves.Demazeau@imag.fr

Abstract. Multi-agent simulations aim at representing the dynamics of complex systems as resulting from multiple interactions between autonomous entities encapsulating their own perception of local environment. From our point of view, this approach would also require to take into account individualized perception of time. In this paper, we propose a new way to implement time distribution in multi-agent systems by associating to each agent its own time and rhythm to achieve its own actions. Our synthetic examples are extracted from our specific research project, dealing with a simulator of irrigated systems, where the parallelism of physical processes appears to be an important component of reality.

Keywords: multi-agent simulation, time-representation

1 Introduction

The ideas we deal with in this paper come from the reflexion we follow within the framework of our research project. The latter consists in the integration of different viewpoints on the future of the same geographical region (namely the Ngalenka region in the North Senegal where new irrigated areas are being developed) with regards to the evolution of both ecological land quality (soil salinity, numerical hydrodynamical models, qualitative thresholds on salt contents, etc) and land assessment (empirical rules of prescribed land use, etc). Some of these models already exist and have been developed with different time steps. Other ones are being formalized and their most convenient time step is not known yet. We have chosen to adopt an outsider point of view of the region we work on. This in order not to promote a single mono-disciplinary and specific point of view against another one. Our simulator first represented the main natural objects recognized simultaneously by the multidisciplinary research team working on the area, and we are going on associating progressively to these objects the specific models that rule their interactions at the scale of our study, whatever their time step is. That is why we look for the most flexible representation of time which will provide the most adaptable way to introduce, as one goes along, new components and new scenarii of future land and water management. More generally, this paper focuses on time definition, modelling and management in multi-agent simulation of natural systems. In the first part, we explore different aspects of the time representation issue in the field of multi-agent simulation. Then, we show how one of these aspect (management of different rhythms) is presently addressed in our application. Finally, the third part resumes a more general discussion on rhythms multiplicity and variability.

2 The time issue in multi-agent simulation systems

The representation of time in computer simulation is complex. Different notions of time coexist. Moreover, there are different ways of managing the temporal progression of simulations. We can add to that the issue of diversity and variability in the choices of temporal resolution that endow the simulated processes.

2.1 Notion of real time, virtual time and computation time

In the simulation field, let us distinguish three notions of time :

- there is the real time, i.e. the time in which the real phenomena are observed.
- there is the virtual time, i.e. the representation of real time by the simulator.
- there is the computation time, i.e. the actual time needed by the simulator to run and to achieve its result, that is the execution time.

When a forest growth simulation displays a snapshot representing the forest at the 10th year, it is said that this 10th year belongs to the virtual time, because it has not really happened in the reality, it is a view of what the simulator has calculated to happen according to given assumptions. The virtual time is also called simulation time. It could also be called simulated reality time because it is defined to represent the time going on in the real world. In the following of the paper, we will use the term virtual time as it is often employed in the literature.

2.2 Two ways of implementing virtual time in a multi-agent simulation system

The simulated system is in general associated with a virtual clock that indicates how far the simulation has progressed (the virtual time). This virtual clock can advance in either regular or irregular time intervals [GD95]. Any dynamical simulation can be considered as a succession of state changes of the simulated world, each of these states associated with a virtual date in the world. This virtual time progresses in a discrete manner, from one step to another, in a continuous linear space of time, the computation time [CH97]. There is one absolute rule that a simulation must follow : this is the causality rule which stipulates that the future of the virtual world cannot have influenced the past. That means that, when one event causes a second event, the latter must be processed after the first one in the computation time.

Simulation directed by clock. In a simulation directed by a virtual clock, the virtual time is discretised in a given number of identical interval sizes. The interval size is called time-step. The time is symbolized by one virtual clock of reference that constitutes the mover of the simulation and that allows the starting of any action from any agent in the simulator. In this case, the time approach is a top-down one. At each time-step, there may be no action to perform, only one action, or many actions to perform. In the latter case (many actions), each action is so associated with the same virtual date. The simulator must ensure that the order in which each action is performed will have no influence on the future of the virtual world (synchronous system). There are a lot of multi-agent simulators that cope with time in this way (for example: RIVAGE [PC97], MANTA [DCF93]), because it is the easiest one. But this representation of time is efficient only if each component is known a priori, since one has to choose the time-step of the simulator as the smallest time interval among those associated with every agent. This search for the lowest common denominator in time scaling is similar to the search for the finest spatial grid in space representation. The definition of a single relevant time step is not so easy as noticed by LePage[LG97]. This point will be discussed later in the paper.

Simulation directed by events. In a discrete event simulation (DES), the progression of the virtual time depends on the event occurrences that are triggered with a precise virtual date which allows to sort them. With this approach, when there is an inactivity period, the simulation goes directly to the next significant event. It is the synchronization kernel that manages all the events that happen in the simulation. Its role is important especially when several events have been triggered at the same date, to manage the simultaneity (virtual parallelism).

Distributed discrete event simulation. In a distributed DES, the simulated world is modeled as a group of communicating entities, referred to as Logical Processes (or LP). Each LP maintains a local virtual clock that defines the virtual time for that LP (LVT) and the LPs operate as distinct discrete event simulators, exchanging event information if necessary [Rad97]. The simulator itself is associated with a global virtual time (GVT). Distributed DES attempt to achieve computer parallelism that is to execute events in parallel computation time. The main problem is to ensure that no causality error occurs. To overcome this problem, synchronization between the LPs can be either conservative [Mis86] or optimistic [Jef85].

Conservative synchronization
Under conservative synchronization, events are processed by each LP only when it can guarantee that no causality (out of order) violation will occur. To make sure that only safe events are processed, all LPs that contain no safe event must be blocked, which can potentially lead to deadlock. To prevent deadlock, two kinds of methods have been developed : 1) deadlock avoidance methods and 2) deadlock detection and recovery methods. The latter have the advantage of being easy to implement, but they can not exploit full parallelism of system : LPs behave over pessimistic if the causalities are not frequent [GD95].

Optimistically synchronized simulation
Here the occurrence of causality errors is allowed. To satisfy the causality constraints, some mechanism to recover from a causality violation is defined. The best known is time warp. In time warp, any LP with an event to process is allowed to run without consideration of the progress of the other LPs. Since some LPs will process ahead of others at any given computation time, it is possible for a LP to receive an event from the past, violating the causality constraints of the simulation. In order to recover, the LP receiving these *straggler messages* must rollback to an earlier local virtual time and re-process events in their correct order. Time warp exploits full parallelism of systems : if causalities are frequent, time warp can be more efficient. Nevertheless, this kind of protocol is hard to implement and to debug because it requires complex manipulations and complex data structures [Rad97], [GD95].

Virtual clock and computer clock. In these two ways of implementing time in a simulation system, virtual time is always defined as independent of the computation time. One can imagine to define a virtual time progression founded upon the computation time (e.g. by means of a proportionality coefficient). One can see such a method used in some of the examples illustrating threads use in [Lea97]. It would be interesting to go further with such an approach.

2.3 Multiple variable time-steps or coexisting rhythms

In our project, we are concerned with the coexistence of many different rhythms. The dynamical processes have been modeled according to their rapidity and the frequency of the actions and the events which compose them. The process of evapotranspiration of the culture is a very slow process that we have to link with the irrigation process which is much faster. Moreover, these physical processes may change their rhythm according to external conditions. For example, water will flow faster through the soil according to the height of the water charge put on the ground. Holding on the variability and the diversity of coexisting rhythms is independent of the way virtual time is implemented (by clock or by event). It is a general modelling issue that would need the definition of a computational theory [Mar77]. Here the question is to dynamically define and to control the time-step of the simulation or to manage the way the events are generated [Bur97].

3 Time representation in our application

Time representation in the present version of our system can be put among the conservative protocol of synchronization. As a matter of fact, only safe actions are processed, all LPs that contain no safe event are blocked until the others LP reach the corresponding virtual time.

The simulator is composed by different types of entities. There are passive entities (e.g. irrigated areas) which state evolves according to the action of natural phenomena (rain, climate changes) or human actions (land use or irrigation decision). There are active entities (like natural phenomena, human decisions) that modify the world either by their own will or according to physical determinismes. These natural phenomena and human actions modify the system entities state by triggering processes like percolation, evapotranspiration or irrigation.

For us, a computer process will be a representation of the dynamics which can describe either a natural physical process or a human action taking. Each process acts via the entities methods that are in the world. It starts or ends because of some events which represent special state changes of the simulated world. Entities and processes are endowed by their own independent life rhythm. The passive entities just update their virtual time. During its cycle, one system component will achieve its set of tasks. When these tasks are completed, it goes forward to the following time lag and increases its own life time, whatever the other ones are doing meanwhile. To ensure the causality coherence of the system, we work on two levels :

- we implement scheduler mechanisms to synchronize components which share the same virtual periodicity time,
- we link different scheduler mechanisms to build a global virtual time.

3.1 Own time definition

Each system entity is endowed with an own-time attribute . This attribute value indicates to the agent its actual virtual date. The entity is associated with a scheduler to whom the entity asks to update its date. The scheduler will respond to its demand after all the entities that are associated with it have done the same demand. Here our scheduler plays the role of a conservative LP. In a Petri net representation, the behaviour of a scheduler can be represented as on figure 1.

3.2 Relating different own times

In order to define a global virtual time, we use mechanisms between schedulers. To simplify the problem, we first assume that the synchronisation relations between different rhythms can be materialized by a proportional number. The global virtual time corresponds to one central entity local time, here the irrigated area time, because almost all the processes act on it.

Theoretically, all the time schedulers are linked with the time scheduler of the central entity following the mechanism represented on the figure 2. But as some entities synchronize themselves to others when they process, we choose to link some schedulers to others when their entities interact. This in order to allow more flexibility. After a first reflexion on the subject, we have implemented this time representation on a *clay model* built in Java using the thread mechanisms. In this model the rhythms were first considered as fixed for good.

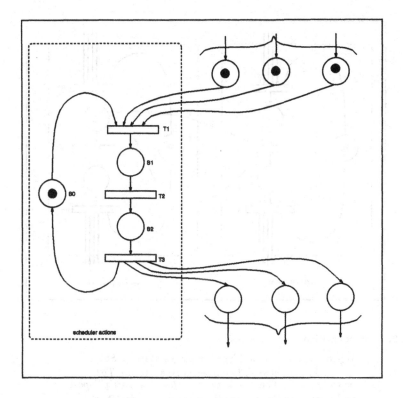

Fig. 1. Petri representation of a scheduler behaviour
T1: waiting for the LPs demand ; T2: one time-step progressing ; T3: releasing of the LPs

4 Taking account of the variability and the diversity of the rhythms when simulating heterogeneous processes

In a parallel direction to the time representation that we are implementing, there is another fundamental issue concerning the introduction of the concept of rhythm variability. Generally, the entities, or processes are equipped with an own rhythm that never changes. We found that under some circumstances it is necessary to add another mechanism to change the entities rhythms. As a matter of fact, the process rhythm represents the time-step associated to a significant action of the process on the world. Thus it may change according to the state of the world. For example we can mention the model of water flow in soil ruled by Darcy-Richards differential equation that describes water transfer between the soil surface and the watertable [PLG97]. The numerical solving of this model by finite differences involves both the spatial discretisation of the soil in a set of superimposed layer and a time discretisation. The time step of this numerical model has to be chosen depending on the input boundaries conditions that the

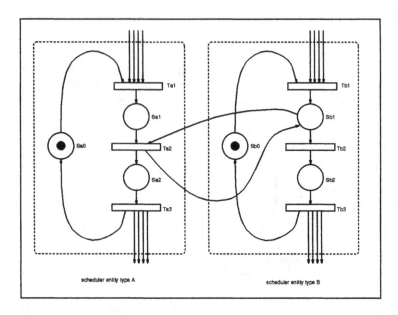

Fig. 2. Synchronization between schedulers

When *sheduler EntityTypeB* changes state to *Sb1*,
it can choose between two alternatives : to fire *Tb2*
or to fire *Ta2*. The link between *scheduler EntityTypeA*
and *scheduler EntityTypeB* represents the fact that
scheduler EntityTypeA associated period unit corresponds
to *N scheduler EntityTypeB* associated period unit,
where *N* is the proportional number materializing
the relation between the two rhythms.

model is going to process. If the water which arrives on the soil has a very high rate, the model is endowed with a rapid time step in order the water flow not to jump from a layer to another one that is not the closest. If this would happen, the model outputs would be biased.

The rate of water that arrives on the soil surface is controlled by the irrigation process which is triggered by the GIE will (the Economical Interest Group composed by cultivators). Since the latter can change it is important to be able to automatically adapt the water flow model rhythm when needed. Conversely, it can also be important to be able to adapt the periodicity or rhythm of decisional processes in order to hold on a priori unknown events that would be triggered by physical processes, for example, to bring moreover water when evapotranspiration has been more important than expected.

4.1 Different types of processes to integrate

The processes that represent the dynamics of the system can be classified in two types.

- There are the continuous processes often described with continuous models. These models can be described by mathematical formula like differential equations. They often represent physical processes. When they are implemented in a simulation tool, there are associated with a period of discretisation or rhythm which can be determined by a sensibility analysis, according to the user choice that can be more or less relevant as regards the system dynamics.
- Some processes are intrinsically dicrete so they are described with models that use their intrinsical rhythm. Human actions are often represented with discrete models. For example, the GIE's meeting that starts different actions on the world (choice of a new culture, choice of the perimeters that will be irrigated).

4.2 Toward an intelligent control of the periodicity of the processes

Considering the above classification, we claim that there exists at least one type of processes or active entities whose rhythm is a variable that one could find interesting to control. We think that this control could be efficiently achieved by the use of control agents that would encapsulate the active entities. These agents would have the general charge of directing the active entities behaviour. In doing this, they would have to know how the other control agents direct other active entities. They would have to be endowed with an internal representation of these others control agents (especially an internal representation of their control capacity). They would also have to be able to communicate with them. For example, to ask them to change their own rhythm when they detect significative changes in the actions of their own process. So the agent notion takes all its meaning. The agent is nor really the physical entity nor the process that rules it. It is rather the computational agent that achieves these dynamics [TPC97]. This kind of mechanism would allow the genericity of our tool. The reflexion must be deepen further in relation with the work that has been already done in the multi-agent architecture field [GBD97],[GB92].

5 Discussion and Conclusion

Multi-agent systems put emphasis upon interchanging asynchronous messages between agents. The latter are so granted with a temporal autonomy (at the level of computation time) generalizing that of the actors (cf. [Bri89], [Yon92])

When multi-agent systems are used to simulate conversations between individuals within a group of human beings, this asynchronous feature of message interchanging among 'pure communicating agents' is very convenient, as in [MIT92]. Simultaneity is not the crucial point, and we can easily manage it. Controling interchange is carried out by protocols of interaction, and beyond that, by mechanisms of internal reasoning within the very agents, without considering any explicit time managing.

However the agents encounter the time question as soon as they have to face a partially changing environment, which evolves independently and introduces temporal constraints. This is the case, for example, when we link a multi-agent system with a real time system [OD96]. The agents have thus to account explicitly for time. That is why questions about temporal logic are so abundantly treated in the literature ([Wer96], [Woo96]).

In the field of multi-agent simulation applied to natural physical systems, the explicit representation of time becomes essential. We have to model the true parallelism of nature, the simultaneity and the different rhythms that we observe. We think that the representation of time (as well as the representation of space) deserves special attention, as far as the notion of environment is studied. In the continuation of this work, we will give special attention to what has been made in Artificial Life (i.e. SWARM) where the problems are similar; from this could emerge ideas or techniques which could be partly included in our project.

In our approach, we consider the world as a set of parallel processes, each one having a specific behaviour, a specific time rhythm, and possibly a specific spatial resolution. In the same way as the spatial resolution means, for spatialised processes, the distance scale from which spatial heterogeneity becomes significant, the time rhythm means, for dynamical processes, the scale of time lag needed by a given process to execute a significant and observable action, as far as the other interacting processes are concerned.

In this paper, we have presented some general principles as regards time implementation that we begun to conceive and to test in the framework of our simulator concerning the evolution of a complex set of irrigated areas. For the moment, our implementation of time representation doesn't take account of the variability of the different rhythms. Nevertheless, it enables subsequent inputs of new entities associated with yet unknown own times, without modifying the existing scheme. Our current reflexion turns on how to hold on variability and diversity of rhythm in a generic way.

References

[Bri89]   J.P. Briot. Acttalk : a testbed for classifying and designing actor languages in the smalltalk-80 environnement. In Y.Demazeau and J.P.Muller, editors, *Proceedings of ECOOP'89*. Eds, 1989.

[Bur97]   Roger Burkhart. Schedules of activity in the swarm simulation system. In *OOPSLA '97 Workshop on OO Behavioral Semantics*, 1997.

[CH97]   Patrick Coquillard and David R. C. Hill. *Modélisation et Simulation d'écosystèmes - Des modèles déterministes aux simulations à événements discrets*. MASSON, 1997.

[DCF93] Alexis Drogoul, B. Corbara, and D. Fresneau. Manta : New experimental results on the emergence of (artificial) ant societes. In C. Castelfranchi, editor, *Simulating Societies Symposium,*, 1993.

[GB92]   Les Gasser and Jean-Pierre Briot. *Distributed Artificial Intelligence : Theory and Praxis*, chapter Object-Based Concurrent Programming and Distributed Artificial Intelligence, pages 81–107. Kluvwer, 1992.

[GBD97] Zahia Guessoum, Jean-Pierre Briot, and Michel Dojat. Des objets concurrents aux agents autonomes. In Joel Quinqueton, Marie-Claude Thomas, and Brigitte Trousse, editors, *actes des Journées francophones d'IAD et SMA*, pages 93–106. Hermes, April 1997.

[GD95]   Zahia Guessoum and Pontien Deguenon. A multi-agent approach for distributed discrete-event simulation. In *DISMAS'95 proceedings*, 1995.

[Jef85] D.R. Jefferson. Virtual time. *ACM Transactions on Programming Languages and Systems*, 7(3):405–425, July 1985.

[Lea97] Doug Lea. *Concurrent Programming in Java - Design Principles and Patterns*. Addison-Wesley, 1997.

[LG97]   Christophe LePage and Vincent Ginot. Vers un simulateur générique des peuplements piscicoles. In Hermes, editor, *Actes des 5èmes Journées Francophones d'Intelligence Artificielle et Systèmes Multi-Agents - JFIADSMA'97*, 1997.

[Mar77] David Marr. Artificial intelligence - a perosonal view. *Artificial Intelligence*, 9:37–48, 1977.

[Mis86] J. Misra. Distributed discret-event simulation. *Computing surveys*, 18(1):39–65, March 1986.

[MIT92] T. Maruichi, M. Ichikawa, and M. Tokoro. Modelling autonomous agents and their group. In Y.Demazeau and J.P.Muller, editors, *Decentralized Artificial Intelligence I*. UCL Press, 1992.

[OD96]   Michel Ocello and Yves Demazeau. Une approche du temps reel dans la conception d'agents. In J.P. Muller J. Quinqueton, editor, *IA distribuee et Systemes multi-agents.JFIADSMA'96*. Hermes, 1996.

[PC97]   Edith Perrier and Christophe Cambier. Une approche multi-agents pour simuler les interactions entre des acteurs hétérogènes de l'infiltration et du ruissellement d'eau sur une surface de sol. In *Tendances nouvelles en modélisation pour l'environnement*. Elsevier, 1997.

[PLG97] Edith Perrier, Christian Leclerc, and Patricia Garnier. Profile-scale simulation of water flow: a computer program to visualize and to estimate soil hydraulic properties effects. In *proceedings of the International Workshop on Characterization and measurement of the Hydraulic Properties of Unsaturated Porous Media. Riverside, USA*, 1997.

[Rad97] Radharamanan Radhakrishnan. Formal specification and discrete event simulation algorithm. Technical report, dept. of ECECS - university of Cincinnati, 1997.

[TPC97] Jean Pierre Treuil, Edith Perrier, and Christophe Cambier. Directions pour une approche multi-agents de la simulation de processus physiques spatalisés. In *Intelligence Artificielle et Systèmes Multi-Agents - 5ème journées JFIADSMA'97*, 1997.

[Wer96] Eric Werner. Logical foundations of distributed artificial intelligence. In John Wiley Sons; editors G.M.P. Hoare and N.R. Jennings, editors, *Fundations of distributed artificial Intelligence*, 1996.

[Woo96] Michael Wooldridge. *Fundations of distributed artificial Intelligence*, chapter Temporal Belief Logics for Modeling Distributed Artificial Intelligence Systems. John Wiley and Sons; editors G.M.P. Hoare and N.R. Jennings, 1996.

[Yon92] A. Yonezawa. *ABCL : An object-Oriented Concurrent System*. MIT Press, 1992.

Author Index

Lecture Notes in Artificial Intelligence (LNAI)

Lecture Notes in Computer Science